I0093197

THE CHALLENGES OF THE
NEW SOCIAL DEMOCRACY

Studies in Critical Social Sciences Book Series

Haymarket Books is proud to be working with Brill Academic Publishers (www.brill.nl) to republish the *Studies in Critical Social Sciences* book series in paperback editions. This peer-reviewed book series offers insights into our current reality by exploring the content and consequences of power relationships under capitalism, and by considering the spaces of opposition and resistance to these changes that have been defining our new age. Our full catalog of *SCSS* volumes can be viewed at https://www.haymarketbooks .org/series_collections/4-studies-in-critical-social-sciences.

Series Editor
David Fasenfest (York University, Canada)

Editorial Board
Eduardo Bonilla-Silva (Duke University)
Chris Chase-Dunn (University of California–Riverside)
William Carroll (University of Victoria)
Raewyn Connell (University of Sydney)
Kimberlé W. Crenshaw (University of California–LA and Columbia University)
Heidi Gottfried (Wayne State University)
Alfredo Saad-Filho (King's College London)
Chizuko Ueno (University of Tokyo)
Sylvia Walby (Lancaster University)
Raju Das (York University)

THE CHALLENGES OF THE NEW SOCIAL DEMOCRACY

Social Capital and Civic Association
or Class Struggle?

RAJU J. DAS, JAMIE GOUGH
AND ARAM EISENSCHITZ

Haymarket Books
Chicago, IL

First published in 2023 by Brill Academic Publishers, The Netherlands
© 2023 Koninklijke Brill NV, Leiden, The Netherlands

Published in paperback in 2024 by
Haymarket Books
P.O. Box 180165
Chicago, IL 60618
773-583-7884
www.haymarketbooks.org

ISBN: 979-8-88890-244-8

Distributed to the trade in the US through Consortium Book Sales and
Distribution (www.cbsd.com) and internationally through Ingram Publisher
Services International (www.ingramcontent.com).

This book was published with the generous support of Lannan Foundation,
Wallace Action Fund, and the Marguerite Casey Foundation.

Special discounts are available for bulk purchases by organizations and
institutions. Please call 773-583-7884 or email info@haymarketbooks.org for more
information.

Cover design by Jamie Kerry and Ragina Johnson.

Printed in the United States.

Library of Congress Cataloging-in-Publication data is available.

Contents

Acknowledgements

Jamie Gough thanks his housemates, friends, and comrades in the 400-strong neighbourhood of Tolmers Square, central London, in 1973–9. Squatting in an area threatened with demolition, we carried out all manner of associationalist initiatives combined with campaigning against property speculation and for social housing. (For an entertaining view, see tolmers.net.) This experience and its many discussions and debates underlies my contribution to this book.

A large part of Raju Das's social capital work was conducted during his tenure in Dundee University, Scotland, where he had arrived shortly after his PhD. He would like to record his gratitude to his former colleagues in Dundee, especially, Allan Findlay, Hester Parr, Fiona Smith, Nick Fyfe, Carlo Morelli and Alan Werritty, who provided a stimulating and comradely intellectual environment to him.

Raju would like to gratefully acknowledge support from the United Kingdom's Economic and Social Research Council (ESRC). A grant from ESRC made it possible for him to collect empirical evidence on social capital reported in the book which is utilized to illustrate the theoretical arguments about the concept. He is grateful to his respondents who freely shared their thoughts about their social lives. He is also grateful to his many research assistants for their invaluable assistance, and especially, Mr. Debadutta Sahu.

All three of us are immensely grateful to Professor David Fasenfest, the editor of Brill's Studies in Critical Social Sciences book series, for his encouragement and editorial feedback.

Figures and Tables

Figures

Tables

CHAPTER 1

Introduction

Raju J. Das, Jamie Gough and Aram Eisenschitz

This book provides a Marxist critique of the dominant contemporary Left strategy for local economic and social development, which we term 'the new social democracy'. It discusses how key elements of this strategy – community ties, cooperation, social capital – can better be taken forward through a locally-based socialist strategy.

Over the last thirty years or so, in both Minority and Majority Worlds (the more developed and less developed worlds, respectively), Left strategy at the local scale has developed a novel form of social democracy. This seeks to build social capital, strengthen civil society, foster community ties and institutions, build a not-for-profit economy, and encourage self-help and voluntary organisations. It seeks to build new participatory forms of local politics which can achieve consensus between different social groups. This strategy goes by a number of names: community development, the social economy, the solidarity economy, the Third Sector, associationism, the commons, and building resilience. Theorized and supported by many left-leaning academics, this strategy is seen as the principal way in which people can improve their economic and social conditions in the face of neoliberal capitalism, and become empowered at personal and political levels.

This new social democratic strategy eschews central elements of earlier social democracy: substantial state intervention into industry, regulation of the private sector to improve employment and working conditions, and public services and state transfer payments in the interest of workers and the poor. The new strategy originates in the post-1970s economic crisis of global capitalism. This caused depression of wages and incomes, higher unemployment, and deterioration of public services, housing and the environment. Earlier social democracy had depended on strong growth and high profits; now these were gone, and social democracy was thrown into crisis. Into its place stepped the new social democracy. Its appeal was that it enabled people to become active in new, local enterprises, initiatives and networks and to provide services and environmental benefits, all without dependence on the state or big capital. It thus promised to overcome isolation and fragmentation, foster social ties and community, and produce immediate, visible results.

Despite its promise and popular appeal, we argue that this approach suffers from major weaknesses. The results of the new strategy tend to be meagre because of the failure to demand control over the major resources of society held by capital, landlords and the state. The new social enterprises typically lead to self-exploitation and subordination to capitalist dynamics, and thus internalise neoliberalism. Accordingly, we argue for an alternative, socialist approach to the local politics of development. This centres on building popular collective organisations in both the economy and social life, which can demand and achieve increasing control over the productive resources of the society. In this approach, social capital, community organisations, local civil society and social economy are not rejected. Rather, placed in their class context, they are seen as potential forms of working class struggle against capital and landowners. This approach makes demands on the local and national scales of the state rather than seeking to by-pass them. And it seeks to link local struggles to those at national and international spatial scales. The book thus presents a critique of the dominant Left strategy for local economic development in both the Majority and Minority Worlds, and advances proposals for a class-based strategy.

1   Capitalism, Class Struggle, Scale and History

This book uses a Marxist approach centred on class relations, the accumulation of capital, their history and geography, and their crisis tendencies (Gough and Das, 2017). Since this book is concerned with local politics and its problematic relation to the national and international levels, we start with a consideration of geographical scale. At the most fundamental level, the social relations and processes of capitalism are, more or less, non-spatial. But as we develop these relations into their more concrete forms, space enters in vital ways. In consequence, capitalist social relations and processes vary 'vertically' across scales, and 'horizontally' across territories (Gough, 1991; 1992). Economy, society and the state are organized at a variety of scales: local, regional/provincial, national and global.[1] In this book we focus on local economic development within a nation, using examples mainly from Britain and India. In doing this, we recognize that the local- and the national-scale processes, both historical and contemporary, cannot be understood in isolation from the processes at the global

---

1   For discussion of geographical scale which have informed our approach in this book, see
    Cox, 1995, 1996, 1998, 2018; Eisenschitz and Gough, 1993; Gough, 2004a, 2004b; Moore, 2008;
    Marston, 2000; Marston et al. 2005; and Taylor, 1987.

scale. Indeed, the world economy is 'a mighty and independent reality which has been created by the international division of labour and the world market', so that 'national capitalism cannot be even understood, let alone reconstructed, except as a part of world economy' (Trotsky, 1931; Das, 2022a).[2] The point applies even more strongly to local capitalisms.

Capitalism is a market society, but quite unlike any previous one. Not only are the means of subsistence (food, shelter, and so on) bought and sold, but so also are the means of production (mines, research labs, factories, call centres, machines, and so on) and, crucially, the ability to perform labour, the co-producer of wealth with nature. Capitalism is characterized by a massively unequal distribution of means of production: the means of production – in their material form and as money-capital – are controlled by a small minority, usually the top 1–10% of wealth owners. So, the majority are forced to rely on wage-work and thus experience what Marx calls 'dull economic compulsion'. Most people lack capital, and most people *must* lack capital: if everyone, or most people, had access to capital (that is enough to make it unnecessary to work for a wage for others), there would be no capitalist and no worker. Capitalists invest money to make more money by buying labour power and productive resources and then compelling workers to create more value than their wage, surplus value. Thus, workers are exploited, whether or not wages are high or low. A part of the capitalist revenue also comes from buying cheap from, and selling dear to, small-scale producers, and from dispossessing them of their property. Thus in capitalism, the interests of capital and those of the majority – wage-earners and petty-producers – are fundamentally incompatible.

This antagonism is for much of the time only latent. Workers tend to accept the rule of capital because of their dependence on profitable firms for their employment, competition between workers for jobs, services and housing, and the appearance of these as the natural and inevitable 'rules of the market' (Marx, 1887; Gough, 2004a: Ch.13; Gough, 2010; Das, 2017: Ch. 12). But class struggle, potential or real, overt or covert, nevertheless breaks out. Class struggle is from both below and above. Class struggle from below opposes the relations of private property, exploitation, dispossession and imperialist subjugation of the South, and their concrete effects such as poverty, inequality, low wages, attacks on union rights and democratic rights. Class struggle from above is when the ruling class counters opposition from the lower classes, wage-workers and non-exploiting small-scale producers. This is partly carried out through the

---

2   The major exceptions were South Korea and Taiwan, which from the 1950s had very rapid productive accumulation and rising wages. This was because of economic autonomy granted by the US, for geopolitical reasons.

coercive apparatuses of the state (Das, 2022b). Countering lower-class struggle may also occur through relatively cheap and revocable concessions in the form of, say, economic development policy with some limited temporary benefits (ibid.). The extent to which the concessions actually benefit workers and the poor masses depend on the strength of capitalist economy and on the balance of power between capital and the lower classes. These concessions can be scale-specific, sometimes national, sometimes local (Eisenschitz and Gough, 1993). Thus, economic development policy directly initiated by the state, or promoted by the state through non-state actors, can be seen in part as class struggle from above, as a response to potential or real class struggle from below.

2   The Capitalist Golden Age, Working Class Struggle, and Traditional Social Democracy

In early industrial capitalism in Western Europe, North America and Australasia, class struggle from below took the form of workers' actions at the level of the workplace or local industry, partly through trade unions which were repressed by the state and the employers. But from the late 19th century, class struggle from below also took the form of social democratic politics organised through mass working class parties, forming an increasing challenge to liberal 'free market' politics. In the 'golden age' between 1948 and 1973, social democracy was the dominant politics in all developed nations, irrespective of the party in government, albeit in very different forms in different countries. This was made possible because of the post-war economic boom: high rates of investment, strong growth of output and productivity, low rates of unemployment, and high rates of profit. Investment and productivity increase were supported by substantial state industrial policies (again, of very different forms in different countries), state-owned utilities and industries, and counter-cyclical fiscal and monetary policies. State spending on public services, social housing and the environment grew. Women's participation in waged labour increased rapidly, supported by expanded public services. Tax revenues from both capital and labour increased strongly, and underpinned state progressive income transfers from rich to poor. All of these processes enabled cooperation between the classes, producing 'the postwar consensus'. In some high-income countries, social democracy operated alongside state-capital corporatism, in which the state cooperates with the major industrial and commercial corporations with negligible input from the working class; this was particularly important in Japan, but also present in continental Western Europe and the US. The social democratic consensus of the postwar period enabled a stabilisation of class relations after the tumultuous class struggles of the interwar period.

At the other pole of global capitalism, the Majority World, from the 1930s to the 1970s the dominant class-political strategy was national developmentalism organised by the state (Das, 2022b: Ch. 12). The native capitalist class sought to build itself through weakening the economic control of imperial capital and, in the case of formal colonies, to achieve political independence. To achieve this end, the native capitalists allied with the masses, albeit under the former's organisational control. This led to popular politicisation and increasing economic and democratic demands. The capitalists were inclined to accede to these demands; the Russian and, later, the Chinese, revolutions gave warning of what a purely repressive stance might lead to. To grow, the capitalist class also needed the support of the state, sometimes via state ownership of major industries. Where there was no pre-existing native capitalist class, a section of the traditional elites used political control of the state to enrich themselves and become capitalists. This model, then, included a degree of compromise between the masses on the one hand and the capital and the landed interests on the other. The result was some land redistribution, provisions of healthcare and education, subsidized food, and state-funded employment. Many of these benefits were distributed through clientalist networks which subordinated the poor to political elites. We can see that there are many similarities of this strategy with social democracy and corporatism in the High Income Countries.

But the material gains for the majority of the population in the Majority World were very limited.[3] The most ambitious national developmentalist governments were overthrown by imperialist intervention (Mossadeq, Sukarno, Lumumba). Massive inequality in land distribution and remnants of semi-feudal relations remained. The capitalist classes often preferred rentier activities to productive investment. State industrial intervention was corrupt rather than designed for productive growth, and state funds and assets were appropriated by the political elite. Major assets were taken over by imperial corporations and the profits expatriated. Both domestic and foreign employers imposed intense labour processes, long hours of work, poor employment conditions and low wages. Democratic rights were limited or, under dictatorships, non-existent, and trade unions, residents organisations and rural movements often repressed; the capitalist class and landowners were unwilling to depart from their chosen economic path, and the lack of democratic rights made it difficult for popular pressure to produce a different path. Thus formal independence and an ostensibly nationalist regime were unable to satisfy

---

3   The major exceptions were South Korea and Taiwan, which from the 1950s had very rapid productive accumulation and rising wages. This was because of economic autonomy granted by the US, for geopolitical reasons.

either the economic or the political-democratic aspirations of the mass of the
population.

3   From Traditional Social Democracy and National Developmentalism to Neoliberalism

Capitalist class relations limit the growth of production in a variety of ways. For
example, we have noted how class relations in the Majority World held back
growth in production under national developmentalism. Another instance is
the long waves of growth and stagnation of the capitalist economy. Labour-
saving investment, while raising the profit of individual firms, in aggregate and
in the long term tends to lower the average rate profit across the economy.
As labour is replaced by machines, total capital invested increases relative to
surplus value produced, and surplus value divided by total capital, the rate
of profit, tends to fall (Mandel, 1978; Roberts, 2016). Thus, the average rate of
profit in the largest economies started to fall in the 1950s; it did so not because
investment was too low but because it was too high, propelled by the economic
boom. By the early 1970s, the average rate of profit had reached such low levels
that capital investment slowed dramatically (Roberts, 2016; Volscho, 2017). In
the fifty years since then, the world economy, with the exception of China since
the 1990s, has experienced much lower rates of growth of output, productivity
and wages and higher rates of unemployment and poverty than in the postwar boom. A series of mini-booms of 8–10 year duration have occurred, largely
created by massive increases in corporate and consumer debt and waves of
speculative investment in different sectors and world-regions; but all of these
ended in crashes, culminating in the 2007–8 world 'financial' crisis. The period
since the 1970s can therefore be termed a long wave of economic stagnation
(Mandel, 1978).

The global ruling class reacted to stagnation with a new strategy, neoliberalism, whose central aim was to raise the average rate of profit on capital. This
has two central elements. First, increasing the share of output appropriated
by capital and decreasing the share of labour (in Marxist terms, increasing
the rate of exploitation). The social democratic collaboration of capital and
labour was replaced by an attack on workers' living standards, organisation
and rights – class struggle from above. The second plank of neoliberalism was
to allowing capital to flow from less profitable sectors and territories to putatively more profitable ones (Shaikh, 2016; Volscho, 2017). This took the form
of flows of capital between advanced economies, deepening their sectoral
specialisation; and a flow of capital from the rich countries into mining and

manufacturing in the Majority World.[4] Flows of capital into manufacturing shift between countries, depending on the geography of wages, tax liabilities, environmental and other regulations. In consequence, nationally-based trade union organizations, which had relied on national economies doing well to be able to strike a compromise with national capital, were unable to mount a counter challenge when ownership of production became global. The movement of capital between countries thus helped to drive down wages and conditions in each country.

Ideologues of neoliberalism launched an ideological offensive against the practice and theory of both postwar social democracy and national developmentalism. They argued that the state industrial policy 'feather-bedded' unproductive capital and weakened incentives to innovate; state borrowing squeezed funds for private investment; state benefits undermined the work ethic by developing a 'dependency culture'; and taxation distorted markets and undermined incentives for capital to invest and incentives for workers to work hard. Neoliberals proposed, rather, that the major economic decisions on investment, production processes, products, and trade should be taken by firms and 'entrepreneurs' rather than by the state, since only they know their business in sufficient detail; the state should withdraw from industrial intervention; workers should accept the need for firms to be profitable, and the right of managers to manage production; trade unions should be reduced in power or eliminated since they are a monopolistic distortion of the free labour market; taxes should be reduced, particularly on capital and 'enterprise'; and state spending should be reduced, particularly on public services and the regulation of business.

Over fifty years, attacks on labour, mobility of capital, and neoliberal state policies have failed to ignite a new long wave of growth (Roberts, 2016). Rather, they have produced immiseration. Many workplaces closed; unemployment increased; wages, conditions and job security declined; public services (education, health, social care, environmental services, social housing) deteriorated as governments cut spending and privatised parts of provision; natural and built environments deteriorated; the quality of essentials including food, water and air declined. The psychological toll has also been enormous: ever-increasing anxiety, depression, eating disorders, self-harm and suicide. Stagnation and neoliberalism have produced a questioning of the established order. But they have deepened competition between workers and increased rage and

---

4 Further on neoliberalism, see Duménil and Lévy, 2011; Flew, 2014; Jessop, 2012; Kotz, 2015; Maher and Aquanno, 2018; O'Connor, 2010; Saad-Filho and Johnson, 2005; Springer et al., 2016.

aggression against others, typically organised around race, ethnicity, national-
ity, gender and sexuality. This workers' consciousness has been ably exploited
by capital to shift blame for the crisis on to specially-oppressed sections of the
working class, particularly by the neoliberal authoritarian populists in both
the Majority and Minority worlds – Trump, Modi, Erdogan, Putin, Bolsonaro,
Orban et al. Neoliberalism has thus been an economic, cultural and political
disaster for the majority.

4   From Traditional Social Democracy and National Developmentalism to New Social Democracy

The onset of economic crisis and stagnation in the 1970s was initially met by
strong resistance from trade unions in a number of developed nations. In some
cases this went from resistance to proposing socialist measures, particularly
nationalisation of the major enterprises and banks. But by the late 1980s this
wave had been defeated by capital and the repressive apparatuses of nation
states. The social democratic and communist parties of advanced countries
were organisationally and ideologically thrown into disarray: their strategy of
gradual improvement in working class living standards and democratic rights
through collaboration between labour with capital had been decisively repudiated by capital. Social democratic parties in government increasingly adopted
neoliberal policies: depression of wages, shift of taxation from capital to labour,
cuts to spending on public services, and deflationary monetary policy. In the
Majority World, the parties of national developmentalism such as the Baath
Parties of Syria and Iraq and the Congress Party of India converted themselves
to neoliberalism; new neoliberal authoritarian-populist parties grew such as
the BJP in India and the JDP in Turkey. During the 1970s and 1980s, this move
to the right was exacerbated by the Moscow-aligned Communist Parties in
both the Majority and Minority Worlds: the wish of the Soviet bureaucracy to
placate the West and to reintroduce capitalism led those parties to abandon
any perspective of class struggle from below, let alone socialism.

   Despite the discipline, disempowerment, fragmentation and demoralisation created by neoliberalism, pressure from the working class did not disap-
pear. And the dire consequences of neoliberalism became increasingly obvious
to all but the ruling class. Social democratic activists, politicians and academics responded, developing their strategies against neoliberalism in three distinct directions. First, a restatement of traditional social democracy focused on
action by the national state. Second, productivist syndicalism focused on the
workplace, in which workers are well rewarded for collaboration with management to increase productivity. Third, the promotion of social capital and

associationism within localities and communities. The last two of these we would, following in part Petras (1997), refer to as the 'new social democracy'. This radical reformulation of social democracy has received support from left-of-centre scholars, including influential economists, sociologists and political scientists. (We discuss and critique these theorists in Chapter 2.)

The dominant fractions of capital have generally been uninterested in traditional social democracy and productivist collaboration of capital and labour, preferring the gains they have made from neoliberalism (for the case of Britain, see Gough, 2020). In contrast, associationism and social capital do not present any obvious threat to neoliberalism; indeed, as we shall argue, they internalise important aspects of it. They have accordingly been the most-practised social democratic strategy in recent decades.

4.1   *Social Capital*

'If people cannot trust each other or work together, then improving the material conditions of life is an uphill battle' (Evans, 1997: 2). In recent decades, trust, co-operation and neighbourly relations have been brought together under the concept of 'social capital'. Social capital denotes networks, associations and organisations bound together by norms of trust and reciprocity. These constitute social resources for individuals which facilitate collective action for mutual benefit (Woolcock, 1998). Social capital is located inside civil society and at the interface between civil society and the state, at the local scale.

The literature distinguishes different forms of social capital. 'Bonding social capital' refers to strong ties connecting family members, neighbours and close friends sharing similar demographic characteristics. 'Bridging social capital' denotes the weak ties among members of civic organizations, including clubs and voluntary associations. This form of social capital of the poor is produced in part by their associational life, for example clubs where people of different occupations and different neighbourhoods meet. 'Linking social capital' refers to vertical ties of trust and cooperation between the common people and those in positions of power and influence in formal organizations such as the state (World Bank, 2001). Through these different forms, social capital is supposed to provide a bottom-up approach to poverty alleviation world-wide. The World Bank says that social capital is a necessary condition for long-term development and that social capital is the capital of the poor. Indeed, in the global south, social capital has been seen as a new theory of development (World Bank, 2001).

4.2   *Associationism*

Associationism is another way in which social capital, especially bridging social capital, has been conceived. Associationism focuses on the creation of

an economy of cooperative and not-for-profit enterprises, community organisations, and common ownership. Its aims are in part material – the creation
of waged jobs and the provision of useful goods and services; but it also aims
to change social relations by fostering social capital and community, cooperation and solidarity, thus empowering individuals and overcoming their isolation and alienation. Associationalism focuses strongly on the local scale –
neighbourhoods, towns, districts of cities and rural districts. Its historical roots
stretch back to the 19th century utopian socialists such as Owen, Fourier and
Proudhon, who sought to develop a non-exploitative capitalism . In the last
four decades, a number of terms have been used for this political project: the
Third Sector, community enterprise, community control, the solidarity economy, the participatory economy, the social economy, and so on.

In recent years a number of scholars have embraced the social economy
enthusiastically as both practical measures against poverty and as an empowering alternative 'beyond capitalism', 'post-capitalism', or 'capitalism not as
you know it' (for example Wright, 2014). The most elaborate, and best-known,
theorisation of the social economy has been that of Gibson-Graham (1996;
2006). Adopting a post-structuralist approach, they argue that many different forms of enterprise are possible within capitalism, a continuum of many
hybrid forms. Social enterprises can thus potentially flourish within a capitalist
'environment', and in this way the sector can aim to grow indefinitely. They see
this as a more realistic, and also more empowering, strategy than trade union
struggles or traditional social democracy.

4.3   *Resilience*

Another policy and academic discourse within the new social democracy is
the strategy of building 'resilience'. In Britain, for example, this has become the
guide for local government policy towards poor neighbourhoods. The neighbourhood is expected to use its inner, intrinsic resources to achieve 'normality'.
Social actors within the area are expected to pull themselves up by their bootstraps, with more or less help from the local state. Community organisations
and building of social capital and social enterprise are to play the leading role
in the 'regeneration' of the area, thus producing resilience against future economic adversity. In this way, poverty can be overcome, or at least ameliorated,
without confronting capital and without substantial income transfers from the
nation state.

The differences between the new social democracy on the one hand and
traditional social democracy and national developmentalism on the other are
summarised in Table 1.1 below.

TABLE 1.1   Traditional social democracy and national developmentalism versus new social democracy

Traditional social democracy and national developmentalism	New social democracy
A big role for the state in economy	State role limited to provision of infrastructure, support services and private property protection
Focused on private or state-owned corporations	Focused on small and medium enterprises and not-for-profit social enterprises
Collaboration between capital and labour based on institutional role of trade unions	Workers' empowerment: skill upgrading, participation in governance of employing firms, starting own businesses and social economy
Public services under the direct control of national/local states, provided universally	Public services through varied combinations of the state, private sector and civil society, and differentiated by social group and locality
Limited redistribution of income and social and economic opportunities at the national scale overseen by the state	Self-activity of individuals and particular groups to improve quality of life
Significant social difference is class seen as income differentiation	Class, understood as income differentiation, is one among many equally important social -cultural identities
Rested on actions of national and local legislators and governments elected by citizens who remain passive between elections	Seeks continuous participation in politics through state-sponsored forms and autonomous fora
Concerned with national-scale economic, social and political processes	Focused on local processes, including cooperation, community ties, and social capital

5   Critique of the New Social Democracy

5.1   *Existing Critiques*

At present there is no book-length discussion of the new social democracy from a socialist perspective. The books by Fine (2001; 2010) and Tittenbrun (2013) present some useful Marxist critiques of social capital. But these authors do not cover or critique associationism, the economic and political aspects of the new social democracy, nor discuss the scale of the locality; in this book we discuss social capital, associationalism and localism together to provide a broader and deeper critique. Fine and Tittenbrun do not discuss the socialist potential of social capital, which we develop in this book as 'the social capital of the working class'. Connectedly, these authors do not provide an alternative, socialist strategy to that of mainstream social capital theorists. In contrast, while we criticise the social economy as it is presently practiced, we also show how it could be developed as a part of broader socialist strategy.

Reisman (1991) gives a left critique of the social economy, and Sharzer (2012) a critique of small firm strategy, with which we agree. But they do not critique the wider framework of the new social democracy – social capital, conservative notions of community, and the consensus seeking approach to local democracy. Like Fine and Tittenbrun, they neglect the socialist potential of the social economy, and they do not put forward a socialist strategy for local politics.

Cowley et al. (1977), Lees and Mayo (1985) and Clements et al. (2008) have provided powerful critiques of conservative and social democratic views of 'community', and argued for a class struggle approach to local and community politics. But these books are pitched at a more historically and spatially-concrete level than our book, which is more theoretical and strategic. Nor do they discuss the economic and economic-political processes linked to community.

There is a massive literature on militant community action and local popular resistance to neoliberalism, a class struggle approach which we support (as we explore in Chapter 3 and 7). Some of this literature is essentially descriptive, some analytical and strategic. The literature falls within a number of disciplinary approaches or sub-fields, including community action, resistance in cities to aspects of neoliberalism, 'the Right to the City', anti-globalisation and counter-globalisation, and Marxist studies of urbanism and urban politics. However, this literature does not offer a critique of social capital and associationist localism. Nor does it offer an *overall* socialist strategy for the local scale, although David Harvey's *Spaces of Hope* (2000) contains some discussion of this.

5.2   *Our Critique*

We argue that the new social democracy fails to achieve its own professed goals and, a fortiori, fails as a strategy for socialism. We show that it is based on thin and misleading theoretical foundations.

We have noted that neoliberal globalization has led to scalar shifts in state-economy-society relations from the national towards sub-national (i.e. the local and regional) scales. This intensified local politics is mostly neoliberal or corporatist, which run the risk of working class resistance. The new social democracy poses itself as a progressive alternative, and one that is strongly localist in being focused on small scale, locally-controlled structures. Social capital, as a component of the new social democracy, is presented as offering cohesion between the classes. This promise has been emphasised by Robert Putnam (Putnam, 1993), the author most responsible for popularizing the concept of social capital, who describes his 'communitarian social capital' as a 'superglue' (2000: 23).

The enthusiasts of social capital neglect its class character, in particular how the material conditions of the poor affects their social capital. They think that social capital is an independent variable and poverty a dependent variable. This view mistakenly abstracts from the fact that the economic-political conditions of poor people have an enormously constraining effect on social capital itself and its purported material benefits for the poor. The social capital approach to development can at best produce meagre benefits for the working class and petty producers, and, worse, ties them into neoliberal social relations and paths of development. Because of the unequal relations of power between state actors and the poor, reflecting the class character of both society and the state, the conditions for state–society synergy ('linking social capital') in support of the interests of the poor are also undermined (see Chapters 3, 4 and 5).

Similarly, proponents of the social economy lack an analysis of spatial capital accumulation and its contradictions, and abstracts from class and other fundamental forms of social power. Because they lack capital, social enterprises are limited in their ability to grow. Cooperators are often forced into self-exploitation to survive. Associationism's attempt to by-pass the state rather than subject it to working class control means that the state's resources and regulatory powers are not mobilised in support of social enterprises. Thus we regard the gradual conversion of capitalism to the social economy as utopian; the struggle for workers' and citizens' control of the mainstream economy is still necessary.

Associationists' wish for greater social, economic and political involvement of ordinary people is contradicted by capitalist social relations. Associationism is hemmed in by disciplinary capital and state. Its localism leaves social and spatial uneven development untouched. Associationism seeks to abstract the good elements of capitalism from the bad. But in our view, the better possibilities of capitalism have to be fought for against both capital and the state, through transitional demands that point towards socialist solutions (Das, 2022a). This requires the maximum unity of workers. But this unity goes against associationism's postmodern conception of agency – diverse socially-excluded groups embedded in diverse localities (see Chapters 2 and 6).

Despite these criticisms of the actually-existing practice of social capital and social economy, we believe that aspects of them have the potential, however limited, to be positive parts of a socialist strategy, thus realising their promise as an alternative to neoliberal deprivation. We put forward the notion of 'the social capital of the working class' understood as the social and community ties which can aid in collective action against capital and the state (Chapter 3). We argue for making strong links of the social economy to popular collective organisations and struggles in the mainstream economy and society, where the social economy can provide a radical levening (Chapter 6).

The fostering of 'resilience' in poor districts holds the poor responsible for their own poverty and abstracts from the causes of poverty in capital-labour relations and the socially- and spatially-uneven development of the capitalist economy. It is thereby in the long tradition of conservative understanding of poverty (Gough and Eisenschitz, 2006: Ch.1). Indeed, the promotion of resilience is inherently conservative in that it proposes a return to normality or equilibrium while failing to question the dysfunctional nature of that condition. The unobjectionable idea of resilience seeks to create a consensus within the area between all social actors, including capital and labour, and is thus depoliticising.

The new social democracy poses itself as opposed to neoliberalism. But in its actually-existing form, it internalises many tropes of neoliberalism (Reisman, 1991). People making their own jobs by being self-employed, providing their own reproduction services, pulling themselves up by their bootstraps and achieving resilience echo the neoliberal ideology of the individual being responsible for their own income and welfare. The social economy is to be powered by entrepreneurship, particularly that of disadvantaged groups. Public services are to be taken over by not-for-profits and voluntary organisations with wages and conditions inferior to state-provided employment, achieving exactly neoliberalism's prime aim for privatisations. The social capital research which argues that markets work better when supported by non-market processes such as the state, trust and customs fits in well with the neoliberal agenda of making 'imperfect markets' more efficient. This absorption of ideologically-dominant neoliberal themes is one reason that the new social democracy has achieved its popularity.

Our fundamental philosophical critique of the new social democracy was adumbrated long ago by Marx. Marx criticised those thinkers he called the 'true socialists' (usually now referred to as 'utopian socialists') such as Fourier and Proudhon, whose strategies had many similarities to the new social democracy. Marx remarked that 'true socialism' ceases 'to express the struggle of one class with the other', and represents 'not the interests of the proletariat, but the interests of Human Nature, of Man [sic] in general, who belongs to no class' (Marx and Engels, 1848: 30; see also Das, 2022a: 213). Implicit in the new social democracy is the idea of humankind in general, people apart from their class position and their setting in a particular society, capitalism. The new social democracy abstracts from the nature of capitalism as a class society, and thus does not see the undermining by capitalism of the production of trust, reciprocity and cooperation.

5.3 *Our Alternative: a Multi-scalar Class Struggle Politics*

The new social democracy seeks collaboration and consensus between capital and labour at the local scale to develop new forms of production and social reproduction. In contrast, we present a strategy for local socialist politics which locates it within class struggle and links it to higher spatial scales. The overriding need is to overcome the fragmentation, isolation, alienation, individualism and anomie of workers generated by five decades of neoliberalism. The local scale is a vital one in developing face-to-face networks of workers to confront both production and social-reproduction issues, and to begin to overcome the many types of division within the working class; the local is, then, an essential scale for left politics.

Local socialist strategy addresses both production (the local economy) and reproduction (home life, neighbourhoods, housing, transport, public services), and creates strong links between them. Community and civil society ties, as well as local trade union and workplace organisations, are built as militant and combative organisations. They seek to collaborate with others at higher spatial scales, regional, national and international. In this way, the competition between localities fostered by neoliberalism can be avoided. In this political environment, social enterprises can be built as genuinely empowering, and thus as small scale, partial glimpses of socialism. Rather than by-pass the local state, its resources should be increasingly subject to the demands of the organisations of workers. Demands are made on the local and national state to provide better resources for, and regulation of, production and reproduction.

Local socialist advance then does not take place in a local ghetto but relates to working class struggle at all spatial scales (see further Chapter 7).

We argue for the development of 'working class social capital': mutual relations of trust and cooperation and solidarity, which help the working class and not-exploiting producers to build political solidarity and thus contest the power of dominant classes and the state (Chapter 3). Because of the position of the state in capitalist society, positive cooperation between state officials and common people is difficult, except where there is a pro-poor political organization – working class social capital – putting pressure on the local state. Under these conditions, relations of trust and co-operation between workers and reformist state officials can produce some benefits for the masses (Chapter 5).

But local socialist struggles cannot succeed if they remain purely local. Localities where working class gains are made in, for example, wages and conditions, regulation of private renting or taxation of business, tend to be boycotted by capital (withdrawal from existing investments, lack of new investment), thus undermining those gains. This is because the major resources of society are in the hands of capital which is spatially mobile: money capital is completely mobile, merchant capital can switch spatially subject to production and consumption geographies, and productive capital can switch location in the time span of the depreciation of fixed capital, five to ten years. This spatial mobility is expressed as corporations which operate on national, continental and particularly global scales. The organisation of workers and poor producers needs to match the scale of capital. At the minimum, this means refraining from competition with workers in other localities. Thus trade unions in different sites of a corporation need to prevent the employer from playing the sites off against each other. Socialist-controlled local governments should not compete with other local areas for investment or national-government funding in a race to the bottom. More positively, gains made in one locality should be celebrated and publicised through national and international workers' organisations, to encourage and materially help their achievement elsewhere. In this way, national and international solidarity can stimulate workers' struggles within each locality (see further Chapter 7). Local and international advance are then not counterposed but treated as part of one process.

6   Outline of the Chapters

Chapter 2 describes and critiques associationism in the High Income Countries. It highlights the differences of associationism from traditional social democracy, and analysed how this change was underpinned by the wave of economic stagnation from the 1970s and capital's neoliberal offensive. It describes the diverse initiatives and forms which have been developed 'from below' as a response to the material and psychological depredations of neoliberalism, and examines some of the academic underpinnings of the new social democracy and associationism. It explores some tensions, contradictions and failures in the practice and theory of associationism, explains why the associationist economy cannot expand to replace capitalism. Associationism fails as a strategy for emancipation because it ignores, and seeks to sidestep, the dynamics of capital accumulation and the conflict between capital and labour.

Chapter 3 discusses 'society-centric' and 'state-society relation' approaches to social capital, and critiques these for neglecting class. The conservative political implications of social capital are discussed. The chapter develops an alternative class-based approach to social capital. The chapter develops the concept of 'working-class social capital', which refers to the ways in which social ties can support the collective action of the working class against capital, landowners and the state. The chapter also discusses the different ways in which the working class social capital can be produced within civil society as well as in the structure of relations between workers and 'relatively autonomous' state officials. The chapter concludes that there cannot be a social capital theory of society, because social capital differs between classes in both its resources and its aims, and because the material conditions of class society severely constrain the production of social capital in working class localities. Yet, within a class theory of society, social capital can play some role; how minor that role is depends on the specific issue at hand and is geographically variable.

Based on qualitative interviews in two rural areas in the Indian State of Odisha, and employing the theoretical framework laid out in Chapter 3, Chapter 4 examines whether, and to what extent, poor people of the daily wage labour class benefit from their social capital within civil society. The latter includes the norms and practice of reciprocity, 'bonding social capital', as well their associational life, 'bridging social capital'. The chapter shows how the economic-political conditions under which poor people live and the spatiality of these conditions severely constrain the production of social capital in its different forms. By reflecting on the dialectical relation between social capital and poverty, the chapter problematises the overly optimistic claims about social capital. It shows that it is untenable to posit social capital as an independent variable and poverty as a dependent variable.

Chapter 5 explores social capital at the interface between the state and civil society at the local scale, both conceptually and on the basis of empirical evidence from Odisha, India. Two questions are addressed. First, to what extent are there relations of trust and cooperation between local state officials and poor rural people. Second, what are the factors that explain the observed level of trust and cooperation between state representatives and the poor? It is found what where the power of state representatives and the resulting social-economic inequality between them and the poor exist unchecked, state-society synergy at the local scale is weak. By contrast, where there is a pro-poor local political organization – a possibility that usually falls outside the scope of social capital enquiry – there may be greater levels of state-society synergy with some benefits for the rural poor. The chapter reflects critically on some general conceptual issues regarding the nature of the relationship between the state and society.

Chapter 6 analyses the promise of and constraints on the social economy, and proposes a socialist strategy for it, extending and detailing the critique in Chapter 2. We locate the political ambiguity of the social economy in the contradictions of capitalist accumulation, particularly the contradictions between the socialisation of production and reproduction *and* value relations and class discipline. We show how the theory and practice of social economy have responded to these contradictions. This analysis of the mainstream actually-existing social economy throws doubt on associationists' optimistic view of it. We discuss the tensions between social enterprises' social aims and their economic survival within capitalism. On this basis, we consider how the social economy might fit within a wider strategy for socialism *beyond* capitalism. In particular, with leadership and strategy from the left it can show the potential for increasingly radical and far-reaching forms of socialisation and worker and citizen involvement, and can thus provide an important field for furthering the struggle for socialism. We advocate a strategy for the social economy centred on empowerment, the building of cooperative social relations, and links to the organised labour movement. Such a strategy can go beyond exemplary, isolated, small-scale enterprises of the poor.

In Chapter 7 we argue, contrary to much traditional left thought, that the local scale is vital for organising struggle against exploitation and oppressions. We present strategic ideas and specific politics for socialist politics at the local scale through class struggle against capital and against the state where it channels capitalist power. This contrasts with the approach of associationists and proponents of social capital who seek class collaboration at the local scale. The local scale is a vital one in developing face-to-face networks of workers to confront both production and social-reproduction issues, and in beginning to overcome the many types of division within the working class. Many key issues span production and reproduction spheres, and these are well addressed at the local level. The local state's resources should be increasingly subject to the demands of workers. The strategy of associationists and promoters of social capital, because it does not confront capital, is largely confined *within* the locality. In contrast, a central aspect of our proposed strategy is to develop links between local organisation and larger spatial scales of struggle against capitalism and for socialism.

References

Clements, D., Donald, A., Earnshaw, M., & Williams, A. (Eds.). (2008). *The Future of Community: Reports of Death Greatly Exaggerated*, London: Pluto Press.

Cowley, J., Kaye, A., Mayo, M., & Thompson, M. (1977). *Community or Class Struggle?* London: Stage One.

Cox, K. (1995). Globalization, competition and the politics of local economic development. *Urban Studies, 32*: 213–224.

Cox, K. (1996). The difference that scale makes. *Political Geography, 15*(8): 667–669.

Cox, K. (1998). Spaces of dependence, spaces of engagement and the politics of scale, or: Looking for local politics. *Political Geography 17*: 1–24.

Cox, K. (2018). Scale and territory, and the difference capitalism makes. In A. Paasi, J. Harrison, and M. Jones (Eds.), *Handbook on the Geographies of Regions and Territories*. Cheltenham: Edward Elgar.

Das, R. (2017). *Marxist Class Theory for a Skeptical World*. Leiden: Brill.

Das, R. (2022a). On The Communist Manifesto: Ideas for the Newly Radicalizing Public. *World Review of Political Economy, 13*(2): 209–244.

Das, R. (2022b). *Marx's* Capital, *Capitalism and Limits to the State: Theoretical considerations*. London: Routledge.

Duménil, G., & Lévy, D. (2011). *The Crisis of Neoliberalism*. Cambridge, MA and London, England: Harvard University Press.

Eisenschitz, A., & Gough, J. (1993). *The Politics of Local Economic Policy* Basingstoke: Macmillan.

Evans, P. (1997). Introduction: Development strategies across the public-private divide. In P. Evans. (Ed.), *State- society synergy*. Berkeley: University of California Press.

Fine, B. (2001). *Social Capital versus social theory: Political Economy and Social science at the Turn of the Millennium*. London: Routledge.

Fine, B. (2010). *Theories of Social Capital: Researchers Behaving Badly*. London: Pluto.

Flew, T. (2014). Six theories of neoliberalism. *Thesis Eleven, 122*(1): 49–71.

Gibson-Graham, J.K. (1996). *The End of Capitalism (As We Knew It): A Feminist Critique of Political Economy*, Oxford UK and Cambridge USA: Blackwell Publishers.

Gibson-Graham, J.K. (2006). *A Postcapitalist Politics*, Minneapolis: University of Minnesota Press.

Gough, J. (1991). Structure, system and contradiction in the capitalist space economy. *Environment and Planning D: Society and Space, 9*: 433–449.

Gough, J. (1992). Workers' competition, class relations and space, *Environment and Planning D: Society and Space, 10*: 265–286.

Gough, J. (2004a). *Work, Locality and the Rhythms of Capital.* London: Routledge.

Gough, J. (2004b). Changing scale as changing class relations: variety and contradiction in the politics of scale. *Political Geography, 23*(2): 185–211.

Gough, J. (2010). Workers' strategies to secure jobs, their uses of scale, and competing economic moralities: rethinking the 'geography of justice'. *Political Geography, 29*(3): 130–139.

Gough, J. (2020). Why Labour lost the British 2019 election: social democracy versus neoliberalism and the Far Right, *Class, Race and Corporate Power, 18*(2) Article 2

Gough, J., & Das, R. (2017). Introduction to special issue: Marxist geography. *Human Geography, 9*(3): 1–9.

Gough, J., & Eisenschitz, A. (2006). *Spaces of Social Exclusion.* Abingdon: Routledge.

Harvey, D. (2000). *Spaces of hope.* Edinburgh: Edunburgh University Press.

Jessop, B. (2012). Neoliberalism. *The Wiley-Blackwell Encyclopedia of Globalization.* Hoboken, New Jersey: Wiley-Blackwell.

Kotz, D. (2015). *The Rise and Fall of Neoliberal Capitalism.* Cambridge, MA: Harvard University Press.

Lees, R., & Mayo, M. (1985). *Community Action for Change.* London: Routledge and Kegan Paul.

Maher, S., & Aquanno, A. (2018). Conceptualizing Neoliberalism: Foundations for an Institutional Marxist Theory of Capitalism. *New Political Science, 40*(1): 33–50.

Mandel, E. (1978). *Late capitalism.* London: Verso.

Marston, S. A. (2000). The social construction of scale. *Progress in Human Geography, 24*(2), 219–242.

Marston, S. A., Jones, J. P., & Woodward, K. (2005). Human Geography without Scale. *Transactions of the Institute of British Geographers, 30*(4): 416–432.

Marx, K. (1887). Capital volume 1. *Marxists.org.* Retrieved from: https://www.marxists.org/archive/marx/works/download/pdf/Capital-Volume-I.pdf.

Marx, K., & Engels, F. (1848). *The communist manifesto.*

Moore, A. (2008). Rethinking scale as a geographical category: From analysis to practice. *Progress in Human Geography, 32*(2):203–225.

O'Connor, J. (2010). Marxism and the Three Movements of Neoliberalism. *Critical Sociology. 36*(5): 691–715.

Petras, J. (1997). Imperialism and NGOs in Latin America. *Monthly Review, 49*(7).

Putnam, R. (1993). *Making democracy work.* Princeton: Princeton University Press.

Putnam, R. (2000). *Bowling Along: The Collapse and Revival of American Community.* New York: Simon and Schuster.

Reisman, D. (1991). *Conservative Capitalism: The Social Economy*. London: Palgrave.

Roberts, M. (2016). *The Long Depression*. Chicago: Haymarket.

Saad-Filho, A., & Johnston, D. (Eds.). (2005). *Neoliberalism: A Critical Reader*. Pluto Press.

Shaikh, A. (2016). *Capitalism: Competition, Conflict Crises,* Oxford: Oxford University Press.

Sharzer, G. (2012). *No Local: Why Small-scale Alternative Won't Change the World*. Winchester: Zero.

Springer, S., Birch, K., & Macleavy, J. (2016). *The Handbook of Neoliberalism*. London: Routledge.

Taylor, P. (1987). The paradox of geographical scale in Marx's politics. *Antipode, 19*(3): 287–306.

Tittenbrun, J. (2013). *Anti-Capital: Human, Social and Cultural*. Farnham: Ashgate.

Trotsky, L. (1931). Permanent Revolution. *Mrxists.org*. Retrieved from: https://www .marxists.org/archive/trotsky/1931/tpr/pr-index.htm.

Volscho, T. (2017). The Revenge of the Capitalist Class: Crisis, the Legitimacy of Capitalism and the Restoration of Finance from the 1970s to Present. *Critical Sociology, 43*(2): 249–266.

Woolcock, M. (1998). Social capital and economic development: toward a theoretical synthesis and policy framework. *Theory and Society, 27*(2): 151–208.

World Bank. (2001). *World development Report – Attacking Poverty*. Oxford: Oxford University Press.

Wright, E.O. (2014). Socialism and real utopias. In R. Hahnel and E.O. Wright (Eds.), *Alternatives to Capitalism: Proposals for a Democratic Economy*. London: New Left Project.

CHAPTER 2

Associationism: the New Social Democracy from Below

Jamie Gough

1   The Emergence of a New Centre-Left Strategy

The promotion of social capital among the working class and the poor has in recent decades formed a part of all political-economic strategies in the High Income Countries (HICs), from the 'Big Society' of the neoliberal David Cameron to the 'community cohesion' initiatives of the Centre-Right to community-based militant anti-capitalism of the socialist left. But the political-economic strategy within which social capital plays the biggest role, and the one where its promotion is the most widely practised, is associationism. Associationism here denotes a strand within contemporary Centre-Left ideology and practice, which is distinct from – and constructs itself in opposition to – the 'traditional' social democracy whose heyday was the boom of the 1950s and 1960s. Whereas traditional social democracy (TSD) rested on a large role for the nation state in guiding and subsidising industrial development, including through state-owned industries, associationism limits state industrial policy to provision of infrastructure and support services. Whereas TSD was focused on corporations, whether privately or publicly owned, associationism is focused on small and medium enterprises and not-for-profit social enterprises, which achieve economies of scale through networking and cooperation with each other. While TSD promoted collaboration between capital and labour by giving an institutional role to trade unions, associationism envisages workers being empowered by their skill, by participating in the governance of their employing firm, by starting their own business, and by setting up cooperatives and social enterprises. Whereas TSD built public services under the direct control of national and local states and provided them on a universal basis, associationism sees these services as being provided through varied combinations of the state, private sector and civil society, and as being differentiated by social group and locality. TSD sought to redistribute income and social and economic opportunities by national processes overseen by the state working with capital, whereas associationism emphasises the self-activity of individuals, particular social groups and small collectives to improve their economic and social lives.

In terms of social divisions, TSD privileged 'class' understood as income differentiation, whereas associationism regards income classes as just one among many equally important 'identities' to be addressed, particularly gender, race/ethnicity and location. Whereas TSD rested on the action of national and local legislators and governments elected for a number of years by an electorate which remained passive between elections, associationism seeks continuous participation in politics through both state-sponsored forms and autonomous fora. Whereas TSD was concerned with national economic, social and political processes, associationism is focused on cooperation, community and social capital at the local and neighbourhood scales.

How did this shift in Centre-Left ideology and practice come about? From the late 19C in Western Europe and the US, TSD was an increasing challenge to liberal ('free market') politics. In the postwar boom between 1948 and 1973 it became the dominant politics in all HICs irrespective of the party in government, albeit it in very different forms in different countries. High rates of investment, strong growth of output and productivity, and low rates of unemployment, and, as cause and effect, high rates of profit (all unprecedented in capitalism before and since) enabled strong growth of wages. Investment and productivity were supported by substantial state industrial policies (again, of very different forms in different countries), state owned utilities and industries, and counter-cyclical fiscal and monetary policies. State spending on public services, the environment, and in some countries social housing grew massively. Women's participation in waged labour increased rapidly, supported by expanded public services. Tax revenues from both capital and labour increased strongly, and underpinned state progressive income transfers from rich to poor (Armstrong, Glyn and Harrison, 1991). All of these processes enabled deep cooperation between the classes, 'the postwar consensus'. 'Traditional social democracy' denotes these various enhanced roles of the state, resting on rapid economic growth and class consensus.

But from the 1950s the rate profit fell, undermined by capital accumulation itself; by the early 1970s it had reached such low levels that capital investment slowed dramatically (*ibid.*; Mandel, 1978; Roberts, 2016). In the fifty years since then, the world economy, with the exception of China since the 1990s, has experienced much lower rates of growth of output, productivity and wages and higher rates of unemployment and poverty than in the postwar boom. The new strategy of capital and states, neoliberalism, centred on increasing the share of output appropriated by capital and decreasing the share of labour, and allowing capital to flow from less profitable sectors and territories to (putatively) more profitable ones (Mandel, 1978; Roberts, 2016). Starting in the least profitable countries, the US and Britain, followed by continental Western Europe and, after 1990, by Japan, living standards of the population declined: many large workplaces closed; unemployment increased; wages, conditions and job security declined; public services deteriorated as governments cut spending and privatised parts of provision; ecology and the built environment deteriorated; the quality of essentials including food, water and air declined.

The onset of economic crisis and stagnation was initially met by strong resistance from trade unions in a number of HICs, notably the US, Britain, France, Italy, Portugal and Spain, which in some cases went from resistance to proposing socialist measures, particularly nationalisation of the major enterprises and banks. But by the late 1980s this wave had been defeated by capital and the repressive apparatuses of nation states. The social democratic parties of Europe, Canada, Australia and Japan, as well as the European Communist Parties, were organisationally and ideologically thrown into disarray: their strategy of gradual improvement in working class living standards and democratic rights through collaboration between labour with capital had been decisively repudiated by capital. Social democratic parties in government increasingly adopted neoliberal policies: depression of wages, shift of taxation from capital to labour, cuts to spending on public services, and deflationary monetary policy. Ideologues of neoliberalism (including new recruits in social democratic parties) launched an ideological offensive against postwar social democratic practice and its intellectual underpinnings in Keynesian economics broadly defined and in mainstream sociology. Neoliberal ideologues claimed that social democracy was responsible for the economic crisis: state industrial policy 'feather-bedded' unproductive capital and weakened incentives to innovate; state borrowing squeezed funds for private investment; state benefits undermined the work ethic by developing a 'dependency culture'; taxation distorted markets and undermined incentives for capital to invest and incentives for workers to work hard. (My account of the origins of economic stagnation above indicates the fallacy of this analysis.) Neoliberals proposed, rather, that the major economic decisions on investment, processes, products and their geographical location should be taken by firms and 'entrepreneurs' rather than by the state, since only they know their business in depth (following Hayek); the state should withdraw from industrial intervention; workers should accept the need for firms to be profitable, and the right of managers to manage production; trade unions should be reduced in power or eliminated since they are a monopolistic distortion of the free labour market; workers should no longer rely on unions or state benefits to survive; taxes should be reduced, particularly on capital and 'enterprise'; state spending should be reduced, particularly on public services; and regulation of business should be reduced.

In the face of the neoliberal offensive, both material and ideological, social democratic activists, politicians and academics have developed their strategies in three distinct directions, divergent responses to the difficulties of maintaining social democratic principles in a world dominated by neoliberalism. The first strategy has been to continue to defend TSD and argue for its relevance to the problems of contemporary HICs. Hutton (1995) and Mazzucato (2013) argue for strong state industrial, R&D and training policies, while Stiglitz, former head of the World Bank, argues for Keynesian fiscal and monetary policies. Most proponents of a Green New Deal use TSD arguments for state intervention to guide the private sector towards green production and to safeguard popular interests in the transition to no carbon. The left of social democratic parties in Western Europe, and the left of the US Democratic Party, argue for a decrease in the power of finance vis a vis productive capital (a traditional theme of Keynesianism), strengthened state intervention in production, renationalisation of utilities and public services, and increased spending on public services (Costello, Michie and Milne, 1989, Varoufakis, 2016; Labour Party, 2019; McDonnell, 2018; Adler and Bechler, 2019). They also called for, variously, stronger protections for workers, improved trade union rights, the representation of workers on company boards, and worker profit sharing schemes. Although these ideas were formally similar to TSD, their class content had shifted to the left: in the postwar boom, TSD ideas were supported by capital, whereas since the 1980s few sections of capital have fully supported them (Gough, 2020). TSD was now against the current. While elements of this programme were found in a weak form in government programmes in Germany and Scandanavia and under Socialist Party governments in France, Spain and Portugal, neoliberalism dominated in those countries, and especially in the US and Britain.

Another set of social democratic activists and intellectuals have taken a different path, which we shall call 'post-modern social democracy' (PMSD). PMSD critiques TSD in ways which have many overlaps with and borrowings from the neoliberal critique.[1] They accept Hayek's argument that private enterprises

---

1 Leading proponents of PMSD in Britain have been Stuart Hall and Martin Jacques, their inappropriately-named journal *Marxism Today*, and the highly-influential volume they edited, *New Times* (1989); the public intellectuals Charlie Leadbetter and David Held; the prolific writings of Geof Mulgan (for example 1991) and the think-tank he founded, Demos; social-economists such as Geof Hodgson (1984) and the journal *Economy and Society*. The geographer Doreen Massey, particularly in her post-modern phase (Massey, 2005), and the geography journal *Space and Society* has also been influential in developing PMSD. For a poetic argument for PMSD see Beilharz (1994). For critiques of PSDM, see Meiskins Wood (1986) and Calinicos (1989).

know their own business better than the state can, and the state industrial policy, particularly of a corporatist (Japanese) or dirigiste (French) kind, is 'bureaucratic' and 'inflexible'. A 'flexible', technologically innovative economy requires decentralised decision making and collaboration of labour with capital. PMSD argues that state-run public services (including state-owned broadcasting) tend to be inefficient, bureaucratically managed, and insensitive to the needs of diverse social groups. The trade unions are criticised for their intransigent and futile opposition to technological change and restructuring, for their unwillingness to put forward innovative ideas for improving processes and products; PMSD is hostile to collective action by labour against capital.[2] PMSD argues that the working class is now too fragmented and differentiated to be a coherent analytical category or political actor, and that multiple other social identities (of gender, sexuality, race/ethnicity, locality) are equally important. Rather than the single collective of the working class, multiple identities and social differences require multiple, overlapping collectives which are often temporary and tactical. The theorists of PMSD argue that both Marxism and TSD have been overly concerned with the 'vertical' power of some social actors over others, particularly the power of capital over labour, leading to a strategy of workers seeking greater power over capital or its abolition. In contrast, PMSD seeks to build people's 'power to' through 'horizontal' collectives, networks and associations (Allen, 1999; 2003; Amin and Thrift, 2002). PMSD argues that the modern state, in all its actions, is insensitive to difference and diversity, paralleling the neoliberal idea that the state cannot respond to individual wants. The PMSD solution is not to simply cut back the state, as neoliberals propose, but to 'decentre' it, open it to, and break down its separation from, civil society, and thus democratise it (Laclau and Mouffe, 1985; Allen, 2003). The state thus becomes an enabler rather than a dictator, a participant in discussions and experiments rather than a planner. The PMSD strategy thus claims to be based in qualitative changes in capitalist society since the 1970s, the 'New Times': in economics from Fordism to flexibility; in sociology from class to multiple, intersectional identities; and in politics from passive representation to participation and democracy (Hall and Jacques, 1989; Lash and Urry, 1987).[3]

---

2   After the defeat of the British miners' strike in 1985, the editor of *Marxism Today* placed a poster on his door which read 'We defeated the miners'.

3   Some PMSD writing has its philosophical roots in positivist social science, particularly Weberianism; this includes the economic-and political-institutionalists and most socio-economists. But most PMSD writing has its philosophical roots in post-structuralism and postmodernism. Post-structuralism developed from the 1980s as a critique of Althusserian structuralist Marxism (the main intellectual approach of the European Communist Parties)

PMSD has been developed in two distinct directions which we shall term 'productivist syndicalism' and 'associationism' respectively. Productivist syndicalism seeks to build the power of skilled workers within the mainstream economy, particularly in the private sector. This is not through collective resistance to the employer, but on the contrary through collaboration with them. Workers are to use their skills and knowledge to solve problems in the production process, and thus gain 'voice' within the firm. Cooperation replaces 'old fashioned' conflict (Cooke and Morgan, 1998). This strategy is seen as feasible in the present epoch of capitalism and indeed going with the grain of it. The world economy is seen as in transition from a 'Fordist' model to some kind of 'flexible accumulation' or 'flexible specialisation' (Murray, 1989). Products are no long standardised but varied and fast changing. The production process tends to be more skilled and to require more autonomy for, and reflexivity from, the worker (Piore and Sabel, 1984; Hirst and Zeitlin, 1989; Storper, 1998; Lash and Urry, 1987). The economy is increasingly knowledge-based, in some left accounts because of demands from workers for more fulfilling work (Wainwright, 1994). Corporations no longer control industries, as smaller firms exploit innovations. The Fordist world-spatial division of labour between high level, skilled work in central regions and routine, standardised production in the periphery is giving way to regional agglomeration of each industry. The notion, popular in the 1970s and 1980s, that capitalism systematically deskills work (Braverman, 1974; Gorz, 1978) is turned on its head.[4]

Productivist syndicalism lies within the PMSD strategy in diagnosing a new 'post-Fordist' epoch of capitalism and in rejecting 'Fordist' conflict between

---

which argued, correctly, that Althusser's theory was unable to account for empirically important features of social structures. However, they did not locate this problem in Althusser's lack of dialectics. Rather, some post-structuralists such as Hirst concluded that abstract structures and processes as such should simply be abandoned in favour of empirical description. Postmodernists express the same point in their rejection of all 'grand narratives'. Other post-structuralists such as Wright, Resnik, Woolf and Gibson-Graham acknowledge the existence of structures but located the empirical in 'over-determination' where structures relate externally rather than dialectically through internal relations. This results in an arbitrariness and eclecticism of explanation which is no explanation, and thus empiricism (see Das, 2017: 125–7). Other post-structuralists, particularly neo-Gramscians such as Hall, Laclau, Mouffe, (later) Massey and Jessop, rejected structures other than the ideological-political, converging with Foucault's power-knowledge as the fundamental social structure. These authors have given PMSD a strong strand of philosophical idealism and moralism, in which political ideas exist detached from, and putatively dominating, material social processes.

4   In the Regulationist theorisation of Jessop (1993), a new, post-Fordist epoch is similarly conceptualised as a 'Schumpeterian workfare state' within which technical innovation is the key driving force of capitalism and the state refrains from industrial intervention.

capital and labour. Rather than the nation- or industry-wide structures of post-war industrial relations, its politics is enacted in a fragmented way, workplace by workplace and even worker by worker. Like TSD, it promotes technological change and worker skill, but it does so without a substantial role for the state.[5]

Another strand of PMSD, which we term associationism, has eschewed attempts to subject medium and large scale capital to democratic or worker influence, whether through TSD or productivist syndicalism, and instead focuses on the creation of an economy of cooperative and not-for-profit enterprises, community organisations, and common ownership.[6] Alongside these economic forms, it seeks a widening of political democracy at the local scale, sometimes through a democratisation of the existing local state, sometimes through autonomous fora. Its aims are in part material – the creation of waged jobs and the provision of useful goods and services; but it also aims to change social relations – fostering social capital and community, cooperation and solidarity, thus empowering individuals and overcoming their isolation and alienation. Its aspiration is to be a radical alternative to capitalism, 'beyond capitalism', 'post-capitalism', or 'capitalism not as you know it'. Its histori-cal roots stretch back to the utopian socialism of the 19C of Fourier, Owen, Proudhon and others; hundreds of settlements were founded, particularly in North America, which attempted to implement these principles (though most collapsed within a few decades; for a critical review see Harvey, 2000: Ch.8). In the last four decades, a number of terms have been used for this political pro-ject: the social economy, the Third Sector, community enterprise, community control, commoning, the solidarity economy, the participatory economy. The project focuses strongly on the local scale – neighbourhoods, towns, districts of cities, rural districts, and is sometimes referred to simply (though mislead-ingly) as 'localism'. As we describe in the next section, associationist practice has taken many different forms, a pluralism which is seen as a strength. It is pragmatic rather than programmatic, experimental rather than analytical.

We have seen, then, that the long wave of stagnation which began in the 1970s, and the neoliberal strategy of capital in response to it, has produced a

---

5   For a critique of the thesis of a new epoch of 'flexible production', see Gough (1992; 1996a; 1996b). Eisenschitz and Gough (1996) show the ineffectiveness of the productive syndicalist strategy in its own terms, and argue that its effect is to increase divisions within the work-ing class.

6   Our use of the term 'associationism' as distinct from productive syndicalism might be confus-ing, in that Cooke and Morgan's discussion of the latter strategy names it 'the associational economy'. 'Association' in their work appears as the association of workers within an enter-prise with each other, and the association of those workers with management.

number of reformulations of social democratic thought. We have argued that three in particular have been prominent: a restatement of traditional social democracy focused on the national state; productivist syndicalism focused on the workplace; and associationism practised in localities and communities. Both in theory and practice there have been numerous overlaps and combinations of these strategies; but they are distinct in their respective logics. Of the three, associationism gives the most prominence to the promotion and building of social capital – indeed, this is its central aim. In countries such as Britain associationism has been the most implemented of the three strategies, given that dominant sectors of capital have been uninterested in the TSD strategy (Gough, 2020) and the tradition of authoritarian or 'distant' industrial relations has blocked the development of management-worker cooperation at the enterprise level. The rest of this chapter is therefore concerned with associationism, though linking and comparing it with other strands of social democracy. Section 2 describes the very diverse initiatives and forms which have been developed 'from below' as a response to the material and psychological depredations of neoliberalism. Section 3 looks at some of the academic underpinnings and support for associationism, in addition to the theorists of PMSD already discussed. Section 4 examines the tensions, contradictions and failures in the practice and theory of associationism. The concluding section considers the associationist project as a whole: why the associationist economy cannot expand to replace capitalism; the moralism and idealism of associationism; and how it incorporates and reproduces neoliberalism. We conclude that associationism fails as a strategy for emancipation because it ignores, and seeks to sidestep, the dynamics of capital accumulation and the conflict between capital and labour.

2   The Bottom-Up Practice of Associationism

Associationism has been an ad hoc, fragmented and 'bottom up' response to the long wave of stagnation of the world economy that began in the 1970s. Community groups and activists, social entrepreneurs, groups of workers, and some local governments and local economic agencies have taken small-scale initiatives to create or preserve jobs, provide social services, supply useful goods and services and healthy food to local people, provide low rent and secure housing, and improve the local natural and built environment. For many of the actors, the motivation for these initiatives has not been purely material but also the social relations they seek to construct. Economic stagnation and neoliberalism have fostered (and in turn been reproduced by) a deep individualisation in which each person and household has to 'stand on their own two feet', and an exacerbation of competition for access to jobs, housing and public services. Many people have experienced this regime as isolating and disempowering, producing an epidemic of depression and loneliness (Sennett and Cobb, 1993; Sharzer, 2022). In contrast, associationist initiatives typically involve cooperation and solidarity at a local or neighbourhood scale, and a building of neighbourly and community ties – 'social capital'. They thus promise empowerment and self-esteem, not through neoliberal individual self-promotion and competition, but through building collaborative creativity, altruism and reciprocity, mutual support and friendship.

A social economy of not-for-profit enterprises is developed in variegated forms: worker-owned cooperatives providing goods, services or marketing; community enterprises with waged jobs, workers on trainee allowances or voluntary labour producing commodities; community enterprises contracted by the state to provide public services; enterprises providing environmental clean-ups, home insulation or repairs of consumer durables. For-profit or not-for-profit local enterprises may originate as split-offs of local parts of large organisations, whether of the state or corporations. In addition, conventional privately-owned enterprises such as small firms and self-employment are seen as a potentially empowering alternative to employment by corporations or the state where one controls one's own job, rather than as a means to enrichment (Sharzer, 2012). This private enterprise appears as personally enriching, creative and social to the extent that the product is superior to the mass produced: artisanal brewing, organic farming, craft jewellery, or body- and mind-therapy. Associationists seek to group these enterprises together into community-owned premises, often converted former factories, mills or warehouses, to provide them with cheap rents, enable some joint services, and develop mutual help and friendships.

Collective forms of provision for social reproduction are developed, such as housing cooperatives, co-housing (a dozen or more households living in a block with collective facilities and sharing of care work), collective households larger than the nuclear family (communes), child care and school-run clubs, and mutual therapy associations. Unconventional housing arrangements are difficult in expensive big cities; many are squats or are in remote rural areas. Rural communes may also be units of production in farming, crafts or environmental education. They then embody all the ideals of associationism, bridging the divide between income-earning and social reproduction through collectivity. Voluntary organisations, often with paid coordinators, and self-help groups are developed to provide services such as child care, gardens, park maintenance or support to schools and hospitals; the latter merge with long standing organisations such as Parent-Teacher Associations and hospital visitors. Local churches are often involved given that they are traditional dispensers of charity (a role celebrated by some left commentators: Byrne, 1999; Wills, 2016).

Many initiatives involve food, such as small scale organic farming (including deep green agriculture such as permaculture which requires much labour with low productivity in money terms), retailers who source locally, food purchase and sale cooperatives which cut out intermediaries, community vegetable gardens whether official or 'guerilla', 'free gathering' of fruit growing on public or private land, community or state-owned allotments, and food banks providing donated or recycled food. Another major focus is the environment, such as community gardens, tree-planting, rewilding of derelict spaces, plant and seed swaps, and litter-picking. Some local campaigns aim for a wholesale greening of the locality; in Britain, local activists in Transition Towns aim rapidly to reduce carbon emissions across the town or city.[7]

Associationists seek to keep money within the community or locality through encouraging local purchasing by residents and local sales by businesses. Local currencies may be organised, in which local enterprises may (partially) pay their employees and which are accepted for payment by local consumer services, thus expanding the local money supply (North, 2007). In Local Exchange and Trading Schemes people use their skills to do jobs for each other, accounted in labour hours which the scheme 'banks' – the exchange of decommodified work (Lee, 1996). Locally-based credit unions provide basic bank accounts for the poor, encourage them to save, and provide small loans at low rates of interest to by-pass the loan sharks (Fuller and Jonas, 2002; McKillop and Wilson, 2011).

Despite associationalists' scepticism towards the state, local government has been important in the growth of the sector. Some local state assets have been transferred to community ownership, and some services previously run

---

7 In the last two decades, the largest scale and most ambitious initiatives in production of an associationist type have been in fundamental software and the internet; these include Open Source software as an alternative to Microsoft and Apple, Wikepedia, and projects to develop non-corporate social media. They rely on the unpaid work of software professions, motivated by social good, through international collaborations. Open Source software is now a major part of global basic software. There are nevertheless problems in this form of work (see for example Moore and Taylor, 2009) which are similar to the problems of associationist voluntary work discussed below. We do not consider this form of associationism in this chapter because it is not rooted in localities and does not seek to develop 'social capital'. Another international movement which might be termed associationist is Fair Trade, a not-for-profit which organises better prices for small producers in the Majority World with large purchasers in the HICs.

by the local state (nurseries, schools, social care, park maintenance, swim-
ming pools) have been transferred to not-for-profit community organisations
either to run autonomously or on contract; the latter are regarded as a better
alternative to contracting to the private sector. In recent years, some left local
authorities in Britain (following from widespread practice in the 1980s) have
attempted to channel their purchasing of print, school equipment, and so on
either to local cooperatives or at least to local firms. This 'new municipalism'
has also set up locally-controlled energy enterprises, whether for generation
(solar, wind) (Henley, 2020), home insulation, or energy retailing; because of
the capital requirements these are generally owned by the local state, but are
nevertheless regarded as part of the associationalist mix because of their small
scale compared with the majors (Hatcher, 2021).

Many of these initiatives have been started by individuals or small groups,
or by 'social entrepreneurs' (Leadbetter, 1997), and have remained isolated.
But associationism aims to grow and multiply these initiatives through varied
forms of local socialisation – locally-based networks, support organisations,
and cross-subsidies and synergies between social enterprises. A model has
been the Mondragon network of cooperative enterprises in the Basque country
which now comprises dozens of (mainly) cooperative enterprises, including a
bank, with multiple interlinkages. Development Trusts and Community Land
Trusts are set up using public or charitable funding or transfers from the public
sector to acquire land, build affordable housing, buy out slum landlords, and
build or acquire small commercial units. Over decades, these property trusts
can potentially earn substantial income which is ploughed back into the trust.
They may achieve viability by using unpaid or training-wage labour, drawing
on local good will. State power and resources may be needed to enable community control. The state may buy land and premises to enable communities
to wrest control from the private sector, as in the purchase of expensive land
for social housing at Coin Street in London in the 1980s following a community
campaign (Brindley et al., 1992: Ch.5). In the Dudley Street neighbourhood of
Boston a community coalition was able to make the Redevelopment Agency
apply legislation intended for the hotel industry to allow it to buy out slum
landlords (Medoff and Sklar, 1994). However necessary the state involvement,
however, associationalists wish the *ownership* of the social economy to be
community based. Thus in the Boston case funds were obtained to enable the
social housing to be vested with the community. Community ownership can
enable the accumulation of capital for investment in new enterprises, as has
been done by the South Shore Bank in the black ghetto of south Chicago (Taub,
1994), thereby making the sector more autonomous and innovative. Both community enterprises and small firms may be fostered by local support agencies

funded either by the state or by corporations' 'social responsibility' initiatives; support for such entrepreneurship is often provided specifically to working class and BME people, women and other oppressed groups.

The development of associationism has been strongly uneven between nations and regions in the HICs, depending on their political cultures. The Mondragon federation in the Basque country started in the 1950s as a way of dealing with extreme poverty and lack of political freedom under the Franco dictatorship, building on Catholic paternal philanthropy and Basque nationalism. The extensive network of social enterprises in the province of Quebec, supported by a favourable legal framework, has arisen from its strong social democratic traditions and the solidarity of French-Quebecois nationalism *vis a vis* the Canadian state. From the 1980s, at a time of rising Scottish nationalism, the state in Scotland encouraged the social economy, which by 2001 comprised 2,700 enterprises employing 25,500 people with value added of £200m per annum (Gordon, 2002). Strikingly, in all three cases, associationism was developed through solidarity in the face of a widely-acknowledged external oppressor. In contrast, in other regions and countries, associationist initiatives have been weakly linked with each other and weakly politically supported, as Amin et al. (2002) showed for England.

Associationists are strong supporters of Universal Basic Income (UBI), a minimum income paid by the state to every citizen. In the last twenty years or so, it has become a favourite policy particularly, though not only, of the Centre-Left (Standing, 2017). A commonly cited motivation for UBI is to eliminate poverty by by-passing the state benefits system with its means testing, exceptions and 'bureaucratic' barriers. But it is also promoted as a way of supporting people who wish to develop their skills and aptitudes in ways that are not, or not initially, marketable, or who wish to construct alternative or conventional enterprises, or as a means of subsidising work in social enterprises which are not fully commercial; associationists support UBI particularly for the latter reasons. A central problem of UBI is that, if it is sufficiently large to provide a decent standard of living (comparable to the median wage), and especially if it is genuinely universal rather than means-tested or administered through the tax system, then the cost is enormous. This means that it cannot be funded by local states, as the localist ideology of associationism favours, since in no country does the local state have sufficient tax base. There have been 'experiments' in a number of countries with locally-paid UBI, but the level of payment is wholly inadequate for associationist aims. Associationists are therefore compelled to look to the nation state, or large regional government, for an adequate system of UBI.

These economic and social initiatives often give rise to, or are allied to, particular *political* initiatives in the conventional sense, especially at the local scale. The practices of the state, whether national or local, are perceived as at best as insensitive and crude, and at worst as authoritarian and tyrannous. These traits have of course always between present in the capitalist state, but they have intensified under neoliberalism. People have responded by attempting to create forms of political decision making at the neighbourhood and local scales which involve direct rather than representative democracy, and which encourage participation from people who have not previously been involved in conventional politics (party membership, elections, local representatives and office holders). In a large part, these political initiatives are a modification of established local government rather than its abolition or supersession: public consultations on particular policies and government initiatives; neighbourhood forums to advise on policies affecting the neighbourhood and possibly make policy on them; state-funded development agencies with substantial representation from community groups; and participatory budgeting in which popular assemblies decide on priorities for state spending (Sintomer et al., 2008). Less common are autonomous political fora set up by community activists as alternatives to the local state; these may discuss particular problems such as housing, transport or the environment, or they may seek to develop a new 'vision' or popular plan for the neighbourhood or district in all its aspects (see for example Mackintosh and Wainwright, 1987: Chs 12 and 14).[8]

The ideology of the associationist movement is strongly localist. Negatively, it sees globalised big business and nation states as having failed; positively, it proposes that by building collaborations, social capital and community at the scale of the neighbourhood or locality basic needs can be met, or at least addressed, and ordinary people can overcome their isolation and feel empowered. These collaborations depend on face-to-face meetings, acquaintance and trust, which are impossible to construct at larger spatial scales. Accordingly, associationist activists support decentralisation of economy and state in the name of local control and even local autonomy. Localism and decentralisation are indeed items of faith for most associationist practitoners and theorists (Eisenschitz and Gough, 1993: Ch.1).

---

8   The ideal form of state decision making for associationists is the citizens' assembly. Citizens chosen at random meet for weeks or months, advised by experts, to make recommendations on a particular question. 'Polarised' debate between political parties is avoided, participants are encouraged to listen to each other, and issues can be considered in depth. Citizens' assemblies were used in recent times before the Irish referendum on abortion and the Chilean referendum on a new constitution. But we do not know of any examples at a local scale, probably, in part, because of the large cost to the state.

This sketch of associationism suggests the enormous diversity and eclecticism of forms of the movement, in contrast, for example, to the unified nature of neoliberalism (united around the subordination of labour to capital, the freedom of capital, and raising the rate of profit). And this diversity speaks of a number of potential tensions in the project. Associationism encompasses both community-owned, not for profit enterprises, cooperative-owned enterprises operating in the market, and conventional private firms. It includes both waged work and unpaid 'voluntary work'. Some projects are for production of goods and services, other for trade (e.g. LETS), other for money and demand (local currencies, credit unions). Some initiatives depend on capital or revenue subsidies from the (local) state, while others seek to take services out of the 'dead hand' of the state and thus dissolve the state into civil society. Some political forms of associationism are reforms of the state, or rely on state organisation, while others wish to build an autonomous civil society. There are tensions between pure localism and lobbying national and regional governments. While most associationists abide by the existing laws, others violate private property through squatting, guerilla gardening or free gathering. But the theoreticians of associationism such as Hodgson (1984) and Schemlzer et al. (2022) argue that it is precisely this diversity that gives associationism its strength, since it corresponds to the real complexity and diversity of the contemporary capitalist economy. Aspects of the latter include the diversity of production technologies and products, the different minimum efficient scales of different branches of production, the different kinds of knowledge and skill needed in these different branches, the different customers and geographies of sale, and the complex mixes of types of labour involved in social reproduction (unpaid domestic work, purchase of commodities, public services). Diverse mixes of paid and unpaid work, types and size of enterprise, trade links and finance are therefore needed to attain reasonable efficiency; there is no simple institutional blue print. This is a dynamic process, requiring constant social and institutional innovation and experiment. At the level of politics, this requires pragmatism – attention to what can feasibly be achieved in the given situation with the resources and participants involved, rather than the application of economic-political principles. Some authors have conceived this pragmatism as a principle in itself of associationism (Wills, 2016).

3   Theories of Associationism

While associationism has arisen principally as a practical response to neoliberal austerity through the actions of community activists, social entrepreneurs and local politicians, it has been extensively supported and theorised by academics and public intellectuals. I have already touched on some of the academic arguments for PMSD in general. On associationism specifically, there are a number of writers whose work provides an intellectual backdrop, and others who have presented a full associationist programme. I now briefly examine how these theorists have fed into associationism, and indicate some problems of these theories; some further problems will emerge in my critique of associationism in section 4. My critique is from the standpoint of the Marxist theory of capitalism: the requirement on workers (that is, the 90% who rely on wages for their survival) to sell their labour power to capital, the extraction of surplus value through capitalist control of the labour process, the reinvestment of accumulated surplus value to further expand it, and the multiple contradictions of these processes (Mandel, 1968; Harrison, 1978; Gough and Das, 2017). I shall refer to this theory as 'Capitalist Value Relations'.

Proudhon, as the most influential utopian socialist of the 19C, has been an important reference point for associationists. He supported small scale artisanal capitalism as liberatory for workers and small owners, but argued that it was exploited and limited by bank finance. As Marx pointed out, he ignored the tendency of capital to centralise and concentrate, and he occluded the exploitation of workers by capital – for Proudhon exploitation was an attribute of rentiers not of capitalism as such. The enthusiasm for small producers freed from rentiers is fundamental to associationism. Later in the 19C, Henry George made a similar argument: the central problem of capitalism was not capital accumulation or the exploitation of workers by capital but rather the parasitism of the landowners.

The title of E.F. Schumacher's influential book, *Small is Beautiful: a study of economics as if people mattered* (1974), could be the motto of associationism. Schumacher criticises capitalism for its dominance by profit-seeking, leading to lack of consideration for the creativity and well-being of workers, the quality of products, and the negative impacts on ecology. In social democratic fashion, he proposes a pragmatic balance between profitability and social benefit, between efficiency and well-being, and between private and public sector. His distinctive argument, however, is that these balances cannot be achieved through large production units or the big state; only small scale enterprise can negotiate the detailed trade-offs, and only at this scale can workers and consumers influence the enterprise. Technologies of production should therefore be appropriate for the small enterprise, 'intermediate technologies' which, as a civil servant, Schumacher promoted in the Third World. Large corporations are not open to social influence because they are run in the interests of anonymous rentier shareholders. Schumacher, like Proudhon, ignores the deep tendency towards concentration of capital, and ignores the discipline of labour by capital even (in fact especially) within small firms.

The later work of Andre Gorz, particularly *Goodbye to the Working Class* (1982) and *Critique of Economic Reason* (1988), is a plea for associationism as the sphere of autonomous and creative 'free time', sharply distinct from the tyranny of work in capitalist production. Gorz's early work anatomised the capitalist control of the labour process, deskilling, and the disempowerment of workers (1978; cf Braverman, 1974; Gordon et al., 1982). Implicit was the possibility of workers' self-management at the enterprise level or at the level of the whole economy, socialism. But the defeats of trade unions by capital in the 1970s and 1980s (section 2) led to Gorz abandoning socialism as an aim. His later work justifies this by emphasising even more starkly the disempowerment of workers within capitalist waged employment, both in the 'high productivity sector' of high mechanisation/ automation where workers are the slave of the machine, and the 'low productivity sector' of consumer services where precarious work renders workers as 'servants'. In neither sector can workers influence the production process, let alone control it.[9] The traditional socialist aim of worker's non-alienated labour and creativity therefore need to be realised in the realm of free time. All citizens should be paid the same wage or state transfer payment irrespective of their employment or lack of it, a version of UBI. The amount of free time should be increased by a progressive diminution of the waged-working day, week or year, enabled by increases in productivity through automation; capitalist production of commodities is already sufficient for everyone's needs and there is no need to increase it. The realm of free time can then flourish: hobbies, sports, play and cultural production; artisanal work; not-for-profit enterprises of low productivity; domestic and caring work, no longer a stressful burden but now a creative and valued activity. A further twist to Gorz's argument is to deplore the growth of consumer services, whether private or public sector, on the grounds that they substitute for, and therefore decrease, domestic and caring work in the home, which for Gorz is a realm of freedom. Gorz has an extraordinarily rosy view of this work, which goes against fifty years of feminist scholarship and practice. But it arises naturally from his view of non-waged work as a realm of self-determination and self-realisation.

Gorz's later work shares all the key aspects of theorists of associationism. It illustrates how the defeats of the workers' movement in early neoliberal

---

9   Many people who have not read Gorz assume that 'farewell to the working class' argues a 'bourgeoisification' thesis, that 'we are all middle class now' and content in our working lives, explaining the decline in trade union membership. Gorz's argument is precisely the opposite: that waged workers are completely proletarianised, deskilled and disempowered.

period led to left intellectuals abandoning the goal of socialism. It neglects the essential dynamics of capital accumulation: capital will not agree to an ever-diminishing working week, nor to the transfer of income to the 'low productivity sector' or to non-waged workers. There is no agent who could force capital to accept these arrangements, since he denies that workers within production have any power. Gorz abstains from changing the relations of production, and instead seeks a change the distribution of money-income.

The writing of the US socio-economist Elinor Ostrom on the commons, for which she received the Nobel prize in economics, have been another important inspiration for associationists. Ostrom has done extensive empirical research on small farmers and fishers, mainly in the Majority World, investigating how they have organised governance systems to prevent free riders in forests and seas from depleting the commons – 'the tragedy of the commons'. Her 'socio-ecological systems' framework (Ostrom, 1990) sets out rules for successfully managing these commons: boundaries around who can participate; mechanisms for making collective choices; monitoring; sanctions on violators; scalar hierarchy of organisations; recognition of these organisations by the state. She argues that these need to be underpinned by appropriate social relations – effective communication, trust and reciprocity. Associationism in the HICs does not generally engage with extensive territorial commons. But it has seen Ostrom's work as a guide to dealing with common property of community organisations and the local state, and for governing networks of cooperative enterprises across a locality. Ostrom's formal, rule-based systems have probably seldom been achieved in the HICs; but the mostly face-to-face communication, trust and reciprocity she argues for are exactly the social relations – the social capital – to which associationists aspire.[10] Note that Ostrom's choice of research subjects, small independent producers, means that she does not have to consider the accumulation of capital nor capital-labour relations and their potential to disrupt cooperation and consensus.

The Analytical Marxist Eric Olin Wright (2014) has given an argument for an associational economy, as part of his reconsideration of socialist economics placed within the long tradition of Marxist and Keynesian writing and

---

10   The themes of trust and reciprocity are also central to the productive syndicalism variant of PMSD (section 2). Flexible specialist industrial districts achieve their high productivity and innovation through trusting and accommodating relations between the SMEs in their mutual contracting, their eschewing of cost-cutting strategies, and their willing contribution to collective services; and relations between firms and their (skilled) workers are based on trust and flexible cooperation (Piore and Sabel, 1984; Hirst and Zeitlin, 1989; Storper, 1998).

practice. This work is based in Wright's earlier work on class (2009), which shifts the focus from the exploitation of all workers by capital and analyses the distribution of value among different sections of wage earners, arguing that managers, technicians and skilled workers are able to appropriate a part of surplus value and thus effectively exploit other workers, thus developing hybrid or contradictory class locations. On this basis, Wright argues against the traditional Marxist (revolutionary socialist) aim of wholly publicly owned economy, on the grounds that it is inevitably dominated, in more or less dictatorial fashion, by a managerial and technical elite. Instead, he argues for two strategies within capitalism: a 'symbiotic' strategy, what I have referred to as Traditional Social Democracy; and an 'interstitial' strategy of social, community and not-for-profit enterprises, participatory budgeting and UBI, which I call associationism. Wright's nomenclature suggests the positioning of these strategies in relation to the mainstream capitalist economy, the symbiotic strategy fully engaged in it, the interstitial strategy operating in its margins. The two strategies together constitute a heterogeneous and pluralist economy, mixing capitalism, the state and popular democracy; the aim is for the democratic elements, that is, the influence of the working class, to grow: a return to the class consensus of the postwar boom.[11]

Perhaps the most influential intellectual input into associationism in the last 30 years has been the work of Julie Graham and Kathy Gibson, sometimes writing as J.K.Gibson-Graham. Gibson-Graham, together with Stephen Resnick and Richard Wolff, have developed a post-structuralist, post-modern and 'anti-essentialist' political economy. They reject the Marxist account of capitalism as centred on the extraction of surplus value by *control of workers in their labour within the workplace*; rather, capitalism consists of systems of *redistribution of output/income* between capital, workers and other social actors. They reject the Marxist view that capital is compelled to expand itself without limit through the exploitation of labour, accumulation of surplus value, and its reinvestment in production. For Gibson-Graham, capitalism is not a totality centred on Value Relations but rather a plethora of diverse types of production and relations of distribution: productive and unproductive labour; class and non-class relations; capitalist and petty commodity production; unpaid domestic work; feudal/serf relations. These each exist as a *sui generis*, separate practice; they interact externally (contingently) with each other rather than internally (necessarily) as parts of the capitalist whole; none

---

11   For a detailed exposition and critique of Wright's theory of class and his strategy for democratic capitalism, see Das, 2017: Chs 2 and 4.

is more important than the others. Each individual can play a variety of roles not only over their lifetime but at the same moment: worker, exploiter, shareholder, independent producer, trader, servant/mistress, landlord/tenant, care giver/receiver, thief/victim of theft. Drawing on postmodern discourse theory, Gibson-Graham argue that the economic practices in which the individual is involved do not determine their moral-political nature; rather, individuals can freely construct their own narrative, aims and evaluations which are as important as the material practices.[12] Within this framework, Gibson-Graham argue that a community-collectivist (associationist) economy with progressive aims can grow and flourish. Since any economic practice can be conducted without any substantial constraint from any other, community enterprise can flourish without the constraint of Capitalist Value Relations. If individuals have multiple economic roles, they can chose which ones to practice and not to practice. If the moral-political value of those relations is (at least partly) a subjective matter, then they can choose to validate practices which others might regard as oppressive such as unpaid domestic and caring work. Value Relations are then no longer an objective imposition on every individual and enterprise, by merely an *ideology* which can be rejected as a choice; hence agency is unleashed. Thus an associational economy of cooperative, creative and sharing work can flourish without the constraint of Value Relations.[13]

In the last twenty years or so, a large literature on 'de-growth' has emerged, motivated in the first place by the climate emergency, pollution and waste, and the destruction of ecosystems. For some authors, this has provided another support for an associational economy (Schmelzer et al., 2022: 212–244). De-growth denotes, at minimum, a reduction in material inputs to, and outputs of, production (cf Schumacher). It is often argued to mean, additionally, a reduction in conventionally-measured GDP, that is, the monetary value of capitalist output (cf Gorz). In another variant, the production of goods and non-essential consumer services should decrease, but the provision of caring services (health, education, social care, individual care) should increase, whether or not these are produced by waged labour or by unpaid voluntary labour (contra Gorz). Associationism's focus on environmental improvement addresses the problem of resource depletion and pollution. To the extent that an

---

12   The view that social interests are discursively constructed has been developed in an extreme form by Judith Butler. Social identities and actions are 'performative', that is, freely chosen without material constraint or determination.

13   For a detailed exposition and critique of Resnick, Wolff and Gibson-Graham, see Das, 2017: Chs 3 and 4.

associational economy is associated with reduced money incomes (low wages or trainee state-transfers in cooperatives, UBI, unpaid voluntary work), it leads to lower consumption of goods and inessential services. Associationism's focus on caring work, whether waged (through contracts from the state), through petty-commodity production (e.g. therapists) or unwaged (the voluntary sector) contributes to the shift to caring work. The de-growth literature, however, tends to sidestep the problem that the central aim of capital is the expansion of its value through the expanded use of labour power and production of commodities (cf the comments on Gorz above).

The specifically political aspect of associationism has been underpinned by Jurgen Habermas and, on a different theoretical basis, Ernesto Laclau and Chantal Mouffe. Habermas in his later writings (2014) developed an ideal type of political deliberation and policy-making which he termed 'communicative rationality', based on Enlightenment notions of knowledge and truth. Political deliberation needs to take place in fora which involve members or representatives of all relevant interests or 'stakeholders', and which have the time and resources for a full sharing of knowledge and empirics of the issues to be discussed. Each participant should present rational arguments for their policy stance, setting out not only how outcomes follow from policies but also the moral criteria on which these outcomes should be judged (Kantian reality and morality respectively). Other participants can challenge both aspects of these arguments on the basis of careful listening. On this basis, there can be discursive convergence on a consensus, encompassing both agreement on the likely outcomes of policy and how those outcomes are to be morally evaluated. This consensus then puts pressure on all social actors to conform to collective wishes, whatever their private interests; in this way, local governance can potentially examine, debate and control all and any aspects of society. This politics has been taken up by other scholars: Fung and Wright (2003) term it 'empowered participatory democracy'; Healey (1997) has written extensively on the application of communicative rationality to urban planning and politics. A corollary of this approach, emphasised by Wills (2016), is hostility to political parties: they embody entrenched and fixed *class* positions, and they insist on antagonism and opposition rather than arriving at a consensus.

Laclau and Mouffe (1985) come to a similar political prescription but through post-structuralism and Gramscian politics. They reject Marxist value relations and the existence of two antagonistic classes; individuals can have multiple class and non-class positions (cf Wright and Gibson-Graham); and social identity is not rooted in economic interests but is discursively constructed (cf Gibson-Graham). But Laclau and Mouffe still wish for progressive collective political projects. Rejecting working class struggle, they find such projects in a certain reading of Antonio Gramsci's *Prison Notebooks*. Gramsci argued that politics proceeds through projects within which coalitions of particular fractions of classes (capital, petty bourgeois, workers, peasants) agree a common political strategy which struggles for material and ideological hegemony (dominance). Laclau and Mouffe argue that these conflicting or contrary material interests, since they are themselves discursively constructed, can be united through discourse. In particular, a 'democratic' counter-hegemonic project can be discursively constructed. Mouffe (2000) argues that different, or even antagonistic, views can, and should, be reconciled through 'agonistic' deliberation, which acknowledges the differences and conflicts in initial position, but achieves consensus on progressive policies and strategies. Thus, as in Habermas's approach, inclusive and sustained deliberation can achieve a consensus, which can potentially become hegemonic, that is, be implemented in practice. This approach can lend weight to the associationist project. A counter-hegemonic project for pluralist democracy could take the form of TSD, productivist syndicalism, or assocationism. Agonistic deliberation supports the kind of politics favoured by associationists – pluralist, diverse, but aiming at consensus.

These academic supports for associationism, like those for PMSD considered in the previous section, are highly diverse in their philosophical method and social field addressed. But they share a central feature: they ignore, or positively deny, Capitalist Value Relations. In the next two sections we shall see that this lacuna leads to multiple practical and ideological problems for associationism.

4   The Problems and Limits of Associationism

Associationalist strategy promises to address the ills of neoliberalism and build solidaristic social relations strongly enclosed within localities while skirting round the power of capital; it thereby appears both progressive and feasible, accounting for its popularity with many community activists and left scholars. But the strategy suffers from severe limitations and contradictions. I shall consider both the immediate problems and failures of the practice of associationism considered in section 2, and the problems of its theoretical underpinnings discussed in section 3. I consider three broad aspects of associationism: economic enterprises and organisations; the relation of these to the state; and methods of political decision making.

4.1 Associationist Enterprise in the Capitalist Sea

I consider in turn the distinct problems of three types of associationist enterprise: cooperatives using wage labour; organisations using unpaid labour; and small firms and self employment.

4.1.1 Cooperatives and Not-for-Profits Operating in the Market

Cooperative enterprises using waged labour and producing commodities to sell in final markets are under intense pressures from the surrounding capitalist economy. This is because they are usually competing against capitalist enterprises, while they lack capital for investment in premises, equipment, training and managerial functions. This lack of capital is a necessary feature of cooperatives because of their ownership by workers. These commercial pressures, the expression of Capitalist Value Relations, have a number of negative consequences. First, cooperative enterprises often become financially unviable and collapse (Amin et al., 2002). In the long term in aggregate, this results in failure to produce minimum scale of agglomerations of cooperatives and thus synergies. Collapse can occur even for the largest cooperatives. The Cooperative Bank in Britain, at one time the fifth biggest retail bank and the only major cooperatively owned bank, collapsed after acquiring the Britannia Building Society in an attempt to expand its branch network and thus compete more effectively against the big four.

The problem of lack of capital might seem to be overcome by enterprises owned by local government, which can draw on their revenue or borrowing power to set up not-for-profit commercial enterprises of larger scale than workers' cooperatives. But because they are competing with still-larger capitalist enterprises, these too may collapse (Hatcher, 2021). In the 2010s, a number of British local authorities set up energy retail enterprises to provide better prices to their local citizens. But when world oil and gas prices rose in the second year of the pandemic, these local energy retailers lacked both the hedge of forward contracts and the cash reserves possessed by the big six capitalist corporations and collapsed. Some local authorities set up formally separate enterprises to build social or low rent housing; but these were squeezed by rising land prices and building costs; the two largest such enterprises (Croydon and Slough) collapsed, bankrupting their respective local authorities.[14]

---

14   A number of other British local authorities became large scale commercial property developers, not for social benefit but to increase their revenue in the face of central government cuts, or simply to accumulate. But these were caught by oversupply of commercial space, exacerbated by the pandemic. This bankrupted the respective local authorities because they did not have the massive cash reserves of the major property companies.

Second, lack of capital means that cooperatives often rely on self-exploitation – low pay, long hours, high work intensity. This prevents them achieving their promise of providing good, empowering jobs (see further Chapter 7). A corollary is that workers in these enterprises tend to leave for better jobs once the initial enthusiasm for the association has dimmed.

Third, commercial success of community enterprises typically rely on using individuals' managerial and commercial skills; in capitalist society these are the preserve of the middle class. Indeed, we have seen the emergence of the professional 'social entrepreneur' who designs and initiates community enterprises and organises their often-multiple funding sources. In consequence, localities with a large density of the middle class tend to have a larger and more dynamic Third Sector, while (former) industrial cities and towns have a weaker sector which is much more dependent on (unstable) state patronage (Amin et al., 2002; Wills, 2016). But this contradicts the aim of associationism to empower poor localities.

Fourth, where community businesses are commercially successful, the surrounding capitalist environment produces pressures on them to become capitalist enterprises or be subsumed by them. Larger community enterprises often employ senior managers who are paid high salaries. Shares in successful worker coops become tradeable. Or, like the Mondragon cooperative complex, they may set up subsidiaries which are simple profit maximising enterprises employing non-cooperators.

Fifth, associational enterprises are excluded from most sections of the contemporary world economy by insufficient capital to attain minimum economies of scale and scope. This is obviously true, for example, of mining, oil and gas; vehicle, aerospace, pharmaceutical and electronics manufacturing; software and internet infrastructure; goods transport and logistics; and infrastructure of utilities. Even funding from cooperative banks or from state-owned banks serving cooperatives is wholly insufficient to enter such sectors; they will continue to be the preserve of transnational capital, billionaire investors and nation states.

4.1.2   Voluntary Labour

Community enterprises using wholly or mainly unpaid 'voluntary' labour suffer from different problems. When they start up they can call on people's moral commitment to their socially- or ecologically-beneficial aims. But after a year or two the hard unpaid work typically results in declining participation. The capitalist norm of a wage in exchange for routine and repetitive labour cannot easily be over-ridden by moral will-power and idealism. To the extent that they employ people with physical or learning disabilities in order to provide them with activity that will empower them, the organisation may lack the resources to operate efficiently; this contrasts with state-run production for people with disabilities, which have the funding to provide support and a good working environment and which do not need to have high productivity. Moreover, where these enterprises operate successfully, for example in community shops or cafes employing unpaid university students, they undermine the commercial viability of private sector competitors and put downward pressure on the wages of the latters' employees.

4.1.3   Private Firms and Self-Employment

Associationism supports small for-profit firms and self-employed artisans and practitioners which produce 'high quality' goods and services. But setting up such enterprises is overwhelmingly done by university graduates with the necessary money- and cultural-capital; small firms set up by working class people are overwhelmingly in building trades and car repairs (men) and hair and beauty salons (women), which do not meet the associationist view of socially useful. Moreover, the high quality goods and services are high price; the enterprises producing them need to be located in higher income areas to find customers. These two circumstances again mean that these enterprises benefit the middle class more than the working class and, *a fortiori*, the poor.

Moreover, small for-profit firms have two further problems arising from their capitalist essence. First, they are subject to over-accumulation, where the formation of a new firm results in the bankruptcy of an existing firm because of the given limited market (Eisenschitz and Gough, 1993: 50–54). (This is true also of the cooperative commercial enterprises discussed above.) Secondly, small firms in general have inferior wages, security and conditions of employment, and labour processes compared to large firms, in part because they are much less likely to be unionised (Rainnie, 1985; Sharzer, 2012).

Across these different forms of enterprise, then, capitalist pressures (the need for capital; competition in final markets; over-accumulation; norms of wage labour) severely constrain, or nullify, the idealistic aims of associationism. Note that these capitalist pressures are not simply external impositions: they are internal to the enterprises themselves.

4.1.4   Communes

As I have noted, communes, whether for co-living only or, especially, including income-producing work, are an ideal form of associationism. But their embedding in Capitalist Value Relations produces deep tensions. Differences in initial ownership of property and in incomes of cooperators produce multiple tensions in who pays for what. Incomes are typically low, leading members to leave for better job opportunities elsewhere, particularly in rural communes. Differences in preparedness to do household and caring work create resentments. In a highly unequal society, equality and collectivity are hard to achieve in a small social unit (for a graphic fictional portrayal, see Ducastel and Martineau, 2008). These tensions often result in break up.

4.2   The Relations between the Associational Economy and the State

We saw in section 2 that the associational economy, despite its ideological framing as bottom-up or 'power-to', is deeply affected by the state, both local and national. Community and cooperative enterprises providing social care are usually contractors to local government; they therefore depend on local government budgets and the extent of the discretionary powers of local government in contracting. Community initiatives are often dependent on a sympathetic local authority to provide or compulsorily purchase land and property. The local-state owned enterprises often regarded as part of the associational economy (section 2) are dependent on both the funding and the political strategy of the local government. All associational enterprises are subject to national (or in federal countries, regional) laws and taxation rules which can either facilitate or impede their functioning; this is true of production and housing cooperatives, cooperative banks and credit unions, local moneys, Local Exchange and Trading Schemes, and community rights to buy. UBI is dependent on the funds and the taxation systems of national and regional states. The latter fund or guarantee some important supports of the associational economy such as banks which lend to unconventional enterprises and advice services provided to them.

This dependence on the state should not be surprising. The contemporary state in the HICs, despite neoliberal ideology and practice, is integral to the functioning of the capitalist economy: laws of property, contract and labour markets; taxation; subsidies; industrial policy. The state is a 'moment' in capital accumulation and the relation of capital to labour. This is an implication of Value Relations as they have developed historically. Thus the associational economy is necessarily profoundly affected by the state, for good or ill.

This dependence presents a profound problem for associationist ideology and practice. Associationist ideology emphasises 'power to' and generalised social capital, and minimises 'power over' whether it be the power of the state or the power of capital exercised through the state (section 3). If associationists acknowledged the importance of the state to their aims, they would be moving into the terrain of Traditional Social Democracy, which they see as 'rigid' and 'bureaucratic' (section 1). They would also have to acknowledge that political parties matter: a supportive role of the state towards the associational economy is far more likely to come from a social democratic or socialist government (local or national) than from one of the Right; for example, we have suggested that the supportive attitude of the Quebec and Scottish governments towards associationism is a product of the respective social democratic traditions of those territories. The implication is that the associationist movement needs to involve itself in class politics: the struggle for the interests of the working class where they conflict with the power of capital. But associationism has no interest in organisations such as trade unions or left political parties which seek to unite parts or all of the working class against capital; nor is it interested in collective movements against sexism, racism and environmental destruction which oppose the perpetuation of those ills by capital and the state. Associationists are thereby compelled to accept, or to hope for, whatever policies towards the associational economy local, regional and national governments currently have.

4.3   The Political Organisation of Associationism: Decentralisation and Deliberative Democracy

We saw in section 2 that associationists aim for particular forms of political decision making: inclusive of all classes; deliberative; non-adversarial; aiming to reach consensus; and minimising the role of the (local) state and representative-elected legislatures. Where associationism seeks to work through the state, it privileges local or decentralised levels of the state against the national as inherently more democratic and participatory.

But this approach is problematic since it abstracts from social and economic interests and processes. Transparent communications between social actors which Habermas recommends cannot argue away the conflicts of interest between them, which are rooted in relations of power. The arguments of groups which are socio-economically powerful will tend to win. This is partly because they have more resources to construct and publicise those arguments. It is also because their arguments run with the grain of socio-economic relations: the interests of capital and the petty bourgeoisie, the inviolability of private property, and the equity and efficiency of free markets, are the *common sense* of capitalist societies (Marx, 1972 ed.). Moreover, owners of property do not have to agree to transfer it to others, whereas workers have to exert collective social pressure to achieve gains. Suppose, for example, that the subject of deliberation is that a neighbourhood community association wishes to purchase land from a capitalist owner who does not wish to sell. The landowner wishes to develop a higher-profit use for the land; indeed, as a capitalist they *must* seek the maximum expansion of its value. The landowner therefore cannot be discursively *convinced* by the community's argument that community ownership would reap greater social benefits. The deliberative forum does not have the power to compel the sale to the community since, in this instance, the

local state does not have the necessary compulsory purchase powers: in capitalist societies private ownership is the enforced norm. Thus a Habermasian
consensus cannot be arrived at, and if it were, it cannot be implemented,
because negated by Value Relations.

The agonistic approach of Mouffe might be thought to avoid this criticism,
since it acknowledges that there are contrary material interests involved in
political deliberation. But Value Relations mean that there are contrary class
interests which cannot be reconciled (though they can arrive at a temporary
truce such as in industrial disputes). Moreover, Laclau and Mouffe's denial
that there is a working class which has certain common interests, including
the abolition or supersession of capitalism, thereby declares non-existent the
only social force which can feasibly achieve an egalitarian or socialist society
against the power of capital. Laclau and Mouffe see the construction of (would-
be) hegemonic projects in philosophically-idealist terms as the development
of 'alternative visions' – a popular trope in academic associationist writing.
But alternative visions do not in themselves achieve any substantial socio-
economic outcomes. Most people engage in politics in order to achieve concrete social or economic gains; if these are not achieved, then they withdraw
from political engagement. (Significantly, the same is not true of the professional intelligentsia, who are inclined to engage in political debate because it is
interesting; this layer is the social base of the Gramscian strategy.) It is through
successful struggles starting from their own immediate, perceived interests
that ordinary people develop and change their ideas, begin to see through the
mystifications of capitalist social relations, and see that things really could be
radically different. This is why Marxist politics is based in praxis rather than
the development of pure ideology, as we explore in Chapter 7. But associationists are uninterested in militant collective organisations which oppose power.

The demand of associationists for the decentralisation of the state, from
national to local and from core to dispersed, is equally problematic. Local government is not *ipso facto* more democratic than the national, and fragmented
governance is not more democratic that the core state. This is because of the
state's relation to capital accumulation. Decentralisation exacerbates competition between groups of workers and between sections of residents in different
localities, neighbourhoods and workplaces. Decentralised government cannot plan at larger spatial scales, and dispersed governance cannot plan across
different aspects of society (for example job, housing, transport, public services); they therefore have less purchase over capital's investment decisions.
Thus close-by, decentralised forms of governance and participation can fail to
empower because they cannot achieve influence, let alone control, over the
major resources of the society controlled by capital.

4.4   The Failures of Associationism

There are, then, deep problems with the practice and ideas of associationism across all three of its aspects considered here. The economics of community and cooperative enterprises, 'good' small firms and self-employment run up against contradictions and conflicts of Value Relations. The relations between associationist enterprises and the state is problematic because of the strong dependence of the former on the latter while associationism eschews the only method – unified class struggle – which could influence the state to support the associationist economy. Associationism's preferred methods of political deliberation treat political discourse as a realm in itself, abstracted from the compulsion of capital accumulation, material class interests and class conflict. The promotion of social capital and association is thus not a plausible strategy for overcoming poverty, nor for combatting the ill-effects of neoliberalism on the population as a whole.

In the next and final section I assess the potential and limits of the associationist movement as a whole.

5   The Limits of Associationism

How large could the associationist economy grow? To what extent could it replace capitalism as conventionally defined? The academic proponents of associationism considered above have given quite different answers to this question. The most cautious approach is that of Wright (2014).

As we have seen, he argues for a combination of associationism ('interstitial strategy') and TSD ('symbiotic strategy'). Wright sees the interstitial strategy as inherently hemmed in and limited to a small size by capitalism; but its merit is to demonstrate in practice an *ideological* alternative to capitalism, to 'prefigure' alternative futures. The main part of his strategy is therefore to create a regulated capitalism. Wright does not pretend that this combination abolishes capitalism or creates socialism (an outcome which he anyway sees as unfeasible or undesirable). Rather, he proposes that the 'democratic' elements of popular control can grow. Wright is aware of limitations in this strategy. He thinks that the middle class will play a larger role in these strategies than manual or unskilled workers (cf section 4), so the benefits for the latter, and a fortiori for the poor, are limited. He also concedes that the democratic elements are unlikely to become dominant or the 'core' of the economy because of the continuing weight of capital; so this is not an 'alternative to capitalism' of his book's title, but at best a softened capitalism. But then, the 'prefigurative' role of associationism can bear no fruit: cooperative management, popular planning and engagement, priority to social reproduction and women's equality cannot spread to the whole society, and are therefore *not* 'prefigurative'. Thus despite Wright's analytical approach, his strategy is enmeshed in contradictions: it seeks a dynamic of increasing popular democracy, but states that this can only go so far; it promises cooperation, collectivity and full public participation, but refuses the only society in which these could be generalised and deepened, socialism, and instead delivers capitalism in the style of the postwar boom (see further Das, 2017: 145–149). Moreover, by proposing soft capitalism as the maximum that can be attained, he has no answer to what happens in a crisis of profitability such as the present period, when capital moves to demolish the previous gains which the working class has made (cf section 1).

A very different approach is that of Gorz (1989) and Schmelzer et al. (2022) who propose to grow the associational economy by forcibly squeezing the capitalist economy. Gorz sees the associationist economy growing through the increase in free time resulting from a steady reduction in the waged-working week, sustained by a UBI funded from the mainstream economy. But an ever-decreasing working week runs directly counter to the basic dynamic of capitalism, to expand surplus value production through expanded exploitation of labour power. It could only be achieved by the collective power of the whole working class, particularly workers in production;[15] but Gorz rejects the possibility of such a movement because he sees the working class within waged production as completely subordinated to capital. Schmelzer et al. envisage limiting or eliminating large capital through draconian regulations and social targets to force their reduction or closure, and by declaring that enterprises of a certain size are held in common or publicly owned (2022: 220–222). But capital would not accept its own abolition: this requires the taking of power by the collective working class, but the authors see de-growth as arising from multiple, diverse and fragmented initiatives 'from below'. Thus Gorz and Schmelzer et al. wish for an ever-expanding associational economy from increasing restriction of the capitalist economy, but reject or evade the only means by which this could be achieved.

The most optimistic and ambitious proponents of associationism are Gibson-Graham (1996; 2006). Since they understand capitalism as a system of distribution rather than of capital accumulation and exploitation, the dynamics of capitalism towards indefinite expansion of capital and domination of

---

15   It is possible to imagine an enforced shorter working week in a situation of 'dual power', that is, where the working class is able to dictate some important actions to capital. But this situation is inherently unstable and short lived; for the beneficial actions to be maintained, the working class has to expropriate capital.

workers within production can be forgotten, or rejected as mere ideology. There are then no limits to new forms of enterprise and collaboration which redistribute output in progressive ways. The implication is that the associationism can expand without limit given the political will. This optimism relies on ignoring the multiple barriers posed by Value Relations to the expansion of the associationist economy that I noted in section 4: that most of the contemporary economy in HICs has economies of scale and scope that community enterprises and workers' cooperatives cannot possibly achieve; that many successful for-profit community enterprises become normal capitalist firms; that workers leave community employment because of low or non-existent wages arising, *inter alia*, from their lack of capital; that expansion of the associational economy depends on state regulation and funding which are only obtainable through collective working class struggle which Gibson-Graham reject. Moreover, even if associationism was successful in becoming the dominant form of the economy and society, its achievement would be extremely limited from the standpoint of human liberation. They state their aim in their book's title, 'The End of Capitalism (As We Know It)'. The ambiguity of this aim points to the fact that the associationism they advocate *is still capitalism*, in the sense of accumulation of capital by individual enterprises (for-profits) in competition with each other, and the employment of wage labour (albeit some at very low or zero wages); there is no planning of investment, production, products and wages by the collective producers (that is, the end of capitalism). This society would therefore still be subject to all the crisis tendencies characteristic of capitalism: over-accumulation and devalorisation, social and spatial uneven development, discipline of employers of workers, wage depression and poverty. Gibson-Graham present their theorisations as a 'feminist' reworking of political economy. But their associationist model lacks the key practices which can achieve greater equality for women under capitalism: opening of male-dominated sectors to women; equal pay for equal work; raising wages and conditions in female-dominated sectors; free high-quality nurseries and free care for the elderly and infirm; affordable housing for all households. To improve these things requires class struggle in industries, across the economy, and in the state, which Gibson-Graham eschews; to achieve them fully requires a collectively planned economy which they, like Wright, reject.

We see, then, that the proponents of associationism do not have a strategy for superseding capitalism. This failure is both a result and a cause of its *philosophical idealism* (see note 3). I have discussed how Habermas, Laclau and Mouffe envisage political debate as existing in its own sphere of ideas untrammelled by materially-based social relations, interests and resources. In this exalted sphere, it is possible to reached a consensus. In a Hegelian move, this consensus idea can then be implemented unproblematically in the material realm. Similarly, the central notion of PMSD, the power of horizontal association ('power to'), abstracts from the real power of capital over labour and the material underpinnings of women's and racial/ethnic the real. Gibson-Graham's view of Value Relations as mere ideology is an idealist manoeuvre. The presentation of associationism as prefigurative of a better future can occlude the question of material feasibility.

The practical form of this philosophical idealism is *political moralism*. We have seen in sections 2 and 4 how associationist practice relies heavily on moral exhortation: if a cooperative is squeezed by the market, cooperators should cut their wages or intensify their work because cooperation is a political good; volunteers should stay in a voluntary organisation despite boredom, exhaustion and lack of income because it is working for the social good; participants in setting up a shared housing scheme should endure years of planning meetings in unpaid time and disruption of their existing financial and/or housing arrangements. This moralism can also appear in associationist demands on the state: proponents of UBI do not seriously engage with the material objections to it (overall cost to the state; its repudiation of a social commensuration of the value of work; or a benefit too low to live on) because they regard it as an obvious moral good that all should have the opportunity to live their lives free from supervision by employer or state. This moralism, then, is an idealist response to the material problems and failures of associationist practice which arise from Capitalist Value Relations.

We saw in section 1 how PMSD, and associationism in particular, arose as a response to the defeats of labour by the capital's neoliberal offensive. But by eschewing working class struggle against capital, associationism is in a weak position to advance working class interests. Rather, it internalises many features of neoliberalism: creation your own employment, whether in cooperative or private enterprise; competing in final markets; intensification of work. By taking on work previously done by the state on a contract basis or through voluntary work, it has smoothed the decline of state services.[16] But in our view,

---

16   In 2002 in Britain, Planet Patrol, a not-for-profit organisation, organised thousands of
      volunteers to monitor the water quality of rivers. This achieved the associationist aim of
      collective work and educating people in ecology. But it was only necessary because the
      private water companies are effectively unregulated, and the Environment Agency has
      been subject to repeated cuts in staffing since 2010 and is unable to carry out the moni-
      toring of water quality. The Planet Patrol initiative thus achieves the Conservative prime
      minister David Cameron's 'Big Society' strategy, of voluntary work substituting for state
      employment.

associationism and the building of social capital are not fated to play a marginal role or a soft wing of neoliberalism. In Chapter 3 we discuss the building of social capital of and for working class struggle. In Chapter 6 we explore how associationists can align with, support, and be supported by trade union and other working class struggle against capital. In Chapter 7 we discuss how the appeal and advantages for popular involvement of local scale organisation can be deployed in local collective working class resistance.

References

Adler, D., & Bechler, R. (Eds.). (2019). *A Vision for Europe 2020*. London: Eris.

Allen, J. (1999). Spatial assemblages of power: from domination to empowerment. In D. Massey, J. Allen, and P. Sarre (Eds.), *Human Geography Today* (Pp. 194–218). Cambridge: Polity Press.

Allen, J. (2003). *Lost Geographies of Power*. Oxford: Blackwell.

Amin, A., Cameron, A., & Hudson, R. (2002). *Placing the Social Economy*. London: Routledge.

Amin, A., & Thrift, N. (2002). *Cities: Reimagining the Urban*. Cambridge: Polity.

Armstrong, P., Glyn, A., & Harrison, J. (1991). *Capitalism since 1945*. Oxford: Blackwell.

Beilharz, P. (1994). *Postmodern Socialism: Romanticism, City and State*. Melbourne: Melbourne University Press.

Braverman, H. (1974). *Labour and Monopoly Capitalism*. New York: Monthly Review Press.

Brindley, T., Rydin, Y., & Stoker, G. (1992). *Remaking Planning*. London: Routledge.

Byrne, D. (1999). *Social Exclusion* Buckingham: Open University Press.

Calinicos, A. (1989). *Against Postmodernism: A Marxist critique*. Cambridge: Polity.

Costello, N., Michie, J., & Milne, S. (1989). *Beyond the Casino Economy: Planning in the 1990s* London: Verso.

Cooke, P., & Morgan, K. (1998). *The Associational Economy*, Oxford: Oxford University Press.

Das, R. (2017). *Marxist Class Theory for a Skeptical World*. Leiden: Brill.

Ducastel, O., & Martineau, J. (directors) *Nés en 68,* film, 2008.

Eisenschitz, A., & Gough, J. (1993). *The Politics of Local Economic Policy,* Basingstoke: Macmillan.

Eisenschitz, A., & Gough, J. (1996). The contradictions of neo-Keynesian local economic strategy. *Review of International Political Economics, 3*(3): 434–458.

Fuller, D., & Jonas, A. (2002). Institutionalising future geographies of financial inclusion: national legitimacy versus local autonomy in the British credit union movement. *Antipode, 34*(1): 85–110.

Fung, A. and Wright, E.O. (Eds.). (2003). *Deepening Democracy: institutional innovations in empowered participatory governance*, London: Verso.

Gibson-Graham, J.K. (1996). *The End of Capitalism (As We Know It): a feminist critique of political economy*. Cambridge, Mass.: Blackwell.

Gibson-Graham, J.K. (2006). *A Postcapitalist Politics*. Minneapolis: University of Minnesota Press.

Gordon, D. (2002). The contribution of the community cooperatives of the Highlands and Islands of Scotland to the Development of the social economy. *Journal of Rural Cooperation, 30*(2): 95–117.

Gordon, D., Edwards, R., & Reich, M. (1982). *Segmented Work, Divided Workers*. Cambridge: Cambridge University Press.

Gorz, A. (Ed.). (1978). *The Division of Labour: The Labour Process and Class-Struggle in Modern Capitalism*. Hassocks: Harvester Press.

Gorz, A. (1982). *Farewell to the Working Class*. London: Pluto Press.

Gorz, A. (1989). *Critique of Economic Reason*. London: Verso.

Gough, J. (1992). Where is the value in post-Fordism? In N. Gilbert, R. Burrows and A. Pollert (Eds.), *Fordism and Flexibility*. Basingstoke: Macmillan.

Gough, J. (1996a). Not flexible accumulation: contradictions of value in contemporary economic geography, Part 1: Workplace and inter-firm relations. *Environment and Planning A, 28*: 2063–2079.

Gough, J. (1996b). Not flexible accumulation: contradictions of value in contemporary economic geography, Part 2: Regional regimes, national regulation and political strategy, *Environment and Planning A, 28*: 2179–2200.

Gough, J. (2020). Why Labour lost the British 2019 election: social democracy versus neoliberalism and the Far Right. *Class, Race and Corporate Power, 18*(2): Article 2.

Gough, J., & Das, R. (2017). Introduction to special issue: Marxist geography, *Human Geography, 9*(3): 1–9.

Habermas, J. (2014). *On the Pragmatics of Communication*. New York: Wiley.

Hall, S., & Jacques, M. (Eds.). (1989). *New Times*. London: Lawrence and Wishart.

Harrison, J. (1978). *Marxist Economics for Socialists*. London: Pluto Press.

Harvey, D. (2000). *Spaces of Hope*. Edinburgh: Edinburgh University Press.

Hatcher, R. (2021). The Limitations and Illusions of Community Wealth Building. *Birmingham Against the Cuts*. Retrieved from: https://birminghamagainstthec uts.files.wordpress.com/2021/01/the-limitations-and-illusions-of-cwb.pdf.

Healey, P. (1997). *Collaborative Planning*. Basingstoke: Macmillan.

Henley, J. (2020). Communities working for a greener Europe. *The Guardian* 3 September.

Hirst, P., & Zeitlin, J. (Eds.). (1989). *Reversing Industrial Decline?* Oxford: Berg.

Hodgson, G. (1984). *The Democratic Economy: A New Look at Planning, Markets and Power*, Harmondsworth: Penguin.

Hutton, W. (1995). *The State We're In*. London: Cape.

Jessop, B. (1993). Towards a Schumpeterian workfare state? preliminary remarks on post-Fordist political economy, *Studies in Political Economy 40*: 7–39.

Labour Party. (2019). *Manifesto: For the Many, Not the Few*. London: Labour Party.

Laclau, E., & Mouffe, C. (1985). *Hegemony and Socialist Strategy*. London: Verso.

Lash, S., & Urry, J. (1987). *The End of Organised Capitalism*, Cambridge: Polity Press.

Leadbeater, C. (1997). *The Rise of the Social Entrepreneur*. London: Demos.

Lee, R. (1996). Moral money? LETS and the social construction of local economic geographies in Southeast England, *Environment and Planning A, 28*: 1377–94.

Mackintosh, M., & Wainwright, H. (Eds.). (1987). A *Taste of Power*. London: Verso.

Mandel, E. (1968). *Marxist Economic Theory*. London: Merlin Press.

Mandel, E. (1978). *Late Capitalism*. London: Verso.

Marx, K. (1972 ed.). *Capital Volume 1*, London: Lawrence and Wishart.

Massey, D. (2005). *For Space*. London: Sage.

Mazzucato, M. (2013). *The Entrepreneurial State: Debunking Public versus Private Sector Myths*. London: Anthem Press.

McDonnell, J. (Ed.). (2018). *Economics for the Many*. London: Verso.

McKillop, D., & Wilson, J. (2011). Credit unions: a theoretical and empirical overview. *Financial Markets, Institutions and Instruments, 20*(3): 79–123.

Medoff, P., & Sklar, H. (1994). *Streets of Hope*. Boston: South End Press.Moore, P. and Taylor, P. (2009) Exploitation of the self in community-based software production: workers' freedoms or firm foundations? *Capital and Class 33*(1): 99–119.

Mouffe, C. (2000). *The Democratic Paradox*. London: Verso.

Mulgan, G. (1991). *Communication and Control*. Oxford: Polity Press.

Murray, R. (1989). Fordism and post-Fordism. In S. Hall and M. Jacques (Eds.) *New Times*. (Pp. 38–53). London: Lawrence and Wishart.

North, P. (2007). *Money and Liberation: The Micropolitics of Alternative Currency Movement*. Minneapolis: University of Minnesota Press.

Ostrom, E. (1990). *Governing the Commons: The Evolution of Institutions for Collective Action*. Cambridge: Cambridge University Press.

Piore, M., & Sabel, C. (1984). *The Second Industrial Divide*, New York: Basic Books.

Rainnie, A. (1985). Small firms, big problems: the political economy of small business. *Capital and Class, 25*: 140–168.

Roberts, M. (2016). *The Long Depression*. Chicago: Haymarket Books.

Schmelzer, M., Vetter, A., & Vansintjan, A. (2022). *The Future is Degrowth: A Guide to a World beyond Capitalism*. London: Verso.

Schumacher, E.F. (1974). *Small is Beautiful: A Study of Economics as if People Mattered*. London: Abacus.

Sennett, R., & Cobb, J. (1993). *The Hidden Injuries of Class*. London: Faber.

Sharzer, G. (2012). *No Local: Why Small-Scale Alternative Won't Change the World*. Winchester: Zero.

Sharzer, G. (2022). *Late Escapism and Contemporary Neoliberalism*. Abingdon: Routledge.

Sintomer Y., Herzberg, C. and Rocke, A. (2008). Participatory Budgeting in Europe: Potentials and challenges, *International Journal of Urban and Regional Research, 32*(1): 164–178.

Standing, G. (2017). *Basic Income: And How We Can Make It Happen*. London: Pelican.

Storper, M. (1998). *The Regional World: Territorial Development in a Global Economy*. New York: Guilford Press.

Taub, R. (1994). *Community Capitalism: The South Shore Bank's Strategy for Neighbourhood Revitalisation*. Boston: Harvard Business School Press.

Varoufakis, Y. (2016). *And the Weak Must Suffer What They Must?: Europe, Austerity and the Threat to Global Stability*. London: Vintage.

Wainwright, H. (1994). *Arguments for a New Left*. Oxford: Blackwell.

Wills, J. (2016). *Locating Localism: Statecraft, Citizenship and Democracy*. Bristol: Policy Press.

Wood, E.M. (1986). *The Retreat from Class: A New 'True' Socialism*. London: Verso.

Wright, E.O. (2009). Understanding class: towards an integrated analytical approach. *New Left Review, 60*: 101–116.

Wright, E.O. (2014). Socialism and real utopias. In R. Hahnel and E.O. Wright (Eds.), *Alternatives to Capitalism: Proposals for a Democratic Economy*. London: New Left Project.

CHAPTER 3

Social Capital and Class: a Critical Theoretical Examination

Raju J. Das

[If] people cannot trust each other or work together, then improving the material conditions of life is an uphill battle' (Evans, 1997a: 2).[1] Recently, trust, cooperation and other similar processes have been brought together by scholars under the concept of social capital. More specifically, social capital refers to norms of trust and reciprocity and to networks, associations and organisations which constitute *social* resources for individuals and which facilitate collective action for mutual benefit (Woolcock, 1998).[2]

There has been a large amount of literature on social capital (the other competing concept that has been popular is globalization/neoliberalism). Like globalization, books on social capital began appearing in the early 1990s. From the mid-1990s, the pace increased until about 2005. After 2005, the interest in it has been high but it has flattened or indeed slightly declined (Figure 3.1).

The popularity of the concept of social capital concept partly reflects the growing realization among non-Marxist social scientists that *economic* processes are linked to *social* relations, which in turn affect these processes (Granovetter, 1985).[3] It also reflects the current worldwide neoliberal agenda (more on this later). In particular, the social capital research on how non-market processes such as the state, trust and customs grease the wheels of market fits in well with the neoliberal agenda of making (imperfect) markets more efficient. Underneath the ever-growing popularity of the social capital literature in social sciences is a major problem with it, however. The literature, in general, tends to *under*-stress the class character of social capital.[4]

---

1 This chapter is based on an earlier publication (Das, 2006).
2 This is not the only definition of social capital. But there is a fair amount of consensus on this (Woolcock, 2000). It must be said that the definition of social capital given by Coleman (1988), one of the original contributors to the social capital debate, is more general than the one used in this chapter in that for him social capital is any aspect of social structure that aids human action.
3 On the conceptual history of social capital, see Farr (2004).
4 There are numerous other problems, including the fact that often the literature conflates what social capital is with what it does (Portes, 2010; Fine, 2010).

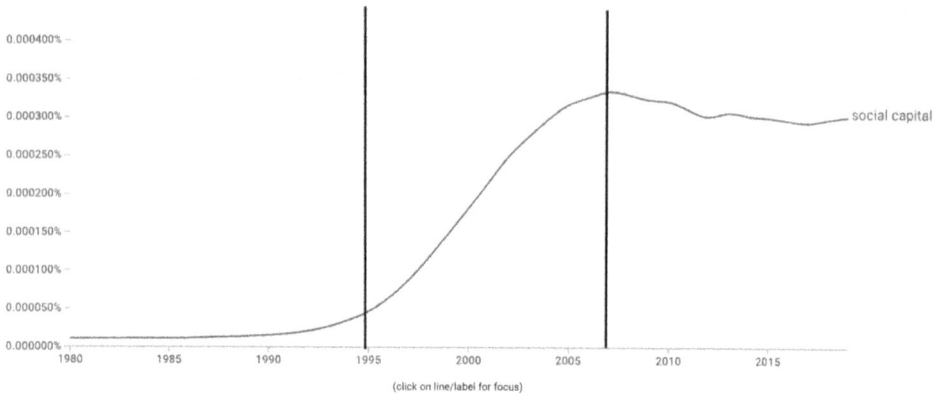

FIGURE 3.1   Popularity of social capital

This chapter is theoretical. It discusses the existing literature on social capital and subjects it to a critique, and then, on the basis of the critique, it seeks
to construct an alternative approach to social capital. This approach sees social
capital as operating in a class-context, and advocates a theory of social capital
in the sense of a social resource placed in the hands of the working class. This
chapter informs the conceptual discussions in the next two chapters where the
elements of the theory presented here are expanded on, which in turn inform
the empirical discussions in these chapters.

The remainder of this chapter has five sections. Sections I and II discuss
'society-centric' and 'state-society relation' approaches to social capital, respectively. Section III critiques these for neglecting class. The next section presents a class-based political economy approach to social capital. In particular,
I discuss the nature of 'working class social capital' and the different ways in
which it can be produced within civil society as well as in the structure of relations between workers and 'relatively autonomous' state officials. The chapter
highlights how the class context of working class social capital constrains and
enables its production in particular places and over space. Contrary to some
'social capitalists' (those who enthusiastically support the idea and the material practice of social capital), the chapter concludes that there cannot be a
social capital theory of society. Within a class theory of society, social capital
can play some role, albeit a very minor role, given the enormously constraining
effects of class relations dominated by the logic of capital on the production
and operation of social capital. Of course, how minor that role will be depends

on the specific issue at hand and is geographically variant. A class critique of social capital is necessary to unveil not only the fact that the concept is without sound reason but also the fact that it has conservative political implications, the implications that are against the long-term interests of the masses. In the final section I draw out the theoretical and political implications of my alternative approach.

1   Society-Centric Approach to Social Capital

In much of the literature on social capital, it is seen as inhering in civil society, but outside the state. We may begin with Bourdieu's notion of social capital which is a part of his typology of capital (Bourdieu, 1986). For him, 'capital can present itself in three fundamental guises'. The first one is 'economic capital, which is immediately and directly convertible into money and may be institutionalized in the form of property rights'. The second form of capital is 'cultural capital, which is convertible, in certain conditions, into economic capital and may be institutionalized in the form of educational qualifications'. Economic and cultural capitals are contrasted to social capital. Social capital is 'made up of social obligations ("connections")' and it 'is convertible, in certain conditions, into economic capital' (p16).[5] 'Social capital is the aggregate of the actual or potential resources which are linked to possession of a durable network of more or less institutionalized relationships of mutual acquaintance and recognition – or in other words, to membership in a group – which provides each of its members with the backing of the collectively owned capital'. Bourdieu says that 'These relationships may exist only ... in material and/or symbolic exchanges which help to maintain them. They may also be socially instituted and guaranteed by the application of a common name (the name of a family, a class, or a tribe or of a school, a party, etc.)'. The establishment and maintenance of material and symbolic exchanges 'presuppose reacknowledgement of proximity' even though 'they are also partially irreducible to objective relations of proximity in physical (geographical) space or even in economic and social space' (p. 21).

According to Bourdieu, 'the network of relationships' that constitute social capital 'is the product of investment strategies, individual or collective, consciously or unconsciously aimed at establishing or reproducing social

---

5   Note that Bebbington (1999: 2029) also talks about natural, human, produced (=financial), social and cultural capitals (or 'capital assets', or simply, 'assets').

relationships that are directly usable in the short or long term, i.e., at trans-forming contingent relations, such as those of neighborhood, the workplace, or even kinship, into relationships that are at once necessary and elective, implying durable obligations subjectively felt (feelings of gratitude, respect, friendship, etc.) or institutionally guaranteed (rights)'. (p. 22).

The social capital literature that has developed *post* Bourdieu makes a series of claims. It is said that social capital (trust, civic norms, etc. in civil society) serves as a non-market means of addressing imperfections/failures of the market by promoting information-sharing through networks and lowering transaction costs, by discouraging opportunistic behaviour, and by helping collective action to (e.g.) manage common property (Serageldin and Grootaert, 2000: 47–49; Mearns, 1996). In a chapter of a book published by the World Bank, Narayan and Pritchett (1999) say that associational life is social, that it is capital and that it is social capital. They say that 'it is capital—in the sense of augmenting incomes' (ibid). And 'this capital is [locally] social, not only in the sense of relating to a social phenomena [non-economic resources], but also social in the economists' sense of containing spillover effects from one household to another within the village' (p. 272). Lin (2001) says that social capital can be measured and suggests various measures such as: size, density, cohesion, and closeness of social networks. There have indeed been several quantitative studies on social capital. Social capital is said to be associated positively with income and income equality (in a sample of 29 market economies) (Knack and Keefer, 1997) and with poverty reduction (in Indian States) (Morris, 1998). Social capital is associated negatively with infant mortality and income inequality in 39 US States (Kawachi, et al., 1997). World Bank researchers assert that social capital of rural households – where social capital is taken to mean networks and associations – is positively and causally associated with household per capita expenditures and welfare in African and Latin American countries (Grootaert et al., 2002; Grootaert and Narayan, 2004). But note that these studies tend to equate correlation to causation. It is also possible that when social capital is treated as one factor operating along with many others, and especially, class related factors such as the strength of working class power, it may have weak association with social outcomes such as health. An empirical study of sixteen wealthy countries suggests that this is indeed the case (Muntaner et al., 2002). Besides, there is also the possibility that both social capital and its purported effects (e.g. economic growth) are a result of a third factor such as state intervention or specific class relations.

Along with the quantitative studies, several case-studies on social capital have also appeared. Putnam's (1993) Italy study claims that: greater degrees of citizens' civic engagement breed trust and co-operation. The latter, in turn, discourage people's free rider attitude and thus resolve the collective action problem involved in monitoring government performance. This makes governments more efficient and more democratic in delivering public goods, causing greater well-being. Kennedy et al's (1998) study finds that in Russia those who lack social capital in the form of support from friends and family are more likely to be vulnerable to economic hardship, caused by the transition to a market economy.

Social capital in the form of entrepreneurial networks is shown to have enhanced the performance of the manufacturing sector by facilitating flows of knowledge between enterprises in Ghana (Barr, 2000) and in Nigeria (Brautigam, 1997). Uphoff and Wijayaratna (2000) report social capital formation in an irrigation scheme in Sri Lanka where ethnic co-operation was demonstrated by upstream Sinhalese farmers sharing water with downstream Tamil farmers (p. 1880). Cooperation among farmers reduced water wastage by individual farmers who earlier had no concern for people lacking water (Uphoff and Wijayaratna, 2000).

These and many other similar studies shed light on social capital of *civil society*, i.e. relations of trust and reciprocity among friends and neighbours, and their local networks and organisations. However, these studies not only under-stress the class dimension of social capital (more about this later) but also generally have a *society*-centric view of it.[6] That is, they tend to overlook the possibility that relations *between* civil society and state officials, and not just relations *within* civil society, can constitute a social resource or social capital. The state is seen as being merely influenced by social capital (Levi, 1996: 50; Booth and Richard, 1998; Unger, 1998).Some scholars even think of the state as antithetical to social capital (Chhibber, 2000: 299).

2   The State-Society Relation Approach to Social Capital

A few scholars attempt to counter this under-conceptualisation of the state. They see social capital as inhering 'not just in civil society, but in an enduring set of relationships that spans the public-private divide' (Evans, 1997b: 184). So, apart from civil society, another locus of social capital is the zone of interaction

---

6   Putnam's conception of civil society misses its 'political' aspects. Putnam's civic community is spontaneous and voluntaristic (and it is also localistic). Such a view is problematic. Civil society is created from above by state-building and broader political associations; and relations between the state and citizens can be conflictual rather than harmonious (Mouritsen, 2003).

between the state and civil society.[7] The state in question is seen as a relatively autonomous, competent state with coherence and credibility. It is sufficiently embedded in civil society, not isolated from it. It has a hierarchical division of labour that allows communities and officials to work out their problems flexibly and imaginatively at the local level without undue interference from above (Evans, 1997b: 194).

Social relations between the relatively autonomous state (officials) and civil society can be characterised as synergy. Following Evans and *pace* Woolcock (1998), one can say that synergy has two aspects: embeddedness and complementarity. Embeddedness refers to (face-to-face) ties of trust between citizens and public officials, who are 'more thoroughly part of the [local] communities in which they work'(Evans, 1997b: 184). Examples of embeddedness include: joint business-government deliberative councils; and, neighbourhood meetings where officials and communities participate to resolve conflicts. Complementarity refers to the fact that the state provides things that the communities do not or cannot have but will complement what they do have (Evans, 1997b). The extra-local scale character of the state and its bureaucratic organisation allow it to provide more effectively certain kinds of collective goods which complement the inputs more efficiently delivered by locally existing private actors. These can be material goods such as the physical infrastructure, including means of transportation and communication, which contribute to social connectedness in a place and across places. To complement the state provision of these goods, citizens contribute their local knowledge and experience.

This broader notion of social capital pointing to a local economic development strategy is exemplified in several empirical studies. Ostrom (1996) shows that poor localities (neighbourhoods) in a Brazilian city had to rely mainly on the government to produce trunk sewer lines which they could not have provided on their own, but they also collaborated in its production. Further, face-to-face interaction between them and officials facilitated the maintenance of the system. Similarly, joint forest management by local communities and state officials is said to have increased village incomes in India's Gujarat State (Serageldin and Grootaert, 2000). A study by two geographers, Bebbington

---

7   Civil society is seen as a) the realm of society in the wider sense, where private interests (especially of the bourgeoisie) rule, or b) as the realm of society which is outside of the state *and* the sphere of capitalist interests, and where social forces pursue emancipatory politics (on the various aspects and meanings of civil society, see Amoore and Langley, 2004; Baker, 2002; Cox, 1999; Hyden, 1997; Howell and Pearce, 2001; Lewis, 2002; Markovitz, 1998; Mohan, 2002; Mouritsen, 2003; Veltemeyer, 2012; Wiarda, 2003; Wickramasinghe, 2005).

and Perreault (1999), shows that state officials with a bias towards indigenous Highland communities in Ecuador formed social capital for these communities by helping them build local organisations and by linking these to organizations at higher geographical scales. These organisations have in turn led to state policies benefiting the Highlanders. Tendler (1997) investigates how in Brazil's Ceara State the government invested in building trust relations between officials and people, the trust relations that increased interaction between them and improved the performance of a public health campaign, reducing infant mortality. These studies show that: social capital is formed through close interaction between people and state officials, especially at the local scale. As Evans says, social capital in the form of trust as well as in the form of '[n]orms of co-operation and networks of civic engagement among *ordinary citizens* can be promoted by public agencies' through their synergy with civil society (Evans, 1997b: 178;184; stress added).

3   A Class Critique of the Social Capital Literature

The idea that what is called social capital is constituted by social relations (Woolcock, 1998) is a useful one. But the social relations that social capital experts talk about are, generally speaking, *not* (explicitly) conceptualized as *class* relations.[8] These are much rather seen as relations between individuals, or aggregates of individuals. Social capital is said to be about 'how *individuals* achieve co-ordination and overcome collective-action problems' (Ostrom, 2000: 173; stress added). The stress on the individual, on the community (a close cousin of social capital) and the local scale on the one hand and the under-theorization of class on the other are two sides of the same coin. Indeed, both approaches to social capital, and especially the former with its link to rational choice theory, under-stress the fact that society, *communities* and places are class-divided, that so-called *ordinary citizens* or individuals belong to particular classes, and that the most important context in which social capital is produced is the *class* context. The relative neglect of class (and especially a relational-conflictual view of class) is expressed in different ways/forms as briefly discussed below.[9]

---

8   These relations are also not conceptualized as relations of race or gender.
9   One may argue that the social capital approach is just a variety of pluralism (see Dahl, 1956; Truman, 1959), since pluralism is about cross-cutting cleavages overcoming any class formation.

Bourdieu's social theory acknowledges class relations in society. His view of social capital does draw attention to its economic basis: 'The volume of the social capital possessed by a given agent thus depends on the size of the network of connections he can effectively mobilize and on the volume of the capital (economic, cultural or symbolic) possessed in his own right by each of those to whom he is connected' (p. 21). Yet, his conceptual approach to social capital is a-historical and pluralistic. As we have seen, his concept of social capital – like that of Bebbington (1999) –is a part of his concept of capital in the plural ('capitals').[10] But he ignores the fact that for there to be forms of capital (economic, cultural and social capitals) in a conceptual sense, one has to know what capital as such is in the first place: multiple forms of a content must presuppose a given content itself. Bourdieu's definition of capital is not particularly precise. For him: properties of capital include: time, ability to produce benefit, use of unspecified form of labour, and so on. Such a view is evident when he says that in its objectified or embodied forms, capital 'takes time to accumulate' and it has 'a potential capacity to produce profits [or some benefits]' (Bourdieu, 1986: 15). Bourdieu's imprecise notion of capital is also evident when he says that 'Capital is accumulated labor ... which, when appropriated on a private, i.e., exclusive, basis by agents or groups of agents, enables them to appropriate social energy in the form of reified or living labor' (Bourdieu, 1986: 15)[11]. In contrast, the Marxist view is that capital is a set of relations between *classes* (mainly capitalists and workers in the modern society) that are expressed in the form of things (e.g. capitalist enterprises or machines, etc.). This is the correct way in which capital is to be conceptualized. Marxism insists on this. But Bourdieu's definition does not say this. Bourdieu more or less operates outside of the Marxist framework (see Burawoy, 2018 on Bourdieu's relation to Marxism).

Bourdieu uses profit, investment, labour, time, etc. in a non-conceptual (= descriptive) sense. 'The *profits* which accrue from membership in a group are the basis of the solidarity which makes them possible' (p. 22; italics added). Similarly, labour (work) in capital-labour relations and in capitalist accumulation, and labour in social capital are treated as the same: 'The reproduction of social capital presupposes an unceasing *effort* [as work or labour] of

---

10   On a recent discussion on Bourdieu's view of capital and capitalism, see Savage et al. (2005) (a favourable view) and Mohseni (2022) (a critical view).

11   'The 'capital' aspect of the [social capital] concept ...is ...fuzzy ...Social-capital writers, at least some of them, are dimly aware of an association of the capital concept with the concept of benefit' (Tittenbrun, 2014: 456). Robison, *et al.* 2002 discusses a Bourdieu type approach to capital without Bourdieu.

sociability, a continuous series of exchanges in which recognition is endlessly affirmed and reaffirmed' (ibid.). 'This work [or labour], which implies expenditure of time and energy and so, directly or indirectly, of economic capital' but such expenditure 'is not *profitable* or even conceivable unless one invests in it a specific competence (knowledge of genealogical relationships and of real connections and skill at using them, etc.)' (ibid.: 22–23). This partly explains why 'the *profitability* of [the] labor of accumulating and maintaining social capital rises in proportion to the size of the capital' (ibid.: 23; italics added). If capital is characterized merely as a resource that produces benefit, as Bourdieu thinks capital does, then society dominated by capital has always existed, so there is nothing specific about a society dominated by the logic of capital. Besides, capital may produce benefit to capitalists, but this benefit, according to Marxism, comes at the expense of workers. So the concept of capital loses its historical specificity when scholars such as Bourdieu see it merely as something that produces benefit.

Social capital scholars emphasize the moral economy aspect of social capital, i.e. reciprocity and self-help at individual and community/local levels. According to Thompson (1971), the concept of moral economy centres on the idea that social relations between elites and common people were grounded in norms of reciprocity and in a socially recognised right to subsistence. Surely, moral economy (especially in the sense of moral responsibility of the rich towards the poor) as a basis for self-help may be economically important in specific places or instances. But moral economy should not be considered in isolation from political economy (i.e. the unequal distribution of material resources between classes and the attendant issues of power). That moral economy or mutual assistance can mean 'narrow and often risky personalized dependencies of people on each other' (Levi, 1996: 51) and especially of the poor on the rich is not systematically recognized. Indeed, by reinforcing the power relation between the rich people who provide some help and the poor people who receive it, moral economy actually undermines the long-term economic interests of the poor by weakening them politically. The rich helping the poor – this is called linking social capital – is conditional upon the poor being subservient to the rich. If their poverty is because of their lack of power, moral economy – as embodied in the system of social capital practices – does nothing to enhance their power.

A few scholars have commented on the neglect of political power in the social capital literature (Foley and Edwards, 1996). But they tend to overlook the *class*-specific implications of this neglect. In particular, it is problematic not to specifically look at the social capital of the working class. For one thing, the working class (in villages, cities and city-regions) has a unique social-political resource in its hands. It is *the* class that produces surplus value on which the entire capitalist society is based and therefore it is *the* class which has the power to stop capitalist production and valorization. It can take on the capitalist class in a way no other class or group can. Capitalism itself is responsible for the political power of labour. One reason is the fact that production in a big capitalist workplace requires many people to cooperate with one another, a fact from which workers learn the value of cooperation in their own social-political life. Relations of cooperation among workers, and relations between them and their organizers and political educators, are an important social resource in the hands of workers. Working class members can share the ways and the means of exercising their unique power among themselves. If sharing and reciprocity are so important to social capital as they are, this class-specific form of sharing and reciprocity cannot be neglected. But it is. Further, the political organization of the working class is a precondition for its economic survival to a greater extent than for the capitalist class whose power lies relatively less in its everyday political organisation and more in their control over productive property (their private political power) and over the state, which itself represents the permanent centralized political organization of the capitalist class. Any neglect of working-class political mobilization is therefore necessarily biased against the working class. Broadening the scope of the concept of social capital in any discussion on the usefulness of social resources to include the state is not enough to counter the neglect of class in the literature. For, the state itself is primarily a class institution with class-specific actions and effects. Most of the social capital scholars, including Evans, tend to ignore this fact in part because of their dominantly Weberian approach to the state.

To the extent that social capital writers do deal with issues of power, their class-specificity is often under-theorized. If Bourdieu who has a socially undifferentiated view of labour as discussed earlier, many other social capital researchers have a socially undifferentiated view of associationalism and solidarity such that there is little or no recognition that political parties, football clubs and bird-watching groups do not have same political effects (see Levi, 1996: 49). They stress 'mutually beneficial coalitions across social and economic divisions' (World Bank, 2001; Putnam, 1993), which are assumed to benefit the society as a whole, as if society does not have class-based conflicts of interest (and other conflicts that class conflicts and class relations tend to cause and/or reinforce).

To the extent that class is discussed at all in the social capital literature, the working class tends to be left out. Much of the literature, including research on industrial districts and on the politics of economic development in geography and development studies, discusses how capitalists and other propertied groups use relations of trust and networks to improve their competitiveness in particular places and to enhance their efficiency and solve coordination problem. Thus when class appears, it does so in the form of mainly propertied classes, including small capitalists and the petty-bourgeoisie.[12] A dialectical-relational view of class is missing.

One may say that I am exaggerating the (working) 'class-blindness' of the social capital literature. Surely, in the literature, there is a discussion on poor people (Morris, 1998; Grootaert and Narayan, 2004), and on how social capital works as the 'capital' of the poor[13] (World Bank, 2001). But even in this discussion, the class character of social capital is not examined. There are at least two reasons for this neglect. For one thing, the class character of the poor themselves is usually left out: the fact that the poor generally belong to a class/classes (wage-earning and semi-proletarian classes) whose material interests are in conflict with the classes having ownership/control over resources (Wright, 1995) tends not be considered. The poor are seen descriptively in terms of income or consumption, etc. In addition, social capital scholars often assume that as social capital of society as a whole develops – i.e. as relations of trust and reciprocity become stronger and as networks and organisations based on trust and reciprocity expand – the poor, as a part of that society benefit and indeed that they benefit from social capital more than the non-poor. This assumption is the social capital version of the neo-classical trickle-down theory of poverty. Not considering the class character of poverty obviates the need to conceptualise how social capital develops in, and is constrained by, the class-context in which the poor men and women live.[14] The neglect of class would be condoned if there was not a literature on the topic to connect to. But there is indeed a large amount of literature on self-help

---

12   The stress on small-scale property owners is seen in the geographical work on social capital and small-scale industrialisation (Bebbington, 1999; Turner, 2007) and in the sociological work on 'ethnic' capitalism (Portes, 2010).

13   Social capital can appear to be social capital of the poor only when social capital's class context is stripped away. It is also true that social capital appears progressive when 'power, securities, and opportunities of the wealthy remain sacrosanct' are abstracted from (Fine, 2000).

14   Similarly, there is a discussion on social capital of peasants (semi-proletarians) (Bebbington and Perreault, 1999). But it is problematic to talk about peasants' social capital without considering the powers and liabilities of peasants as a class (e.g. poor peasants) or peasants as a set of classes whose interests are in conflict with those of, say, the landlords and agri-business companies (and the capitalist state), and how their class position constrains (and enables) their social capital. The concept of peasants merely as a set of individuals/families with small-scale property is deficient.

cooperative, and other related activities within working class communities that *can* correct the missing class dimension in the currently fashionable social capital research (Bourke, 1994; Farr, 2004; Morriss and Irwin, 1992; Short, 1996; Thompson, 1964).

Social capital enthusiasts' uneasiness with class is very well expressed in the following quote. 'If a community is riven by conflicting interests, the nature and meaning of social capital becomes more complicated' (Evans, 1997b: 196; also Duncan, 2001: 75). But just because a process is complicated does not mean that it should not be examined. There is a method of analyzing the complex processes: it is called the method of abstraction. The method of abstraction involves, among other processes, the task of separating the more concrete or contingent aspects of a complex object from those aspects that are necessarily related to the object under examination (Sayer, 1992).

One purpose of this chapter is to develop a class-based, political economy approach to social capital to unpack opportunities of, and, *more importantly*, limits to, social capital as they are rooted in class relations in specific places and over space. The question I address is: *to the extent that* social capital is a useful category, what is its class character?

4   Towards a Class Approach to Social Capital

Underlying the political economy approach to social capital is a specific approach to class relations and to the state. Class is a structure of relations of, and processes (re-)producing, inequality in the distribution of means of production and the resultant relations/processes of exploitation between classes (Camfield, 2004; Wood 1998; Wright, 2005, 1989).[15] Class structure defines limits within which certain outcomes are more likely than others. Class structure is both enabling and constraining (Callinicos, 1988: 235). In terms of the relation between social capital and class, class limits within which social capital is produced and it has effects on different classes (and on other relations). Within the limits of class, certain ways of social capital production and certain effects of social capital are more likely than others. Social capital is produced and used by particular classes. Social capital is about norms of reciprocity and networks/organizations which foster these norms. Cultural and political norms always presuppose material resources. Without these resources, the social resources of norms as well as networks/organizations considered to be

---

15   For more recent discussions on class, see Das (2017), and O'Neill and Wayne (2017).

social capital have limited causal powers.[16] And access to material resources is influenced by class relations, *more than* any other set of social relations.

I will look at the social capital of the working class only.[17] The latter is defined here as the class, which is excluded from the ownership of, and control over, means of production and whose main source of income is the sale of labour power.[18] I use 'working class social capital' advisedly.[19] I use it primarily as an investigative category to look at the ways in which the working class (re)makes and lives its life (Thompson, 1964) and creates its history and geography (Herod, 1997; Harvey, 1982). In struggling for better economic-political conditions in particular places within the limits defined by class structure and the state, workers employ several strategies. One of them is their own social resource (advisedly called social capital here) – trust, norms of reciprocity, connections, networks and organisations. Workers use this resource not only to directly bridge the gap between the amount of subsistence resource that a particular family has and what it needs, but also to resolve their own collective action problems and to build connections with certain state actors and with one another over space in order to improve their economic condition. Working class social capital, like social capital in general, exists within civil society ('micro level') and in state-society relations ('macro level').[20] Its production is enabled *and* constrained by processes broadly derived from its class context.

'Micro level' working class social capital is the social capital of the working class inhering in civil society. It refers to norms of trust and reciprocity and to

---

16   Strictly speaking, these social *resources* are not *capital*. If I am referring to these as capital, this is because the term has been used in that sense. Capital proper refers to an exploitative relationship between capital and labour; resources *become* capital within this relationship. Ideally, every time I use the word social capital, I should say 'what is called social capital' (or, I should put the term under quotation marks). I return to this matter – my reservations about social capital – in the conclusion.

17   Space constraint will not permit a discussion of the propertied class social capital.

18   The working class thus defined includes semi-proletarians (labourers with small amounts of means of production) on the basis of the assumption that their main contradiction is with capitalists rather than with any other class/group.

19   As already indicated, I am acutely aware of the problematic nature of 'social' in what is called social capital by the enthusiastic supporters of the concept. 'Social' in their social capital implies that 'capital' is not necessarily social, when in fact it is. It is also useful note that I am not saying that there is a common pool of social capital of which the working class must have a share like the capitalist class. To a large extent, relations of connections and trust and their causal powers are specific to classes (and genders and ethnic groups). Relations of connection among the capitalist class people constitute *their* social capital, and will have little use *for* the working class, given that the interests of these two classes are fundamentally incompatible (see note 16 above).

20   'Micro' and 'macro' are used entirely for the convenience of labelling.

networks and organisations among working class people. Working class micro social capital has class-specific effects. Norms of trust and reciprocity can discourage free rider behaviour and facilitate collective actions such as: building of physical and social infrastructure in working class communities (e.g. community house; roads; library) which can enhance their social connectedness; launching political action against employers paying low wages; or monitoring corrupt officials implementing anti-poverty policies. Norms of trust and reciprocity can lead to informal mechanisms of support within working class communities. These can take such forms as: informal borrowing of food and other items of necessity; worker-managed eating-places; micro credit groups as well as sharing of information/tacit knowledge between (propertied) labourers.[21] Working class people also use relations based around family and kinship as survival strategies (Argyle, 1994: 79). Self-help (e.g. food sharing; informal credit) is particularly important during strikes as it can increase workers' staying power vis a vis employers.

The production of working class social capital is enabled and constrained by class processes. First consider the enabling class processes. Useful here is the concept of 'organicity of classes', a crucial concept in contemporary class theory (Bodeman and Spohn, 1986). It refers to 'the primordial relations, the particular [class-specific] ways of life and culture, the common outlook and the interpersonal ties within which ... [the working class is] embedded' (ibid.: 10). This concept counters the idea of what Bodeman and Spohn call 'naked proletarian' – that the working class is without traditions, ties of family, kinship and neighbourhood.[22] As E. P. Thompson aptly said, the working class is a social and cultural formation, like capitalism itself. Commenting on the influence of religion on class struggle, he referred to the processes which connote social capital: 'the working class community injected into the chapels *its own values* of mutual aid, neighbourliness and solidarity' (1964: 392; italics added). Indeed, *mutual aid and neighbourliness* are important social resources. In his famous Preface to *A Contribution to the Critique of Political economy*, Marx (1859) says that the contradiction-ridden material conditions under which people live generally structure their 'social consciousness' and political organization. If this is true, then it is not difficult to argue that common class-specific ways of life of working class families can create a specific type of bond between them, or what is known as 'bonding social capital' in the social capital literature, i.e. social relations and norms of reciprocity among people of similar

---

21 These are the labourers who supplement their wage, the main source of their income, through small-scale entrepreneurial activities.

22 Primordial relations can also create disunity in the working class.

socio-economic status (Putnam, 2000: 22–23). Marx says in *The 18th Brumaire* that to be a politically organised class, workers must have a *community*, a national *bond*, and a political *organisation.* Community, bond and organisation are indeed keywords in the social capital literature.

Portes, a sociologist, says that a source of social capital is 'bounded solidarity' (Portes, 2010). Bounded solidarity emerges from a common situation people find themselves in, rather than from norms of trust and reciprocity one has learnt during childhood. Actors' altruistic dispositions are not universal. Much rather, these 'are bounded by the limits of their community' (Portes, 2010: 33). 'Other members of the same community can then appropriate such dispositions as "their" source of social capital' (ibid.). This concept, Portes says, is best exemplified by Marx's analysis of the rise of working class consciousness. 'By being thrown together in a common situation, workers learn to identify with one another and support one another's initiatives' (Portes and Sensenbrenner, 1993: 1325). 'The weapon of the working class in this struggle is precisely its internal solidarity born out of a common awareness of capitalist exploitation' (p. 1324–1325).[23] Workers' solidarity is based on an emergent sentiment of we-ness among them as they face similar difficult situation, a sentiment based on moral imperative rather than rational calculations of costs and benefits (ibid.: 1327–8; see also Callinicos, 1988: 199–203). Indeed, their common experience of the social crisis – the crisis of reproduction of a healthy life – caused by capitalism, including relative (and for many workers, absolute) poverty, is a potential basis for reciprocity and network. Portes says that 'If sufficiently strong', emergent sentiment [of we-ness] will lead to the observance of norms of mutual support [e.g. exchange of gifts], appropriable by individuals as a resource in their own pursuits' (p. 1325). This is similar to the support that newly arrived ethnic minority immigrants get from existing ethnic minority immigrants who have a sense of solidarity based on their perception that they are discriminated against (ibid.).[24]

---

23   Marx says in *Poverty of Philosophy* that the domination of capital creates the common situation and common interests of the working class.

24   Thus workers' micro social capital is produced by ties among individual workers and among groups of workers. Some of these ties are ties of kinship, family, location, and so on. Social capital that can be produced by these ties among workers can contribute to their unity, and provide temporary forms of material support for them to cope with the social crisis they always experience. More importantly, these ties come from their 'emergent sentiment of we-ness' or 'bounded solidarity', a limited form of class consciousness, and which is, in turn, reinforced by these ties and associational life. Further, workers' social capital is not the same as class consciousness but can be helped by the latter. Workers' social capital is also not the same as their political solidarity but can be based on solidarity and reinforce it. Working class social capital is also not necessarily the same as,

Workers' class position not only enables the production of workers' micro social capital. It also constrains it. Given their class position, most workers (and small-scale producers) have limited material resources to share among themselves. And, without *resources* to share, informal *rules* of sharing in a place (e.g. in a neighbourhood) and over space (e.g. between neighbourhoods) are difficult to sustain for long (in their active form). Social resources of the working class, its networks and connections, tend to be indeed socially and spatially limited. So, the working class has 'less' social capital than other classes. This is confirmed by a few empirical studies. In Britain, for example, there are 'deep differences in the connections that people in different class situations have to the community', and this is evident from the fact that 'On average, people in the middle class have twice as many organisational affiliations as those in the working class' (Hall, 1999: 438).[25] In addition, a higher proportion of working class people 'suffer[s] from a complete absence of social support' than other classes (ibid.). Also, the nature of working class social capital is different from that of other classes:

> [W]hile social clubs and trade unions dominate the associations to which working class members belong, those in the middle class develop affiliations with a much wider range of organisations. ... The patterns of informal sociability of the working class are [also] more likely than those of the middle class to revolve around close contacts with kin and with a small set of friends.[26]
>
>   ibid.

A major factor underlying these class differences in the stock and nature of *social* resource which is given the name, social capital, is the fact that the working class is excluded from, and relatively deprived of, *material* resources (especially, means of production) of society. A fundamental aspect of the working class life is also *insecurity*, not just *exclusion* from material resources. Because

---

but is a part of, working class collective action in the sense that the former (and especially macro social capital) works *within* the limits of the class structure whereas the latter can and must be aimed at *transcending* class relations.

25   This is consistent with findings from Britain that people in disadvantaged positions are more likely to draw social capital from weak ties and those in more advantaged positions are more likely to draw social capital from formal civic engagement and networks (Li et al. 2005).

26   Although classes in Hall's study are defined following the Weberian methodology, the results are broadly indicative of the class differences in social capital that this chapter is discussing.

the working class has been separated from means of production, its access to means of subsistence, generally, depends on securing wage work, which, however, is not guaranteed. One never knows how one is going to get through to the end of the week, a fact which indicates the severity of social crisis.[27] The material *insecurity* of the working class can undermine the conditions for the reproduction of social norms of self-help and reciprocity, which presuppose a sense of *security*, an expectation that when one is in difficulty, one's relations with others can certainly act as insurance. Indeed, in a recent work Putnam himself recognizes this: as more and more workers are joining the contingent labour force (part-timers, people with insecure jobs, etc.), the conditions for connectedness at work are being undermined (Putnam, 2000: 88).[28]

Further, given their separation from means of production and subsistence, working class people are more likely to face social crisis which is partly manifested as poverty than almost all sections of the propertied class. There is also much competition for jobs. Now, too much poverty and intra-class competition can adversely affect norms of reciprocity (Brehm and Rahn, 1997: 1009). There is also the issue of identity. Reproduction of the structure of social relations partly depends on agents' perceptions of them*selves* and of their 'others', the perceptions that underlie the formation of identities. Workers' cross-cutting identities (ethnicity, gender, locality, etc.) *can* weaken their social capital in the form of their social networks (Callinicos, 1993: 50). White labourers may unite *with* white property owners in one area *against* minority (non-white) workers in the same area. Place-bound cross-class alliance is also important: labourers in a city enter into alliance with capitalists in that city to attract inward investment but that might hurt workers elsewhere (Fitzgerald, 1991; Harvey, 1982; Cox and Mair, 1988). These divisions often are enduring as the capitalist class often uses them to control the working class (Wright, 1982: 539).

Now consider 'macro' social capital of the working class. I define this as norms of trust and reciprocity and as networks and organisations, all located in the zone of interaction between the working class and 'relatively autonomous' actors of the capitalist state – i.e. the officials and the actors who manage

---

27   Even in the richest country on earth (the USA), where social capital research has gained much popularity including in the form of Putnam's work, a survey found out that 63% of respondents would not be able to cover, out of pocket, an emergency expense of $1,000 such as an emergency room visit or the cost of repairing a broken down vehicle, without either cutting down on expenses elsewhere, borrowing or resorting to credit (Barrickman, 2016)

28   Of course, this recognition is not more than an after-thought in his overall framework that treats social capital as an independent variable.

the affairs of the state at different geographical scales, including the local.[29] It refers to the 'synergy' between them (Evans, 1997b; *pace* Woolcock, 1998).[30] The synergy refers to the provision of collective goods by the state in working class communities such as infrastructure and material assistance to the poorer workers. The synergy also refers to state's embeddedness in these communities, i.e. to the ties, based on trust and reciprocity, between state officials and working class communities under their jurisdiction. Their participation in the daily lives of the working class communities can enhance the latter's trust in pro-poor officials. This also can make it possible for these communities to shame and censure the officials when they are found working against workers' interests.

Macro-level social capital in the form of synergy between the state and the working class, like micro level social capital, is both enabled and constrained by class-processes. First of all, synergy is made possible by the existence of common grounds, common interests, between the state (officials and politicians) and the working class. To the extent that the state represents capitalists' *common* interests, the common grounds between the state officials and the working class partly reflect those between the capitalist and working classes in particular places. Where these common interests also coincide with the relatively independent interests of the state (officials), chances for co-operative action by the state and workers are maximized.

There are several possible common grounds or interests. Firstly, both capitalists and workers, generally, have an interest in the weakening of pre-capitalist class structures and political relations (Rueschemeyer et al., 1992). Weakening of traditional structures of political domination also helps the state's penetration of society and exercise of what Mann (1984) calls 'infrastructural power' (including that of rule-making). A local history of workers-state alliance against the traditional elites can contribute to workers' macro social capital.

---

29   It is important not to include the state *as such* as a part of workers' social capital. What is included here is only the relation of trust and cooperation between workers and relatively autonomous pro-worker officials who may be present, especially, at the local scale.

30   I am deliberatively excluding, from macro social capital, the relations of trust and community between workers and managers/capitalists or what Greene et al call 'phychological contract'. The features of psychological contract include: workers identifying themselves with companies; face-to- face communication between managers and workers on the shop floor and in informal parties in the community, outside of work; joint decision making and consultative committees; workers' expectation of managers to play a paternalist role; and a sense of community at the workplace (Greene et al. 2001: 229–231). A mainstream writer believing in social capital as a glue may include, under social capital, Greene's 'psychological contract'.

Secondly, an improvement in the material standard of living of the working class can be compatible with (and sometimes even might promote) capitalist economic growth. This will especially be where economic growth is based on the production of wage goods in the domestic market. The state has also an interest in growth because of its own conjunctural or derivative 'dependence' on that from which it receives its revenue (conjunctural or derivative because the 'dependence' is a product of a more fundamental attributes of the state – i.e. its class character).[31]

Thirdly, sometimes the common grounds between the working class and the state can be due to *intra*-capitalist class differences. For example, factions of the capitalist class can reap place-specific super-profits by paying below-subsistence wages to nominally free labourers and/or by using unfree labour (Brass, 1999). So, state-workers synergy (through, for example, pro-worker legislations made possible by reformist officials) can make possible some increase in wages but will leave the conditions for average, competitive profit rates of the capitalist class intact. The abolition of unfree labour in the same process will benefit labour but will not be *in*compatible with the interests of the capitalist class *as a whole, which* generally presupposes free labour. Abolition of unfree labour in so far as it allows greater spatial mobility of the working class might indeed benefit some capitalists, especially those located in areas of labour shortage.

These common grounds – and there are others (see Wright, 2000) – exist *structurally*. They are to be translated into relations of cooperation between workers and the state through individual and collective *agency*. I see the state fundamentally as an institution that reproduces class relations and the dominance of capitalist class through a variable combination of administrative/ physical coercion, ideological education/socialization (consent formation) and minor and revocoble economic concession. This is the logic of the state. Within the limit of this logic, the state is also a socio-spatial site of contradictory class presences, a site where both dominant and subordinate classes, directly or through their representatives, are present at different geographical scales, although quite unequally and with vastly unequal amounts of influence. There *are* parts of the state, especially at the local scale of state-society relations, where pro-working class elements (e.g. politicians/officials representing working class interests) may be present, albeit more in some localities and less in others. Indeed, as Poulantzas says, dominated classes are present in the state 'in the form of centres of opposition to the power of the dominant

---

31   On this, see Das (2022: 4; 51; 185).

classes' (1978: 142; 148), even against the will of the latter. They can take a reformist stance, within the overall logic of the state.[32] The relations of trust and cooperation between the working class and the reformist officials, including those who may have working class background and ideology, can become a form of macro social capital of the former. These elements can, within limits of capitalism, employ the structurally given 'relative autonomy' of the state and use resources at their disposal to build connections with workers and try to empower them materially and politically, as they sometimes do for peasant/semi-proletarian communities (Fox, 1996; Bebbington and Perreault, 1999). The possibility that conflicts over wages and working conditions can be resolved (even if temporarily) in favour of the working class in specific places is enhanced by the presence of pro-worker reformists within the state.

Heller (1997) indeed shows how social capital was produced in India's Kerala State by both labour mobilization and supportive state action. In particular, government action supported workers' mobilization and offered institutional resources that allowed militancy to become compatible with accumulation. The implication of the synergy is that it made labour realise the need for discipline as well as the need for reconciling redistribution with capitalist growth. Persistent political competitiveness led to a situation where almost all parties, whether in or out of the government, were, more or less, committed to political mobilisation and construction of encompassing organisations among working class people.

But there are severe limits to synergy between the state and workers that is supposed to produce macro social capital for workers. Firstly, the state, as just mentioned, is a fundamentally class institution, whatever else it may be (Barrow, 1993; Clarke, 1991; Jessop, 1990).[33] Given its class character which is partly expressed, at a relatively concrete level, as what Offe (1987) calls the institutional separation of the state from the capitalist economy, may not have the resources for the reformist officials to make available to the working class. Even if it does, it may be simply constrained from providing material benefits to the working class as happens under neo-liberalism. Without resources being used for workers, norms of reciprocity between them and state actors will weaken.

---

32   I am using 'reformist' to indicate that these officials try to provide some temporary relief to workers within the constraints of capitalism/class. Whether their *intention* is to remain just reformist is beside the matter here.

33   Recent works on the state include Aronowitz and Bratsis (2002) and Pressman (2006). On a recent discussion on the class character of the state as a (socio-spatial) structure of social relations, and of those who manage the common affairs of the state from a standpoint that is critical of the relative autonomy thesis, see Das (2022).

In fact, with neoliberalization of state officials, many of them refuse to inter-act with common people; rather they integrate themselves with the capitalist class. While the personnel of the state before the onset of neoliberalism, often drawn from lower strata of society (e.g. petty-bourgeois strata), maintained some distance between them and the capitalist class, now the personnel of the state revel in their connections with the business class. The state actors in pre-neoliberal times 'were generally skeptical about, and even to a degree hostile to, the capitalist class' (Patnaik, 2007: 12). Officials of the neoliberal state are different: they differ fundamentally from the personnel of the pre-neoliberal state, 'not just in their ideological predilections, which are closely aligned to the views of the Bretton Woods institutions, *but also in their being deeply enmeshed with the world of finance and big business'* (ibid.: 12; italics added). Their motivation 'is no different from that of the big bourgeoisie and financial interests', so they have 'no compunctions about being closely integrated with the latter' (p. 13). Patnaik adds: 'The matter relates not just to anti-poverty pro-grammes. The personnel of the neo-liberal State have little interest in running the public sector' which has typically provided employment and other benefits to the segments of the population. Such neglect of the public sector is a reason why it 'becomes financially unviable over time, and provides grist to the mill of those who want it privatized'.

Neoliberalization of state officials has an interesting implication for social capital formation. On the one hand: not carrying out normal government func-tions, the bureaucracy is 'more interested in networking with patrons in the world of corporates and foreign donors, or in attending World Bank-sponsored training programmes, than in the nitty-gritty of administration' (Patnaik, 2007: 14); it thus develops its own (linking) social capital. On the other hand, neo-liberalism constrains the social capital of common people (in the form of, say, linking social capital), as we have seen. Indeed, the neoliberalism agenda itself has been conducive to the popularity of social capital as a concept which reflects such agenda. Interestingly, in a paper prepared for a conference on economic reforms (=pro-business, pro-market reforms) in the late 1990s spon-sored by the IMF, that neoliberalism-promoting global institution (Mueller, 2011), Fukuyama (2001: 18), a cheerleader for global capitalism, says that social capital, understood as 'an informal norm that promotes co-operation between two or more individuals' (p. 7), not only reduces costs of free-market trans actions but also 'promotes the kind of associational life which is necessary *for the success of limited government and modern democracy'* (italics added). Fukuyama warns that 'states can have a serious negative impact on social capi-tal when they start to undertake activities that are better left to the private sec-tor or to civil society' (p.18), i.e. when states go against the neoliberal agenda.

He adds that: 'There are ... good reasons why countries should restrict the size of their state sectors for economic reasons. On top of this, he says, one can add a cultural motive of preserving a sphere for individual action and initiative in building civil associations'. (ibid.). This sphere is, of course, the sphere of social capital that can compensate for poor people's lack of productive resources and for the reduced level of state's welfare for them.

The second reason why there are severe limits to synergy between the state and workers is that: even if the state provides collective material and intangible goods, it can do so in a bureaucratic manner which can disrupt micro social capital in the form of workers' trust in officials and their own local initiatives and organisations (e.g. their self-help networks). This, in turn, can hurt prospects of macro social capital formation. Bureaucratic distribution of benefits unequally among working class members (or areas) can fragment the working *class* into individual citizen-*clients* competing for benefits from the paternalist state. Further, formal equality before law and citizenship can, paradoxically, fragment the working *class* into individual *voter-citizens*, thus undermining *class-based* identity and solidarity. These possibilities have indeed been observed in several countries such as Mexico and India (Fox, 1996; Das, 2000).

Thirdly, the structure of the state itself makes synergistic interaction between the state and workers problematic. The state is not a neutral instrument equally accessible to all social forces. It is fundamentally the state of the capitalist class, with the degree of its operational autonomy being a conjunctural matter, and not the essence of the state. It has an in-built structural bias that makes it more open to dominant class influences than to the exploited classes, with the question of the *degree* of the state being open to ruling class influences a conjunctural matter. The state becomes a structurally selective terrain which tends to insulate it from working class influence on, and surveillance over it. This problem is compounded in the less developed nations by the fact that their states become particularly repressive as they lack the resources with which to buy consent from the working class.

Finally, and this point applies to both micro and macro social capital of the working class, when working class social capital increases workers' material and political power beyond a level that dominant classes will tolerate, the latter will try to counter that by using their own social capital, including their ties with state officials. Beyond certain limit, dominant classes and their state (and it is essentially *their* state) will not tolerate co-operative action between reformist officials and workers, for the state's primary task is to reproduce conditions of class exploitation and class domination. Neither will relations of cooperation within the working class, which can promote their unity vis a vis dominant classes, be supported by dominant classes. The latter will create or reinforce divisions based on gender, race, caste, religion, education, location, etc. There are therefore practical as well as epistemological limitations of the concept of social capital.[34]

Within the limits of capitalism, a variable amount of working class social capital can be tolerated by the capitalist class and its state. This is partly because given the capitalist nature of the state, the state has 'some autonomy', and therefore everything that state actors do is not reducible to capitalist interests. This should not blind us to the fact that the class context of social capital severely limits the state-society synergy in the interest of the working class. This means that the usefulness of social capital as a concept and as a social practice is rather limited.

If the function of social capital is social cohesion, if it is 'a glue that holds societies together' (Serageldin and Grootaert, 2000: 44), working class social capital as conceptualized here cannot be the social capital of social capital researchers. This is because to the extent that one can talk about social capital of the working class, its aim must be to help it challenge the social order and not hold it together, while one most fundamental objective of the state is to reproduce disunity – separation – among the working class. Indeed, social capital of the working class as conceptualized in this chapter – i.e. relations of reciprocity and solidarity that can help the working class challenge the state and the class relations it protects – may be called, in the language of mainstream social capital literature, negative social capital or 'the dark side of social capital' (Putnam, 2000: 350–363).

5   Conclusion

Social capital has become a key concept in major social science disciplines. Its popularity partly reflects the current neo-liberal agenda. Its popularity is surprising given that the concept has major problems one of which has been the focus of the discussion here: class character of social capital is not discussed. It would be, of course, wrong to say that the class character of social capital

---

34   To the extent that social capital writers discuss the limitations of social capital as a practice (not as a concept), as, say, in the discussion of the dark side of social capital (e.g. mafia social capital), the limitations are only contingently related to the social capital practice. In the class approach taken here, the limitations are, however, a necessary aspect of the social capital practice. It is also the case that some social capital writers such as Putnam occasionally recognize some of the limitations I discuss but then proceed *as if* these do not exist.

has been totally neglected. Indeed, a few scholars do attempt to incorporate the class dimension (Bourdieu, 1986; Duncan, 2001; Portes and Sensenbrenner, 1993). This chapter seeks to critically extend and contribute to that work.

The chapter identifies and discusses two major approaches to social capital in the literature ('society-centric' and 'state-society relation' approaches). In critiquing these approaches for its neglect of the class character of social capital, the chapter unpacks the different forms that this neglect of class has taken. Subsequently, it seeks to develop a class or political economy approach to social capital. In particular, it discusses the nature of 'working class social capital' and the different ways in which it can be produced within civil society as well as in the structure of relations between workers and 'relatively autonomous' state officials. The chapter highlights how the class context of working class social capital constrains and enables its production.

Working class social capital, as conceptualized in this chapter, is about mutual relations of trust and cooperation within working class places or communities, the relations which can act as a social resource in promoting working class solidarity and therefore help the working class contest the power of dominant classes and/or the state. It is *also* about relations of trust and co-operation between workers and reformist officials with sympathy for the working class. Working class social capital in both these senses can provide *some* material benefits to the class at a local scale and more or less temporarily.

In contrast to, but also complementing, much of the class struggle literature, which focuses mainly on the struggle between capital and labour, the approach in this chapter allows one to look at *opportunities* for and *constraints* on a) collective action and co-operation within the working class and b) co-operation between the working class and state actors. In contrast to the approaches to social capital that generally under-theorize the class character of the social resource called social capital (norms of reciprocity, networks, etc.) and overlooks the literature on working class self-activity, including self-help, this chapter has attempted to show that social capital (like all socio-cultural practices) must be seen in its class context. This approach also leaves open the possibility that workers can/do use social capital produced in a class-*neutral* context, that is, the social capital as it is generally conceptualised in the literature, and this may give the semblance of similarity between working class social capital and social capital per se. But my approach is distinctive from non-class approaches in recognizing the severe *limits* to working class social capital formation, the limits as defined by the class structure. Social capital scholars for whom social capital is a matter of networks/organisations that *cut across* class cleavages (Putnam, 1993: 175) do not have to worry about these limits. Social capital seen in a cross-class context is potentially very conservative.

This form of social capital – cross-class social capital – is constituted by mutual relations of trust and connections between, say, the capitalist class and the working class or between landlords and semi-proletarians (peasants), and is supposed to produce small benefits for the subordinate classes in specific places while helping to reproduce the overall class structure at the national scale. On the other hand, social capital seen in a class context as indicated by the concept of working class social capital, prioritizes class conflict, and has the potential for producing working class solidarity *vis a vis* dominant classes.

I have argued that class is enormously constraining of social capital. This is often neglected in the literature on social capital which treats social capital as an independent variable and a solution to social ills. Therefore, it is absolutely problematic to try to construct a new theory of social capital of poverty, of health or crime (Woolcock and Narayan, 1999). There cannot be a social capital theory of society. Within a class theory of society, social capital can play only a very minor role. Of course, how minor that role will be depends on the specific issue at hand and can be place-specific because the balance between class-constraints and class-opportunities mentioned earlier will vary geographically. As well, those who valorize social capital's favourable impacts on the poor neglect the fact that: because of the overall class structural context and the consequences of that context (as expressed in various forms of social crisis such as poverty), people have to rely on small amounts of help available through social capital (e.g. self-help, etc.).

The approach outlined here is potentially open to some criticisms. For example, a Marxist, whether they support the social capital idea or not, can argue that the state, given its class character, cannot do much for the benefit of the working class. However, underlying my approach to social capital is a specific approach to the state. In this approach, as far as workers' *immediate interests*, as opposed to their *fundamental interests* are concerned, state policies vary in their classness to a certain extent and at a relatively concrete level.[35] This means that some policies are more pro/anti-working class than others and that *within* limits of capitalist property relations and logic of accumulation, state's actions are generally a product of, and reflect, not only the longer-term interests of the capitalist class in the existence of a working class that is relatively well-fed, relatively healthy and that has the skills to contribute to the process of production and exchange, but also working class struggle and bargaining strength. Within the limits of class structure, therefore, certain

---

35 'Fundamental interests' are defined *across* modes of production (e.g. interests in capitalism or socialism). 'Immediate interests' are defined *within* a mode of production (Wright, 1982: 541).

synergistic relations between the working class people and reformist state actors are temporarily possible (especially at the local scale of state-society relations). Further, capital depends on the state to protect exploitative property rights. The need to protect exploitive relations, in the face of potential and actual opposition from below, might make the capitalist class tolerate certain amount of working class (macro) social capital which can contribute to its solidarity and which can produce small amounts of benefits for that class.

Secondly, one could argue that my approach is reformist. My response would be that my approach is not automatically inconsistent with working class radicalism. There is nothing necessarily reformist about stressing the importance of the relations of trust and reciprocity *among* individual workers and *among* groups of workers. A class approach to social capital and the attendant stress on working class social capital which exists *only in the sense of social resources of the working class* may indeed have some potential for radical politics. To the extent that working class people perceive that possibilities for reform within capitalism exist un-exploited, that perception can impede its struggle over its fundamental interests, i.e. struggle for socialism.[36] An important underlying aim of my approach is to make it possible for one to see the severe class-structural limits not only to working class members practicing self-help within civil society but also to the synergy between workers and the state actors and to the amount of assistance the state can provide to them. Another implication is that the construction of what is called working class social capital itself is a part of the process of the production of political awareness of the working class in the sense Lenin, apart from Marx and Luxembourg, recognized. According to Lenin (1964: 53), working class political awareness is raised through political parties and also through 'those institutions, societies and associations—even the most reactionary—in which proletarian or semi-proletarian masses are to be found'. These institutions include 'cooperatives', 'sick benefit societies' and educational institutions (ibid.: 48, 191, 384) as well as mutual aid societies, libraries and reading groups, etc. (Das, 2011). As mentioned above, the relations of trust and cooperation among working class people, especially if these are informed by class consciousness and supported by working class institutions, provide a foundation for political solidarity. Given the neo-liberal attack on the working class, it is very important that all avenues of promoting working class political awareness and organization be employed in particular places and

---

36   This is the 'political' counterpart to Marx's (1859) 'economic' claim that 'No social order is ever destroyed before all the productive forces for which it is sufficient have been developed, and new superior relations of production never replace older ones before the material conditions for their existence have matured within the framework of the old society'.

across places. Working class social capital (as a social resource including informal networks and associations of this class) is only one of them. It is not more important than formal working class organizations such as councils of workers and small-scale producers (Soviets), rank-and-file committees, militant democratically-functioning trade unions that make use of both minimal and transitional demands, anti-capitalist parties, etc., although working class social capital *can* contribute to the formation of these organizations. Capitalists use their social capital, i.e. their informal connections with one another and with state actors, in their mutual struggle and in their struggle against the working class. So, the working class must also use its own form of social capital.

As I have said, much of the social capital literature reflects the current worldwide neoliberal agenda, although it is the case that not all social capital enthusiasts are necessarily neo-liberals.[37] Indeed, social capital is a part of new social democracy as explained in Chapter 1. For one thing, the stress in the social capital literature on mutual assistance and self-help, which NGOs (with support from international agencies such as World Bank) tend to fetishize and promote, reflects and reinforces the neoliberal-capitalist idea that the burden of reproduction of working class families, whose jobs are lost through capitalist restructuring and/or whose wages are below the value of labour power, should be borne by themselves, through such processes as self-help. It should not be borne through the reduction of the share of the capitalist class in the total social product which workers produce. In particular, in the neoliberal framework, the burden of the reproduction of the working class should not be borne by the state, whose welfare role must be curtailed (Wills, 2000: 646) nor by the capitalist class whose profits must be protected. A major argument in this chapter is that there are severe limits to the reproduction of norms of reciprocity among working class people and to their practices of mutual aid actually. This argument undermines the neoliberal idea that the working class people under the onslaught of neoliberal attack can bootstrap themselves through mutual aid, an idea that is very dear to many NGOs and post-Marxists (Petras, 1997).

Further, social capital research on how non-market processes such as mutual trust and customs grease the wheels of market by reducing transaction costs (Serageldin and Grootaert, 2000: 48) fits in well with, and generally, supports, the neo-liberal agenda of making markets more efficient and thus producing more profits for the capitalist class. Neoliberalism by destroying working

---

37 Anarchists, 'populists' and other progressives with anti-neoliberal views may be sympathetic to social capital of the social capital researchers.

class lives and places through such processes as job loss and withdrawal of the welfare provisions by the state has created a potential for class confrontation (Zeilig, 2002 Petras, 1997). Social capital as cross-class social capital as a glue – indeed Putnam describes it as a 'superglue' (Putnam, 2000: 23) – can be very helpful to avoid this situation, potentially making social capital believers great social engineers or new social democrats.

However, the class approach to social capital taken here is different. It draws attention to the fact that the class context in which people live not only requires them to resort to social capital as a survival strategy but also to the fact that the class context enormously constrains the production of social capital that is beneficial to the working class. It emphasizes how it is that *working class* norms of reciprocity and working class associations, i.e. working class social capital, can serve as 'an oppositional social capital' (Body-Gendrot and Gittell, 2003: xiii) which can be used to promote working class political solidarity vis a vis dominant classes and the state.[38] Working class social capital as conceptualized here is not a sociological superglue that holds conflicting elements of society together. To the extent that it is a glue for the working class communities, it is one that can, to some extent, promote *unity* among working class people furthering their ability to confront the capitalist class and the state, and to build a socialist movement. And to the extent that it is a grease, it has some potential to grease the wheels of not the capitalist market but of class conflict.

As we have seen some social capital scholars themselves say that 'the nature and meaning of social capital becomes more complicated' in a situation where there are 'conflicting interests' (Evans, 1997b: 196). If this is so, why not take conflict and its underlying theoretical underpinnings including, especially, class as starting point rather than social capital, and why not discard social capital altogether? I have been extremely critical of the concept myself, so why do I still use it? What is the rationale for using the language as well as the concept of social capital in spite of my strong criticisms? Could I not theoretically (and later in the other chapters, empirically) examine 'the social capital mechanisms', i.e. norms of reciprocity and social-cultural-political associations, operating in the lives of working-class people, without using the social capital language at all and indeed by using 'social resource' or some such term? My answer is: yes! Then why use social capital? If indeed social capital is neither new nor a powerful factor in resolving capitalism's social crisis manifested as poverty, etc., why resort to the theory of social capital at all?

---

38   '[W]e can conceive of building social capital as a way to empower [people]...' (Warren et al., 2001: 6).

Very briefly, there are two potential answers to this question. One comes from some social capitalists themselves, including some of those associated with the most ardent promoter of social capital, the World Bank. For example, Bebbington et al. agree that much of the social capital discussion has been 're-treading classical social science themes' and thus 'there is clearly much wheel-reinvention going on' in this discussion (2002: 17–18, 36). But they argue that social capital promotes conversations across disciplines. And more importantly, it opens up space for development theory and for development agencies such as the World Bank (or at least some parts of this institution) to engage with issues of power, participation, empowerment and so on.[39] Consider also the work of the sociologist, Portes (2010). He is critical of many aspects of the social capital research and yet he says that 'Social capital is arguably one of the most successful exports from sociology to other social sciences and to public discourse during the last two decades' (p. 28). He also says that 'Economic sociology has in social capital one of its most valuable explanatory tools' (p. 47). One could also say that the sorts of conceptual and empirical issues I have raised in this chapter (and in the next two chapters) could be accommodated within the social capital literature. Indeed, many social capitalists, including Grootaert (1997), Woolcock (1998) and Bebbington, would accept some of these criticisms of the social capital literature that it does not (adequately, if at all) take into account issues of power, conflict and class, but would still get on with the social capital business, treating it as a central category in development thinking and indeed as a new theory of international development.

All this indicates that, as Fine says, 'even dissent within the social capital enterprise seems to strengthen rather than to weaken it' and that 'social capital's ready accommodation of opposition represents a highly successful form of legitimizing repressive tolerance' (undated, 14). Social capital literature 'incorporates and neutralises dissent' (Fine 2002a: 799). Fine therefore says that 'The most appropriate answer to social capital is to reject it altogether' (Fine, 2002b: 20). This is the second approach adopted by those who are critical of social capital (see also, Fine, 1998, 2000 and 2001; and Arrow, 2000; Robison et al., 2002; Tittenburn, 2014).[40]

---

39   The extent to which it succeeds in doing so depends on the discursive battles within the Bank between pro-market scholars and those who are inclined towards political economy, says Bebbington et al. (2002: 17, 37). That does not mean that the Bank is a class-neutral site. It is in fact a prominent site of ruling class hegemony. It is a major imperialist institution.

40   Interestingly, Kenneth Arrow, the economist, also 'would urge abandonment of the ... term "social capital"' (2000, 4), but on different grounds than Fine's. Also, the Polish sociologist, Tittenbrun (2014: 459) says: 'social capital...does not deserve its name. First, it does not

The suggestion that the social capital thinking must be discarded altogether does have merits. But I take a *slightly* different route (a 'critical support approach'). Ben Fine calls this 'a less acceptable alternative' to discarding social capital altogether: in this approach, social capital is used as an investigative category. So, I use the term synonymously with social resource in the form of trust and reciprocity, etc., and I push the social capital thinking to its limit. I do so by 'demanding' that it be directed to take account of economic power and class context. Instead of rejecting altogether the social capital as a term and indeed social capital as a concept, my strategy is to engage (with) the social capital literature critically, and in the process to conceptually (and later in the book, empirically) demonstrate to social capitalists the extremely limited causal power of social capital as a concept as compared to that of class as a concept. My aim is therefore to suggest that social capital as social capitalists talk about is really not worth spending much time on. To make this point, one has to theoretically and empirically engage with the social capital literature *on its own turf*.

My strategy *might be construed* as consistent with Bebbington's suggestion that 'political economy ... [can give] context and sense to any discussion of social capital' and that 'notions of social capital ... [can give] greater specification to our conceptualization of the links between politics and economy' (Bebbington 2002: 801). But such a construal would be mistaken because according to me there is nothing in this view of social capital that says that we must *necessarily* place it in its political economy or class context. Indeed, as Bebbington, a prominent and thoughtful contributor to social capital research, says, 'the structure of an actor's set of social relationships [which potentially constitute social capital] maps neither easily nor automatically onto class ... or other positions' (Bebbington 2002: 801). This echoes Evans' point noted earlier that in a conflict situation social capital becomes a very complex issue. My strategy on the other hand is really to argue for a much more circumspect use of social capital than is the case with Bebbington et al. More specifically, my strategy is to firmly place the concrete objective practices that the concept of social capital refers to (e.g. reciprocity, self-help, associational life, etc.) within a class framework. This is especially necessary for any examination of the relation between social capital and common people's lives. Given the enormously

---

refer to any real, i.e. economic capital, at all; and, second, its definition of social captures only some of the possible social relations, leaving out of the picture the remaining, at least equally important ones. Conclusions are self-evident. Misnomers, even if they are such buzzwords, should be banned from science, and there is no reason why social science should not be subject to this rule' (see also Robison et al., 2002).

constraining power of class on the usefulness of social capital as a resource, social capital as a concept will have a minor role, although *how* minor it is – *how* constraining class is – will be a geographical/contextual question.

Epistemologically speaking, in terms of the term-concept-reality triangle, social capital is a *term* (one could use a substitute term such as social wealth), and it is a *concept* too in the sense that it refers to *actually-existing processes/ relations* (reality) reflected in our thinking: social capital mechanisms do exist and have effects. For example, in some neighbourhoods, children can play freely on the street or in the park while neighbours make sure they are safe without asking for a monetary compensation; people can informally borrow from one another to meet their needs without an interest or collateral; and who one knows can sometimes help one land a job without the job-seeker necessarily paying a fee. Whether we use social capital or social resource or another term is beside the point. Criticizing *the term* does little to challenge the concept itself which points to the existence of things (e.g. relations of trust, informal networks, etc.) that the concept reflects. Of course, one can point out the fact that a given term, or a given part of a term (e.g. 'capital' as in 'social capital'), means different things in different contexts, thus creating confusion: if capital in social capital means reciprocity, and if capital invested in a factory means money invested to make more money on the basis of the appropriation of surplus value, what is common to the two usages of the same term (capital), and what is the underlying conceptual motive behind such usages?[41] But then we are challenging the referents of capital as a term, rather than the term itself: i.e. we are challenging capital as a concept.

Whether the mechanisms that a term refers to exist, how they operate and whether they operate as the term describes, and so on depends not on the term that is used to describe the corresponding concept. By using the same term as the social capitalists use, and by examining some of the processes that the term refers to, I have wanted to show the severe inadequacy of *the concept of social capital* as used by social capitalists: I accept that social capital mechanisms matter, but how it matters and how much it matters – or the ways in which these mechanisms are said by social capitalists to matter – cannot be understood except in their class context where people are seen as bearers of class interests rather than merely as sociable beings or social-capital-bearing people. Even the question of why people even depend on social capital (local

---

41   Non-Marxists use class, capital, state, socialism, etc. just as Marxists use these terms. Marxists cannot say to others 'Don't use these terms because these terms belong to us'! Marxists can, however, challenge the legitimacy of the concept that a given term refers to and how the concepts are causally connected.

norms of reciprocity, etc.) cannot be explained in abstraction from the class context.[42] And when the class context is introduced, social capital mechanisms matter a lot less than social capitalists say they do. The only thing that the social capital language in my view does is that it is a *descriptive* umbrella concept that brings different social practices together (reciprocity, associational life, trust, and so on), which exist independently of the concept/theory that are used to describe/explain these and which allow an individual or a group of individuals to achieve something, or to do something together, *which they would not otherwise be able to*.[43] Clearly, in the light of the conceptual issues I have raised (especially the idea that class and consequences of class such as social crisis manifested partly as poverty are enormously constraining of the production of social capital, which makes treating social capital as an independent variable very problematic), I reject some World Bank scholars' contention (Woolcock and Narayan 2000) that social capital offers a *new theory* of international development. Any theory of international development that does not put the primacy on the destructive effects of capitalism and of imperialism is simply to be rejected. What the poor need is not social *capital* (as a social resource). Much rather, what they need is the development of their own class-power to challenge the class-power of the owners of capital, where the latter – capital – embodies the relations of exploitation under the logic of capitalism, as Marx (1867) explains. In this process, if workers' social capital can help a little, that would be a positive thing. I hope that this theoretical strategy, if followed by many, will lead to the social capital obsession withering away on its own. Whether this is a better strategy than the one that Ben Fine suggests is, of course, subject to debate. He is critical of my approach. According to him:

> Das ... explicitly rejects my advice that the concept of social capital be jettisoned altogether and, instead, seeks to endow it with a 'class-based,

---

42   A poor wage worker will know many other poor wage workers and norms of reciprocity among them mean nothing. Poverty is an absence of the conditions needed for a normal life, and a reciprocal exchange of such a negative condition means nothing: it has no chance of producing any positive impact on the people doing the act of reciprocal exchange. Similarly, there are limitations to the informal vertical exchange (e.g. trust relations between state actors and the poor people). The absence of such relations is not the fundamental cause of poverty; indeed, if anything, poverty of common people – which implies unequal power relations between them and the officials with some decision-making power – explains the lack of trust relations.

43   Bebbington also gives this reason to explain his interest in social capital ('social capital is a sort of linguistic device'). But note that this is clearly not his *main* reason for using social capital (Bebbington 2002: 802).

political economy' content. [In his study of the working class social capital] the appendage of social capital is at best superfluous and at worst unduly homogenizing across specificity in lieu of appropriate attention to detail (although Das does offer detailed case studies).

Fine continues:

[The] dispute is not simply about whether social capital is capable of offering an acceptable analysis on the basis of an individual contribution. Rather, whilst a Marxist (or other) version of social capital might deliver appropriate insights, these would certainly be lost amongst the orthodox juggernaut of contributions that dominate the literature ... Das might be interpreted as having fallen into this trip, with class, political economy, conflict, power, the state, and so on being appended ... Whatever the intentions of individual authors in this regard, the overall effect across the literature is to legitimise the notion of social capital as truly universal and well founded. Look, it can deal with things like class, and even Marxists are able to accept it'.

FINE, 2010: 155–156; square brackets added

The risk that Fine alerts us to is real: the Marxist study of social capital from a vantage point that is opposite to the one taken by mainstream social scientists can contribute to the legitimization of the study of that topic in spite of its serious problems. But one can only hope that a) in the light of the study of social capital as a social resource conducted in this and next two chapters and similar studies and critiques conducted by others, the existing views of social capital, including as a significant solution to all problems of society, will be problematized, and b) attention will be diverted from social capital to serious considerations of political economy including the dynamics of society dominated by the logic of capital as embodying exploitative relations. The use of the social capital *language* from a class-theoretical standpoint really shows that any public policy or any attempt in civil society to promote social capital, will take society nowhere. If common people suffer from social crisis, they do so not because they lack social capital. They lack social capital partly because they suffer from social crisis. Indeed the lack of social capital is heavily caused by the class context in which people live. People suffer from social crisis because those who own the real capital exploit them and subjugate them. So the solution to society's problems is not the infusion/promotion of what is called social capital, but the development of a mass movement towards a democratic society beyond the rule of capital.

References

Argyle, M. (1994). *The Psychology of Social Class*. London: Routledge.

Amoore, L., & Langley, P. (2004). Ambiguities of global civil society. *Review of International Studies, 30*: 89–110.

Aronowitz, S., & Bratsis, P. (Eds.). (2002). *Paradigm Lost State Theory Reconsidered*. Minneapolis: University of Minnesota Press.

Arrow, K. (2000). 'Observations on Social Capital', in Partha Dasgupta and Ismail Serageldin (eds.) *Social Capital: A Multifaceted Perspective*, Washington, D.C.: World Bank.

Baker, G. (2002). Problems in the theorisation of global civil society. *Political Studies, 50*(5): 928–943.

Barr, A. (2000). Social capital and technical information flows in the Ghanaian manufacturing Sector. *Oxford Economic Papers, 52*(3): 539–559.

Barrow, C. (1993). *Critical Theories of the State*. Madison: University of Wisconsin Press.

Barrickman, N. (2015). Survey finds a majority of Americans unable to pay for major unexpected expenses. Wsws.org.; https://www.wsws.org/en/articles/2016/01/09/surv-j09.html.

Buttigieg, J. (1994). The concept of civil-society in Gramsci and the debate on civil-society. *Argument, 36*(4–5): 529–554.

Bebbington, A. (1999). Capitals and capabilities: A framework for analyzing peasant viability, rural livelihoods and poverty. *World Development, 27*(12): 2021–2044.

Bebbington, A. (2002). Sharp Knives and Blunt Instruments: Social Capital in Development Studies. *Antipode. 34*(4): 800–803.

Bebbington, A., & Perreault, T. (1999). Social capital, development, and access to resources in Highland Ecuador. *Economic Geography, 75*(4): 395–418.

Bodeman, Y., & Spohn, W. (1986). The organicity of classes and the naked proletarian: towards a new formulation of the class conception. *The Insurgent Sociologist, 13*(3), 10–19.

Bourdieu, P. (1986). The forms of capital. In J. Richardson (Ed.). *Handbook of Theory and Research for the Sociology of Education*. New York: Greenwood.

Booth, J. and Richard, P. (2012). Untangling Social and Political Capital in Latin American Democracies. *Latin American Politics and Society, 54*(3), 33–64.

Brass, T. (1999). *Towards a Comparative Political Economy of Unfree Labour*. London: Frank Cass.

Brautigam, D. (1997). Substituting for the state: Institutions and industrial development in eastern Nigeria. *World Development, 25*(7): 1063–1080.

Brehm, J., & Rahn, W. (1997). Individual-level evidence for causes and consequences of social Capital. *American Journal of Political Science, 41*(3): 999–1023.

Body-Gendrot, S., & Gittell, M. (2003). Empowering citizenship to social capital. In S. Body-Gendrot and M. Gittell (Eds.), *Social Capital and Social Citizenship*. Lanhem: Lexington Books.

Burawoy, M. (2018). The poverty of philosophy: Marx meets Bourdieu. In T. Medvetz and J. Sallaz (Eds). *The Oxford Handbook of Pierre Bourdieu*. Oxford: Oxford University Press.

Callinicos, A. (1993). *Race and Class*. London: Bookmarks.

Callinicos, A. (1988). *Making history: Agency, Structure and Change in Social Theory*. Ithaca: Cornell University Press.

Camfield, D. (2004). Re-orienting class analysis: Working classes as historical formations. *Science and Society, 68*(4): 421–446.

Chhibber, A. (2000). Social capital, the state, and development outcomes. In P. Dasgupta and I. Serageldin (Eds.), *Social Capital: A Multifaceted Perspective*. Washington, D.C.: World Bank.

Clarke, S. 1991. *The state debate*. London: Macmillan.

Cox, K. and Mair, A. (1988). Locality and Community in the Politics of Local Economic Development. *Annals of the Association of American Geographers, 78*(2): 307–325.

Cox, R. (1999). Civil society at the turn of the millennium: prospects for an alternative world Order. *Review of International Studies, 25*(1): 3–28.

Dahl, R. (1956). *A Preface to a Democratic Theory*. Chicago: University of Chicago Press.

Das, R. (1996). State theories: A critical analysis. *Science and Society, 60*(1): 27–57.

Das, R. (2017). *Marxist Class Theory for a sceptical World*. Leiden/Boston: Brill.

Das, R. (2000). State-society relations: the case of an anti-poverty policy. *Environment and Planning C: Government and Policy, 18*(6): 631–650.

Das, R. (2006). Putting Social Capital in its Place. *Capital and Class, 92*: 65–92.

Das, R. (2022). *Marx's Capital, Capitalism and Limits to the State: Theoretical Considerations*. London: Taylor and Francis.

Duncan, C. (2001). Social capital in America's poor rural communities. In *Social Capital and Poor Communities*. New York: Russell Sage Foundation.

Evans, P. (1997a). Introduction: Development strategies across the public-private divide. In P. Evans. (Ed.), *State-Society Synergy*. Berkeley: University of California Press.

Evans, P. (1997b). Government action, social capital, and development. In P. Evans. (Ed.), *State-Society Synergy*. Berkeley: University of California Press.

Farr, J. (2004). Social capital – A conceptual history. *Political theory, 32*(1): 6–33.

Fine, B. (1998). The Developmental state is dead – long live social capital? *Development and change, 30*(1): 1–19.

Fine, B. (2000). Social Capital: A Critique. WDR 2000/1 Discussion, wdr@lists.world bank.org.

Fine, B. (2001). *Social Capital vs Social Theory*. London: Routledge.

Fine, B. (2002a). The F**k You Up Those Social Capitalists. *Antipode 34*(4): 796–799.

Fine, B. (2002b). It Ain't Social, It Ain't Capital and It Ain't Africa. *Studia Africana*, No. 13, 18–33.

Fine, B. (2010). *Theories of Social Capital: Researchers Behaving Badly*. London: Pluto Press.

Fitzgerald, J. (1991). Class as community – the new dynamics of social-change. *Environment and Planning D, 9*(11): 117–128.

Foley, M., & Edwards, B. (1996). The paradox of civil society. *Journal of Democracy, 7*(3): 38–52.

Fox, J. (1996). How does civil society thicken? The political construction of social capital in rural Mexico. *World Development, 24*(6): 1089–1103.

Fukuyama, F. (2001). Social capital, civil society and development. *Third world Quarterly, 22*(1): 7–20.

Granovetter, M. (1985). Economic action and social structure – the problem of embeddedness', *American Journal of Sociology, 91*(3): 481–510.

Greene, A., Ackers, P., & Black, J. (2001). Lost narratives? From paternalism to teamworking in a lock manufacturing firm. *Economic and Industrial Democracy, 22*(2): 211–237.

Grootaert, C., Oh, G., & Swamy, A. (2002). Social capital, household welfare and poverty in Burkina Faso. *Journal of African Economies, 11*(1): 4–38.

Grootaert, C., & Narayan, D. (2004). Local institutions, poverty and household welfare in Bolivia. *World Development, 32*(7): 1179–1198.

Hall, P. (1999). Social capital in Britain. *British Journal of Political Science, 29*(3): 417–461.

Harvey, D. (1982). *Limits to Capital*. Chicago: Chicago University Press.

Heller, P. (1997). Social capital as a product of class mobilization and state intervention: Industrial Workers in Kerala, India. In P. Evans (Ed.).

Herod, A. (1997). From a geography of labour to a labour geography: Labor's spatial fix and the geography of capitalism. *Antipode, 29*(1).

Howell, J., & Pearce, J. (2001). *Civil Society & Development: A Critical Exploration*. Boulder: L. Rienner Publishers.

Hyden, G. (1997). Civil society, social capital, and development: Dissection of a complex Discourse. *Studies in Comparative International Development, 32*(1): 3–30.

Jessop, B. (1990). *State Theory: Putting Capitalist States in their Place*, Cambridge: Polity.

Kawachi I, Kennedy, B., Lochner K. and Prothrow-Stith D. (1997). Social capital, income inequality, and mortality. *American Journal of Public Health. 87*(9): 1491–8.

Kennedy, B, Kawachi, I., & Brainerd, E. (1998). The role of social capital in the Russian mortality crisis. *World Development, 26*(11): 2029–2043.

Knack S., & Keefer, P. (1997). Does social capital have an economic payoff? A cross-country Investigation. *Quarterly Journal of Economics, 112*(4): 1251–1288.

Li, Y., Pickles, A., & Savage, M. (2005). Social capital and social trust in Britain. *European Sociological Review, 21*(2): 109–123.

Levi, M. (1996). Social and unsocial capital: A review essay of Robert Putnam's Making Democracy Work. *Politics and Society, 24*(1): 45–55.

Lewis, D. (2002). Civil society in African contexts: Reflections on the usefulness of a concept. *Development and Change, 33*(4): 569–586.

Lin, N. (2001). Building a Network Theory of Social Capital. In N. Lin, K. Cook, and R. Burt (Eds.), *Social Capital: Theory and Research*. New York: Routledge.

Markovitz, I. (1998). Uncivil society, capitalism and the state in Africa. *Commonwealth & Comparative Politics, 36*(2): 21–53.

Marx, K. (1859). A Contribution to the Critique of Political Economy: Preface. https://www.marxists.org/archive/marx/works/1859/critique-pol-economy/preface.htm.

Marx, K. (1867). Capital volume 1. *Marxists.org.* Retrieved from: https://www.marxists.org/archive/marx/works/download/pdf/Capital-Volume-I.pdf.

Mearns, R. 1996. Commons and collectives: the lack of social capital in Central Asia's land reforms, Paper presented at the Sixth Conference of the International Association for the Study of Common Property, Berkeley, California, 5–8 June, 1996. Available at: https://opendocs.ids.ac.uk/opendocs/bitstream/handle/20.500.12413/3344/WP40.pdf?sequence=1.

Mohan, G. (2002). The disappointments of civil society: the politics of NGO intervention in northern Ghana. *Political Geography, 21*(1): 125–154.

Mohseni, A. (2022). The Idea of Capital in Bourdieu and Marx. *Philosophical Papers, 51*(2): 265–293.

Morris, M. (1998). *Social capital and poverty in India.* IDS Working paper, University of Sussex, No. 61.

Morris, L., & Irwin, S. (1992). Unemployment and informal support – dependency, exclusion, or participation. *Work Employment and Society, 6*(2): 185–207.

Mouritsen P. (2003). What's the civil in civil society? Robert Putnam, Italy and the Republican Tradition. *Political Studies, 51*(4): 650–668.

Mueller, J. (2011). The IMF, Neoliberalism and Hegemony. *Global Society, 25*(3): 377–402.

Muntaner, C., Lynch, J., Hillemeier, M., Lee, J., David, R., Benach, J., & Borrell, C. (2002). Economic inequality, working-class power, social capital, and cause-specific mortality in wealthy countries. *International Journal of Health Services, 32*(4): 629–656.

Narayan, D., & Pritchett, L. (1999). Social capital: evidence and implications. In P. Dasgupta and I. Serageldin (Eds.), *Social Capital: A Multi-Faceted Perspective.* (Pp. 269–295). Washington: The World Bank.

O'Neill, D. and Wayne, M. (2017). *Considering class.* Leiden: Brill.

Ostrom, E. (1996). Crossing the great divide: Coproduction, synergy, and development, *World Development, 24*(6): 1073–1087.

Ostrom, E. (2000). Social capital: a fad or a fundamental concept. In Dasgupta and Serageldin (Eds.).

Patnaik. (2007). The state under neoliberalism. *Social Scientist, 35*(1/2): 4–15.

Petras, J. (1997). Imperialism and NGOs in Latin America. *Monthly Review, 49*(7): 10–27.

Portes, A. (2010). *Economic Sociology: A Systematic Enquiry.* Princeton: Princeton University Press.

Portes, A., & Sensenbrenner, J. (1993). Embeddedness and immigration: notes on the social determinants of economic action. *American Journal of Sociology, 98*(6): 1320–1350.

Poulantzas, N. (1978). *State, Power, Socialism.* London: New Left Books.

Pressman, S. (Ed.). (2006). *Alternative Theories of the State.* New York: Palgrave MacMillan.

Putnam, R. (1993). *Making Democracy Work: Civic Traditions in Modern Italy* Princeton: Princeton University press.

Putnam, R. (2000). Bowling Alone: The Collapse and Revival of American Community, New York: Simon & Schuster.

Robison, L., Schmid, A., & Siles, M. (2002). Is Social Capital Really Capital? *Review of Social Economy, 60*(1): 1–21.

Ruschemeyer, D., Stephens, E., & Stephens, J. (1992). *Capitalist Development and Democracy.* Cambridge: Polity.

Savage, M., Warde, A., & Devine, F. (2005). Capitals, assets, and resources: some critical issues. *British Journal of Sociology, 56*(1): 31–47.

Serageldin, I., & Grootaert, C. (2000). Defining social capital: an integrating view. In P. Dasgupta and I. Serageldin (Eds.).

Short, P. (1996). Kinship, reciprocity and vulnerability: social relations in the informal Economy. *Australian Journal of Social Issues, 31*(2): 127–145.

Tendler, J. 1997. *Good government in the tropics.* Baltimore: Johns Hopkins University press.

Thompson, E. (1964). *The making of the English working class.* New York: Pantheon Books.

Thompson, E. (1971). The moral economy of the English crowd in the Eighteenth century. *Past & Present, 50*: 76–136.

Tittenbrun, J. (2014). Social capital: Neither social, nor capital. *Social Science Information, 53*(4): 453–461.

Turner, S. (2007). Small-Scale Enterprise Livelihoods and Social Capital in Eastern Indonesia: Ethnic Embeddedness and Exclusion, *The Professional Geographer, 59*(4): 407–420.

Truman, D. (1959). *The Governmental Process.* New York: Knopf.

Unger, D. 1998. *Building social capital in Thailand.* Cambridge: Cambridge University press.

Uphoff, N., & Wijayaratna, C. (2000). Demonstrated benefits from social capital: The productivity of farmer organizations in Gal Oya, Sri Lanka. *World Development*, 28(11): 1875–1890.

Veltemeyer, H. (2012). Civil society and development. In P. Haslam, J. Schafer and P. Beaudet (Eds.), *International Development*. Don Mills, Ontario: Oxford University Press.

Warren, M., Thompson, J., & Saegert, S. (2001). The role of social capital in combating Poverty. In S. Saegart, J. Thompson and M. Warren (Eds.). *Social Capital and Poor Communities*. New York: Russell Sage Foundation Press.

Wiarda, H. (2003). *Civil Society: The American Model and Third World Development*. Boulder: Westview Press.

Wickramasinghe, N. (2005). The Idea of Civil Society in the South: Imaginings, Transplants, Designs. *Science & Society*, 69(3): 458–486.

Wills, J. (2000). Political economy II: the politics and geography of capitalism. *Progress in Human Geography*, 24(4): 641–652.

Wood, E. (1998). (1986). *The Retreat from Class*. London: Verso.

Woolcock, M. (1998). Social capital and economic development: toward a theoretical synthesis and policy framework. *Theory and Society*, 27(2): 151–208.

Woolcock, M. and Narayana, D. 2000. Social Capital: Implications for Development Theory, Research, and Policy, *The World Bank Research Observer*, 15(2): 225–49.

World Bank. (2001). *World Development Report – Attacking Poverty*. Oxford: Oxford University Press.

Wright, E. (1982). Race, class and income inequality. In A. Giddens and D. Held (Eds.). *Classes, Power and Conflict*. Berkeley: University of California Press.

Wright, E. (Ed.). (1989). Rethinking, once again, the concept of class structure. In E. Wright (Ed.), *The Debate on Classes*. (Pp. 269–348). London: Verso.

Wright, E. (1995). The class analysis of poverty. *International Journal of Health Services*, 25(1): 85–100.

Wright, E. (2000). Workers' power, capitalist-class interests, and class compromise. *American Journal of Sociology*, 105: 4.

Wright, E. (Ed.). (2005). *Approaches to Class Analysis*. Cambridge: Cambridge University Press.

Zeilig, L. (2002). *Class Struggle and Resistance in Africa*. Cheltenham: New Clarion.

CHAPTER 4

Social Capital in the Spaces of Civil Society

Raju J. Das

Social capital is said to provide a bottom-up approach to poverty alleviation (Woolcock 1998).[1] The World Bank (2001: 129) says that social capital is necessary for long-term development and that it is the capital of the poor. This chapter argues that much of the literature on social capital is too sanguine of its benefits for the poor. It is, of course, important to look at the extent to which social capital – norms of reciprocity and networks/associations – can help the poor. But how the conditions of the poor can affect social capital is equally important to examine. This has often been neglected by 'social capitalists'.

Based on qualitative interviews in two villages in eastern India and focusing on poor daily wage labourers, this chapter examines not only the extent to which wage labourers benefit from their social capital but also the mechanisms in which their economic-political conditions affect their social capital. By seeking to unpack the dialectical relation between social capital and poverty, the chapter aims at problematizing the overly optimistic claims about social capital, especially the 'communitarian' social capital of Robert Putnam (Putnam, 1993), the person most responsible for popularizing the concept. It shows that it is untenable to posit social capital as an independent variable and poverty as a dependent variable because the economic-political conditions of poor people have an enormous constraining effect on social capital itself and its purported material benefits for the poor.

In the first of the following sections, I briefly review the literature on social capital and poverty to set the context for my own study. I expand on some of the points raised in chapter 3. Then I discuss the empirical context of my research on social capital. The next two sections deal with the empirical material on social capital. The second section discusses the norms and practice of reciprocity – 'bonding social capital' – of wage-labour families. The third section examines their associational life, a form of 'bridging social capital'. In the concluding section, I return to the literature on social capital and link it to the empirical discussion in the chapter.

---

1   This chapter is based on an earlier publication (Das, 2004).

1   Literature on Social Capital and Poverty: a Brief Review[2]

As mentioned in the previous chapter, social capital refers to norms of reciprocity and networks/associations which can promote cooperative actions and which can be used as social resources for mutual benefit (Putnam, 1993: 167; 2000; Woolcock, 2000). I will deal with reciprocity and associations in turn.

Reciprocity is of two types: specific (also known as balanced) and generalized (Putnam, 1993: 172). Specific reciprocity refers to a simultaneous exchange of items of equivalent value (e.g. workmates exchanging holiday gifts). Generalized reciprocity, which is of interest here, refers to 'a continuing relationship of exchange that is at any given time unrequited or imbalanced' (Putnam, 1993: 172). Each individual act of generalized reciprocity (henceforward reciprocity) is usually characterized by a combination of short-term altruism and long-term self-interest: 'I help you out now in the (possibly vague, uncertain and uncalculating) expectation that you will help me out in the future' (Taylor in Putnam, 1993: 172). The norm of reciprocity serves to reconcile self-interest and solidarity. This norm is a highly productive form of social capital, according to Putnam. Reciprocity is at the heart of self-help associations that help people cope with economic insecurities. As a part of the reciprocity network, people exchange labour, capital and consumption goods (Putnam, 1993). 'Social relations', says Uphoff (2000, 226), 'create value through reciprocity' in the sense that 'many things that we want and need cannot be created simply by our own efforts'.

The second component of social capital is the networks of civic engagement – networks of interpersonal communication and exchange – among people of equal socio-economic status (Putnam, 1993: 172–6). These are also known as horizontal associations (as opposed to vertical associations exemplified by patron–client relations). Networks of civic engagement such as neighbourhood associations, cooperatives, sports clubs and mass-based parties represent horizontal interaction. Based on his Italy study, Putnam suggests that these networks foster norms of reciprocity among members, facilitate the flow of information about trustworthiness of members, increase the potential costs of defection and help members cooperate for mutual benefit (Putnam, 1993: 173–4). He says that areas with more social capital have greater levels of economic development. The geographical work on inter-firm relations and new industrial spaces in developed and less-developed countries also makes use of concepts of trust, embeddedness and networks, which are all part of

---

2   Some of the conceptual issues raised in Chapter 3 are elaborated here.

the social capital concept (Molina-Morales et al. 2002; Buck 2000; Pinch and Henry 1999; Christerson and Lever-Tracy 1997; McDade and Malecki 1997; Gertler 1995). This work, like social capital research generally, rightly suggests that 'economy and society are incorrigibly intertwined' (Thrift and Olds 1996, 314; see also Biggart and Castanias 2001). But both Putnam's work on interpersonal relations and geographical work on inter-firm relations tend to neglect, or pay lip service to, not only issues of class but also poverty and related issues that constitute the social crisis (the crisis of livelihood and of the reproduction of a healthy life) of common people. In this chapter I investigate therefore the relation between social capital and poverty of the wage-earning class.

Since the publication of Putnam's 1993 book, there has developed a specific literature on social capital and poverty, in which a typology of social capital has been developed. In this typology, there are different types of social capital in relation to the poor people: bonding, bridging and linking social capital (World Bank 2001; Gittel and Vidal 1998).[3]

'Bonding social capital' refers to strong ties connecting family members, neighbours and close friends sharing similar demographic characteristics (World Bank 2001, 128). Norms of reciprocity and mutual help tend to be strong among people with strong ties. On the other hand, weak ties among members of civic organizations, including clubs and voluntary associations, constitute 'bridging social capital' (Gittel and Vidal 1998). Bridging social capital refers to horizontal connections, i.e. connections to people with 'broadly comparable economic status and political power', but with different demographic, ethnic and geographical backgrounds. This form of social capital of the poor is produced at least in part by their associational life (e.g. clubs where people of different occupations and different neighbourhoods join).

Some scholars say that the poor have plenty of bonding social capital but only a modest amount of bridging social capital (World Bank 2001; Holzmann and Jorgensen 1999). That is, the poor people in a place typically know many people like themselves in that place and may have some scattered connections to people in other places. Bonding social capital and bridging social capital roughly (but not entirely accurately) correspond to reciprocity and network components of social capital discussed earlier (see Woolcock 2000: 11).

Both forms of social capital can potentially benefit the poor. Bonding social capital – the strong ties connecting social groups such as family members and neighbours – offers 'immediate practical support' when misfortune strikes. It

---

3 Linking social capital refers to vertical ties between the poor on the one hand and people in positions of power and influence in formal organizations (such as the state) on the other (World Bank 2001). I will deal with this topic in the next chapter.

can be a source of informal safety net (Narayan and Pritchett 1999, 284). The study by Kennedy et al. (1998) finds that in Russia those who lack social capital in the form of support from friends and family are more likely to be vulnerable to economic hardship, caused by the current transition to a market economy. Kozel and Parker (1998) report that social groups among poor villagers serve vitally important protection, risk management and solidarity functions in rural north India.

Bridging social capital on the other hand can be a powerful means by which poor people address problems requiring collective action (e.g. maintaining roads). The World Bank (2001: 129) says, 'social networks and organizations are clearly key assets in the portfolio of resources drawn on by poor people to manage risk and opportunity'. The rich people do advance their interests through clubs and associations but 'their relative importance is greater for poor people' (ibid.). In this sense it is argued that social capital is the capital of the poor. Narayan and Pritchett (1999) indeed show a positive correlation between associational life (e.g. density of associations) and income. More specifically, they show 'increase in village social capital increases the income of all households in the village by ... an impressively large amount' (ibid.: 274). Associational life reduces poverty by facilitating information-sharing and cooperation to address community problems (p. 276).

The conceptual distinction between bonding and bridging social capital has, to some extent, addressed the problem of clarity about the relation between social capital and poverty. Yet the literature has several problems. Some of these problems have been recognized by the World Bank itself and by academic scholars outside of the Bank. For example, social capital can lead to an overload of demand on resources of more well-off groups from less well-off groups; social capital emerging from group membership benefits only group members and not society at large, and so on. These and other problems have been discussed extensively by geographers and others, so I will not reiterate these here (see Harriss 2002; Mohan and Mohan 2002; Fine 2001; DeFilippis 2001, 2002; Harriss and De Renzio 1997). I will deal with just one issue: the causal relation between social capital and poverty – where poverty is one aspect of the social crisis of common people – is much weaker than Putnam and his followers, including World Bank scholars, think. Statistical studies such as those by Narayan and Pritchett do not make it sufficiently clear though whether the statistical correlation implies causation. Also the direction of causality might be much more problematic than the study assumes. For one thing, many social capitalists fail to recognize that mutual assistance, an important aspect of social capital, can mean 'narrow and often risky personalized dependencies of people on each other' (Levi 1996: 51). Clearly, Putnam's claim that social capital can be more important than physical capital (1993: 183) is highly problematic.

More important from the standpoint of this chapter is the following point I make: those who make optimistic claims about social capital often fail to consider how the conditions under which the people earn their living – their class position in short – can shape the production of social capital itself.[4] On the one hand, the conditions under which working class people live can contribute to the production of social capital. As discussed in Chapter 3, Portes identifies four sources of social capital. One of them is 'bounded solidarity' (Portes and Landholt, 2000: 534). This solidarity is based on an emergent sentiment of we-ness among members of the working class (and other groups) who face similar difficult situations. It is a sentiment based on moral imperative rather than rational calculations of costs and benefits (Portes and Sensenbrenner, 1993, 1327–8; see also Callinicos, 1988, 199–203). If sufficiently strong, this emergent sentiment will lead to the observance of norms of mutual support [e.g. exchange of gifts], appropriable by individuals as a resource in their own pursuits. (Portes and Sensenbrenner 1993: 1325)

On the other hand, social capital production can be constrained. Putnam (1993: 178, 163–4), who takes a rational choice approach to social capital, seems to suggest that the only obstacle to cooperative action is that people are self-interested. Such an approach neglects the fact that pressing social conditions (e.g. class constraints) can prevent people from exhibiting cooperative behaviour including reciprocity. There is now a small and growing literature which conceptually *and* empirically shows that this is indeed the case (Beall, 2000). This chapter seeks to make a contribution to that approach, i.e. to a political economy or class-based approach to social capital.

A major issue underlying the class character of the stock and nature of *social* resource in the form of social capital is the fact that the working class is excluded from, and relatively deprived of, *material* resources (especially, means of production). Given their class position, workers have limited material resources to share among themselves. And, without *resources*, informal *rules* of sharing in a place and over space are difficult to sustain for long (in their active form).[5] Further, self-help and mutual aid are based on an expectation of certain degree of *security*: that when one is in difficulty, one expects that one's relations with others will act as an insurance and that one can get

---

4   This neglect of class in the social capital literature reflects the neglect of class in the social sciences as such, and particularly in the post-modernist literature (Wood, 1997; Das, 2017).

5   This applies with greater force to low-wage economies of the global capitalist periphery and to working-class poor communities in wealther core countries.

help. Yet, a fundamental aspect of the working-class life is *insecurity*, not just exclusion from material resources. Because the working class has been separated from means of production, its access to means of subsistence, generally, depends on securing wage work, which, however, is not guaranteed. One never knows how one is going to get through to the end of the week. The *insecurity* of the working class, as a part of the working class social crisis, can undermine the conditions for reproduction of norms of self-help and reciprocity, which presuppose a sense of *security*.

Thus class relations, and poverty as a consequence of these relations, can contribute to social capital, but they can undermine its production. In the following section, I will broaden out the constraining forces on social capital to include not only the economic conditions of daily wage earners but also their political conditions. I will show that economic and political conditions in which they live have an enormous effect on social capital and limit any beneficial role. The constraining role of these conditions can be much more powerful than their enabling role, thereby limiting any possible causal role of social capital in poverty alleviation that many social capitalists assign to it.

2   The Empirical Context

The empirical context of the chapter is the Odisha State of India (It used to be called Orissa). Odisha is indeed a part of India's vast contiguous poverty belt. At least half of the population of 32 million is below the official poverty line (in early 2000s). Close to 85 per cent of the population lives in villages, and agriculture contributes to more than 50 per cent of Odisha's income. Half the population is illiterate, and in contrast to Kerala or West Bengal, upper castes/ classes dominate the political and economic spheres, while the lower classes are not sufficiently well-organized to be able to influence the operation of the state, except in some isolated pockets.

If this is the situation, it would be interesting to see how the poor live their lives there, how they use, for example, their 'social capital' to make ends meet, and how Odisha's political economy might be an obstacle to the poor labouring people trying to develop an associational life and more generally 'civil society', which can play a role in their (future) political empowerment.

Empirical data were collected in Odisha through 71 in-depth interactive interviews and seven focus-group discussions, supplemented by questionnaire surveys (with 149 respondents), in two village-clusters (*Gram Panchayats*), Remuna and Chasakhanda, in the early 2000s with wage labourers and others (e.g. politicians) (Figure 4.1). The fieldwork was conducted with the help of

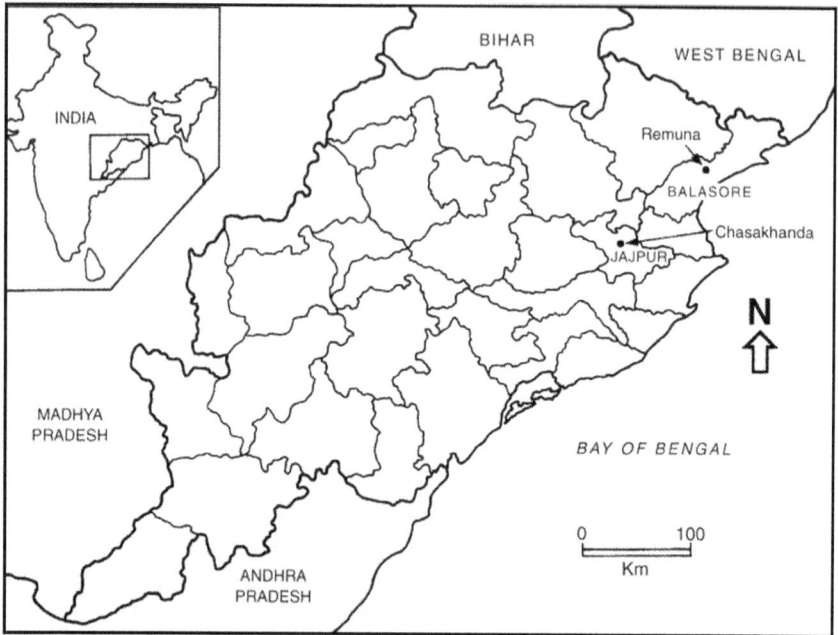

FIGURE 4.1   Study sites in Odisha, India

a team of Research Assistants from December 2001 to April 2002 and from 6 December 2002 to 10 January 2003. A large number of respondents came from the class of daily wage earners.[6] A typical member of this class is a poorly paid and unskilled/semi-skilled man or woman with limited security of employment and very low level of autonomy at work. The selection of respondents from this class was done to ensure that they represented different segments (e.g. workers in agriculture and outside of agriculture). In addition, landowners, entrepreneurs as well as politicians from different political parties and government officials who are in day-to-day interaction with wage labourers were interviewed. Such interaction happens at different geographical scales [hamlet, (administratively-defined) village, *Gram Panchayat*, which has many villages in it, and Development Block, which comprises several *Gram Panchayats*].

---

6   Although class has been defined in several ways [Sheppard and Barnes 1990; Thrift and Williams 1987; Wright, 1989; see also Patnaik's (1999, 211–13) work on the labour exploitation criterion of class identification], I define the working class here in a simple way: as the people whose control over the means of production is non-existent or very limited, so their main source of income is the sale of labour power for a wage that covers no more than the average cost of maintenance (in reality, the wage falls way below the cost of reproduction).

Remuna is in Balasore district and Chasakhanda is in Jajpur district (which until recently used to be a part of Cuttack district) (Figure 4.1). In many respects their socio-economic levels of development are more or less similar but there is some unevenness (see below).[7] But their local politics is different. Whilst Jajpur is traditionally known in Odisha for clientelist politics based on patronage, Balasore – at least, large parts of it – is by contrast known for left-wing or progressive politics.

In Chasakhanda *Gram Panchayat* of Jajpur district, the level of working-class political solidarity is very low as compared to Remuna of Balasore district, which is partly indicated by a very weak electoral presence of the Left parties there (Table 1). Indeed, in the last local election, while the parties on the political left polled less than 13 per cent of votes in Chasakhanda, they polled more than 22 per cent in Remuna. Both at the level of State Assembly constituency of which Chasakhanda is a part and at the level of Chasakhanda *Gram Panchayat* itself, political power lies in the hands of centre/centre-right politicians, although there are pockets of working-class solidarity within the *Gram Panchayat*.

By contrast, Remuna Gram Panchayat has a tradition of a peasants' and workers' movement organized by one of the Left parties [i.e. the Communist Party of India (Marxist)], Remuna has also greater number of civic organizations, including more self-help groups per thousand population than Chasakhanda (3 in Remuna and 1.82 in Chasakhanda). The area is a part of an Assembly constituency which has elected a Left politician to the State's Legislative Assembly in the past. The elected Head of Remuna *Gram Panchayat* is also from CPI(M).

Remuna and Chasakhanda are villages where cultivators depend mostly on unirrigated farming. Rice is the main crop in both areas, but Remuna produces some vegetables and pulses as well. Some of the villagers in Remuna work in nearby factories. Chasakhanda, however, has no industries close by. In terms of economic development, Remuna is a relatively better-off area than Chasakhanda, as indicated by the differential agricultural productivity: the per hectare paddy yield is 2,700 kilos in Remuna, but only 1,900 in Chasakhanda. Another indicator of uneven development is the percentage of inhabitants from scheduled castes and tribes to the total population.[8] In Remuna

---

7 On Odisha's inter-District disparities, see Sahoo and Paltasingh (2019) and de Haan and Dubey (2005).

8 These groups are among the poorest and the most deprived in India, including in Odisha (Mohanty, 1990). The vast majority of them are landless labourers or poor peasants, and their presence in an area is taken as a proxy indicator for the level of development.

it is below 30, but in Chasakhanda it is more than 43 (the Odisha average is 38).[9]

The vast majority of the respondents for qualitative interviews were those who actually interacted with one another causally (state officials, politicians and labourers). They were selected one by one as the research proceeded and as the understanding of causal group was built up (see Sayer, 2000: 20). My aim was to interview a relatively *small* number of individuals about a *large* number of properties/issues related to social capital to unpack the causal mechanisms that link social capital to the economic-political conditions under which wage-earners live. Groups of wage labourers were invited for focus group discussions in specific places such as community centres, schools and places of worship where they normally meet. An average interview lasted for about 40 minutes. During the interviews, a series of questions based on the social capital-and-poverty literature was used to facilitate discussions. Interviews were conducted in Odia language. The author translated the majority of the transcripts; a few were translated by a professional translator, whose translations were randomly checked by the author.

3   Bonding Social Capital of Poor Wage Labourers in Odisha

3.1   *Stock and Benefits of Bonding Social Capital*

For several months in a year, labouring families, whose main source of income is daily casual labour, are short of food. Therefore, the informal exchange of food on a reciprocal basis (or, informal interest-free borrowing and lending of food) is widely practised and is an important aspect of Putnam's generalized reciprocity. For daily wage labourers (unless otherwise noted, the respondents are daily wage labourers), the norm/practice of reciprocity is crucial to their survival. One of them said: 'My family did not have anything to eat for lunch today. We asked a neighbour of ours for some rice. He gave us some rice ... This person is also a poor person like us'. Another said: 'If I don't have rice, I can borrow for a week and survive'.

---

9   With regard to income distribution, in both places the top 5 per cent of households earn a monthly income of more than Rs.4,000, while 85 per cent earn less than Rs.2,500. If income inequality is measured in terms of the coefficient of variation, Remuna's income seems to be slightly more unequally distributed than that in Chasakhanda; Remuna's coefficient of variation being 1.19, compared to 0.79 for Chasakhanda. In terms of education, the two areas are very similar: close to 30 per cent of the questionnaire respondents are illiterate, and 40 per cent have had some school/college education.

Next to food, medical emergency is the most important area where a lot of reciprocity is observed. Ill-health in rural areas means the need for transportation to hospitals located in towns. It also entails expenditure on medicines, etc. A respondent said: 'We help each other. If somebody needs medical emergency help, we take him to the hospital'. If the nature of medical emergency is very serious, help at the larger social-spatial scale (e.g. community level) is mobilized, not just from a few neighbours. A poor writer who leads a cultural organization, added:

> I was very sick on October 12. Villagers took me to the hospital [which is 5–6 hours by bus]. They contributed from Rs.5 to Rs.10 or Rs.50 each. They collected Rs14 000–15 000. I didn't have money to buy an ordinary medicine. They helped me without expecting anything in return. They are also helping others ... Sometimes they are helping by cutting down their own food expenditure.

As these quotes and others below suggest, there *are* strong norms of reciprocity in both the study areas. People help each other in both monetary and non-monetary terms.

3.2 How Class/Economic and Political Conditions Affect Norms/Practice of Reciprocity

Where are these norms coming from? The fact that everyone depends on wage work and that everyone is poor, or at least not well-off, sustains a norm of reciprocity among the labouring families. This is evident from the following comments from respondents:

> Those who are daily labourers trust me and I trust them. When he is in difficulty I will help him a little. ... There is sharing among us. If I borrow something from him today, I will return in two days or tomorrow. Otherwise, he will be in difficulty. ... We fifty or so labourers [in our hamlet] help each other. But those who are of higher status, they don't interact with us and we don't interact with them.
>
> I share my food with other labourers. Because I think I have experienced deprivation (*abhaba*) before. We were poor. We have worked very hard. Our mother used to feed us boiled *matharanga saga* (a wild spinach-like plant). I even pay for medicines when people are in hospitals. I have even donated blood. I think if I need blood this person will give blood for me in future.

A labour organizer, who belongs to a Left party, said: because labourers are all one class, within that class, there is a relationship, there is giving and taking, there is mutual help and sympathy.

It is quite clear that class solidarity growing out of common class position is an important factor underlying reciprocity. Some labourers have a class consciousness, however under-developed. That is, they are conscious of the fact that they are a class which is excluded from the ownership of means of production (e.g. land) and whose livelihood therefore depends on wage work. Reciprocity is partly based on this consciousness and the empathy it generates. As a respondent from Chasakhanda said: 'Our neighbours are like us. They depend on wage work. We help each other in times of need'.

Labourers' structural class position, the fact that they depend on wage work for their livelihood, is one thing. Concrete consequences of their class position are another. Insecurity and poverty, two major aspects of the social crisis of the working class people, are major consequences of their class position. Everyone knows that he/she will be without work and therefore without food or without money to pay for healthcare, etc. for many days in a year. But no one knows which days they will or will not get wage work and therefore will or will not have food to eat. This insecurity seems to sustain the norm and practice of reciprocity. Each act of helping implies a 'guarantee' that the person who helps will need and get help in future. Helping is based on an expectation of return help. A labour organizer in Chasakhanda said: 'People feel "if I help someone, I will get help in future"'. A participant of a focus group discussion in the politically active Remuna shared this view too:

> We are neighbours, my house is next to his. Suppose I have things [to eat] today. You don't. I give you today. Tomorrow you give me. Why is this feeling there? Because we all belong to one category of people. Today I am in want, there is no guarantee that tomorrow that person will not be in want. He will surely be in want. So good relations exist. Because if I depend on him today, tomorrow he will need help from me. Because of this, good relations exist.

A lender today might turn a borrower tomorrow. This awareness of each other's vulnerability helps develop a relationship of cooperation and trust.[10] It is

---

10   Class consciousness on its own or in combination with neighbourliness underlies reciprocity to a much greater extent in the left-leaning locality than in the more conservative one.

the combination of insecurity and poverty that underlies the norm and practice of reciprocity among labourers.

Although I had expected that objective class relations as such would be a much stronger basis for reciprocity, this is not what I found. Between class relations and consequences of class relations (e.g. poverty, etc.), the latter are more important factors underlying norms of reciprocity. Labourers are more conscious of the consequences of their class position, i.e. their poverty and insecurity, than of their class position itself. There is a reason for this. The extent to which labourers are conscious of their class position as such is limited in the two localities (as in most places in India and other countries), although this consciousness is stronger in Remuna than in Chasakhanda.

The role of class and consequences of class in sustaining reciprocity cannot be seen in abstraction from the spatiality of class. To some extent, norms of reciprocity among poor working class people exist also because of the feeling that labourers live together in a locality. And neighbourliness (which signifies spatiality of class) and class-based norms of reciprocity exist together. Class and location both influence norms of reciprocity. A participant in a focus group with CPI(M) members in Remuna reinforced this view by saying that people belonging to the same economic category live in the same neighbourhood, and they are fully aware of each other's difficulties.

While class and class-related aspects of labourers' lives can promote reciprocity, these can also undermine that. There are at least three different aspects of the class character of labouring families that actually undermines the practice of reciprocity and its effectivity for relief from poverty. Firstly, poor labourers have very limited ability to help their neighbours of the same class. A member of a focus group in Remuna said: There is solidarity among the poor class people. Suppose I am sick today, our wage-earning folks will surely help me. But they don't have the means, wealth. They will do whatever they can.

This is supported by a respondent from Chasakhanda when he said:

> Often we have to borrow. Instead of eating three times a day, we eat two times and save a little so we can return the money we have borrowed. ... I am in want, how shall I help you? ... You see, I am getting Rs30 a day, and he is getting Rs30 a day. His wage is not enough for his family. Mine is not enough for my family. We don't have any surplus to help each other.

Not only do poor people have limited ability to help each other. It is also the case that poor people cannot get much help from their poor neighbours who might be only slightly better off (or from other people, for that matter). A lady politician said:

> If you have a good relation with me, I will give you, you will give me ...
> that's all. ... Who cares about very poor people? No one cares. Because
> they cannot return. No one trusts them. Those among the poor people
> who are trust-worthy ... if they are working for me, they can return what
> I give them, then I will help them.

This view was echoed by another:

> My neighbours will lend me something if they think I have the ability to
> return. If someone is extremely poor and has absolutely nothing, then
> they won't lend him anything. They won't give him anything.

And a member of a focus group in Chasakhanda added: 'When we ask for some
money, people don't trust us. They think we are daily wage workers and live
hand to mouth, how will we return the money?'

Thus given the social crisis of reproduction they constantly face, the poor
labouring families cannot provide much material help to others (in spite of the
existence of strong *norms* of reciprocity). Nor can they get much help: those
who need help the most are the ones who are excluded from the networks of
reciprocity. How can there be reciprocity when a family is always in need and
cannot help others?. Apart from the fact that not everyone is a part of the network of reciprocity, it is also the case that – and this is the third aspect of how
class constrains the practice of reciprocity – when people do help each other,
the amount of help people give and receive from one another is not much.
A school clerk explained:

> A lot of give and take is there (in rice, etc.). But when one needs a heavy
> amount, it is not possible to get help ... This is also not a permanent solu-
> tion. This is temporary help. How many times will one help?

If wage labourers are poor, how is the norm of reciprocity practised at all?
As a person called NSM said, 'not everyone in our village will run out of food
at the same time'. That means that at the community level, on a given day,
there may be some surplus of food which can be shared, if there are strong
norms of reciprocity. Some families can have some surplus above their minimal consumption level for a few days. The circulation of rice, etc. in the form
of mutual help comes out of this *temporary* 'surplus' which is *really* a part of
labourers' consumption fund. This is shared with families not having food with
the strong expectation that it will be returned when needed. But this also suggests that because of lack of any surplus on a long-term basis, there is a very

weak *material* basis for the *norm* of reciprocity. That is why, when one borrows but cannot return as promised, the relationships turn bitter. The continuity of the practice of reciprocity is under threat because the trust underlying that is eroded, often not intentionally. As one person said: 'If I borrow something from you and can't return, I will procrastinate, relations get bitter. Relations of trust weaken because of want (*abhaba, anatana*)'.[11] Sometimes relations break down. When one family borrows from another but does not return, or does not return, as quickly as expected, they quarrel. Thus trust and reciprocity, the basic ingredients of social capital, can cause limited and temporary relief from absolute poverty. But the practice of trust and reciprocity can be constrained, and the norms underlying that practice are weakened, by poverty.

Spatiality of class understood in terms of neighbourliness can also have a constraining effect on reciprocity. Social capital presupposes social interaction. And 'social interaction usually takes place in a localised spatio-temporal context' causing people's 'local dependence' (Cox and Mair, 1988: 312; Das 2001 on local dependence in Odisha villages). With respect to social capital, for example, 'mutual aid [which is an important aspect of social capital] is with particular neighbours', as Cox and Mair say. It is generally the case that by being in the particular place – or by being a part of place-based social support networks – do people get help or can help others. As one respondent (a low-caste government official living in a low-caste labourers hamlet) said: 'Suppose I don't have rice to eat, I will get from my neighbours, I won't get from *outside* of the village' (italics added). One reason for the geographical boundedness of mutual help is that mutual help presupposes trust, and trust relations take time to develop through routinized place-based interactions characterized by what Giddens (1987) calls 'co-presence'. Norms and practice of reciprocity indeed tend to be spatially bounded: these tend to happen in limited geographical spaces. This can potentially make people vulnerable. People have access to resources of the place-based networks of which they are a part, but these resources are limited not only because of class and its consequences such as poverty. Resources are limited also because the networks stretch across geographically limited areas.

I am dealing with labouring families as constituting the working class, families who depend on daily wages for living. This class is not homogeneous. There are economic-cultural differences within this class. And, these have a bearing

---

11   These views were echoed by many. One person said: 'Some people borrow but don't return. When this happens, neighbours are reluctant to help each other'. Another said: 'If someone borrows something from someone else, the borrower does not want to interact with that person too long, lest he would have to return what has been borrowed. He wants to avoid that person. He wants to establish relationships with other people'.

on the practice of reciprocity. Some of these families have a person with a government job (e.g. clerk) with a salary (e.g. a family where parents work as daily labourers but their son works in a government office). These working-class families are slightly better off than the families who are totally dependent on daily wages. These two categories of families, although often they are of the same class and caste, do not get along well, and often are not engaged in mutual reciprocity. One person said: 'There are some people in our *harijana* [lowest caste] community, they have got government jobs, they don't like us. They don't want even to come to our houses'. This view was shared by another:

> [T]hose among our *Harijan* caste who have become well-off ... hate their own caste people who are poor. Earlier tràditionally even landlords used to have some sympathy with the poor people. But these people [the richer sections among the *harijans*] hate us.

There are important occupational-cultural differences within the working class. Some are farm labourers and others are factory labourers. This sort of difference is very important in Remuna, but not in Chasakhanda, because Remuna is close to an industrial town and it itself has some industries. A senior government official in Remuna, RJS, said:

> [There are factory workers and agricultural workers]. If a factory worker takes [someone] for work to a factory, there will be competition between the two types of workers. [Some] factory workers get Rs 60–70 a day whereas agricultural labourers get Rs 50. Factory labourers wear trousers and shirts but agricultural labourers wear *gamuchha* (a thin and long cotton towel). [Some] factory labourers get a salary [but agricultural labourers are daily labourers]. Agricultural labourers want to work in factories, but factory workers are not encouraging them. Rarely do factory labourers help agricultural labourers find a job in a factory.

In part because of occupational differences, there are some income differences within the working class. When all are poor and struggling to survive, a little bit of economic difference among them – even the luxury of some people having some food to eat everyday while others have little or nothing – causes ill-feelings, feelings of jealousy which can undermine norms of reciprocity. A respondent said: 'If I am earning Rs 50 in a place and if I don't call my neighbour to work there, he gets angry with me. ... Because we all are in want, there is a feeling of jealousy among us'.

There are also political differences within the working class, i.e. the differences along political party lines. This has several implications. Reciprocity or mutual help is often practised within a group following a specific party.

> If during the election there was a fight between two people, when one goes to work as a part of a team, they do not call the other person to join the work-team. When government help comes, often it is circulated within circles defined by party loyalty. If someone of the Congress Party got some assistance (following a natural calamity such as a cyclone), they would share it all with other Congress people depriving non-Congress people of the assistance.

This view is supported by not only poor daily wage labourers but also by slightly better off people (e.g. a government clerk and a government clerk-cum landowner). The former said: 'A Janata party person will not help a poor person supporting the Congress party'. The latter generalized by saying: 'People think, 'He belongs to that party. Why should I help?'"

Thus the practice of reciprocity is often confined to groups defined by common political loyalty. If one is outside specific groups, one may not get the help one needs from people who can help.

4   Bridging Social Capital of Poor Wage Labourers

4.1   *Stock and Benefits of Bridging Social Capital*
Associations/clubs – labourers' associational life – represent a form of bridging social capital. It is social capital at a larger social, and often spatial, scale than the norms of reciprocity (or bonding social capital). There are a large number of civic organizations, such as cultural associations, self-help groups, youth clubs, development associations, religious associations, in both the localities under study. These associations, many of which are located in working-class hamlets and dominated by working-class members, seem to promote relations of trust and cooperation among poor people. One explained:

> There was a lot of conflict between *dhoba* and *kandara* on the one hand and *pana* castes on the other [these are all 'ex-untouchable' castes]. We [i.e. the low caste labourers] established *Pallee mangala yuvaka sangha* (Rural welfare youth association). Even when dogs from different neighbourhoods used to fight among themselves, that used to divide the

neighbourhoods. Because of the club, younger people from different hamlets sat together. People are no longer quarrelling among themselves. When I went and sat there in the club, would my father quarrel with other people there? ... Earlier we were not sitting together, we were not doing things together. Now we are sitting in one place. The attitude to help each other developed. Earlier high caste people did not interact with *harijans*. Now they are interacting with them. Now we are all eating together, sitting together. We gossip together.

Clubs and associations then promote social capital in the form of trust and cooperative relations. The latter in turn can produce tangible benefits. As one said, youth clubs help 'in digging the village pond and tube-wells' and provide 'help to people in difficulty' and help students. Similarly, someone who leads a cultural organization said: 'We tidy up village roads. Clean ponds. Provide help to people during medical emergency. We also help people with their daughters' marriage. We have also dug a pond'.

And the benefit of association is not just material. Lots of people join informal religious associations for sociability and spiritual purposes. When asked why he is a part of his religious association, an old wage worker, BBJ, said, 'To worship our deity. To enjoy. We are all poor people. This gives us an opportunity to sit together and enjoy'.

As mentioned earlier, Remuna is a part of an area with a much greater stock of bridging social capital than is Chasakhanda. Indeed, Remuna is a part of eastern Odisha, which has a long tradition of peasant movement against landlords. Remuna itself has a strong organization of the CPI(M), a Left party, which is involved not only in political organizing but also in providing help during distress (e.g. clothes after the super-cyclone that hit Odisha). As mentioned earlier, Remuna, unlike Chasakhanda, is close to an industrial centre and itself has small factories, a large number of people from Remuna are industrial workers. Thus relations within the village are reinforced through relationships at work in the nearby factory areas, which makes it easier for them to form associations. But although Remuna has a greater tradition of strong civil society than Chasakhanda does, the production of bridging social capital like that of bonding social capital is adversely affected by the economic and political conditions in which labourers live in both the places. It is to these that I now turn.

4.2 *How Do Class/Economic and Political Conditions Affect Labourers' Associational Life?*

People need money to run associations. And, money is something that daily labourers do not have much of. They start fighting over who will contribute how much to these associations. Apart from money, people have to contribute labour as well. But daily labourers are busy with their work. If they do not labour, they don't get to eat. They leave home at around 8 in the morning and return in the evening very tired. The problem of the lack of time is compounded by the fact that increasingly they have to travel miles to get work. Two people spoke to this issue of time:

> People are too much concerned about their survival. I have five members in my family. Will I first take care of them or will I go to a club or association?
> Suppose you call me to spend some time for the club, I first think of wage-work. If I have money for six months to support my family, if I am needed for the club or any organization, I can sit and talk, I can give time for the organization.

As a local politician who knows many labourers, said:

> If everyone has enough to eat, there will be no jealousy. If people have enough to eat, they will say 'let's do this or that together'. Because of lack of money, people are not keen on cooperating to do things together. Everyone is looking after his [or her own] interest.

Associations do function as bridging social capital in that it links wage labour families of different locations/hamlets and different castes. Bridging social capital links families that mainly depend on farm wage labour and families that depend on low level government jobs. But they are not bridging the 'gaps' between these families and richer families. When asked if associations enhance relationships between the rich and the poor, a wage labourer, CJ, who also does petty business, said: 'The rich even do not want to interact with us much. They think if there is a lot of interaction, we might ask them for help'. Wage labourers' poverty keeps their associations away from (those of) the rich.

As if poverty, which is a part of common people's social crisis, behind which are class relations, is not enough to undermine the conditions under which these associations can thrive, political factors add to their problems. As I said earlier, labourers, like others, are deeply divided along political party lines, thus limiting the amount of social capital that is produced. Sometimes, people cannot even sit together. A government clerk remarked:

> We have a community house for meeting, etc. But if people from one party come one day, people from another party don't go that day, they come the next day ... Sometimes, they will be together, they will work

together [for wages], go to the shopping area, etc., but when it comes to building an association, there are differences.

Often politicians deliberately weaken these associations. Numerous respondents shared this view. One said:

> Cultural associations would enhance trust relations. But politicians are destroying trust. Poor people can be united [through cultural associations] but politicians are dividing them ... They will not benefit without creating conflicts. They cannot enter our village without dividing us.

A respondent from the landowning class also had similar views: 'Some people had established a youth club. They participated in the election. After that the club collapsed. Now there are party feelings among them'.

It is clear that poor labouring people trying to build voluntary associations are in a dilemma. If they align themselves with a specific party, they might get some (government) money from politicians and thus address their monetary problem I referred to earlier. But in return, politicians want electoral support of the members of that association. And, when an association extends support to politicians of one party, politicians of another party try to put pressure on some members of the association and buy their support, thus creating conflicts within the association. When an association is loyal to a specific party or of a faction of a party, the quality of social capital is compromised: the association will do things only for the benefits of one section of the labouring community (e.g. for labourers supporting a specific political party or leader). On the other hand, when an association decides to keep itself away from the influence of political parties, and in this sense, remains apolitical, it is starved of monetary support from politicians. As the leader of the cultural organization mentioned earlier said: 'Other associations and groups get money [from/through parties] but our cultural association did not because we operate on a cross-party basis. Younger people from all parties are with us'.

It was clear from the interviews that any civic association of people is potentially a vote bank. When one party thinks a particular association is a potential vote bank *for* the opposition, it tries to capture it (or at least some influential members) as soon as possible as a pre-emptive measure. And, in many instances, poorer people are vulnerable to politicians' attempts to co-opt them through one or more of the following: bribery; promise of wage work on government-sponsored projects; promise of government benefits; and support in local/family conflicts. There is an additional issue. As politicians are rightly seen as pocketing government money meant for the labouring families, local-level cultural and social associations can potentially play a counter-surveillant role vis-à-vis the politicians. These associations are therefore potentially a threat to politicians of all hues. Controlling an association through patronage, or at least controlling a few members, is a useful way of disorganizing the people and/or curbing their critical attitude. As the secretary of an NGO in Remuna, said: 'The more disorganized the people are, the better for the politicians. Politicians will prevent their organization' (see Table 4.1 for summary information).

Indeed, because of political party differences, conflicts arise and mutual trust erodes, which prevent people from doing things together. Politicians are not just trying to break associations once they have been formed. Indeed, by eroding trust and creating conflicts, they are undermining the conditions that should be conducive to forming associations and engaging in collective activities. There is a near consensus among the respondents of different classes and occupations in both the places that politicians and political parties are the major source of conflict (at the local scale).

TABLE 4.1   The study areas in eastern India

	Remuna	Chasakhanda
1. Total population (2001)	10 669	9064
2. Scheduled castes and tribes[a] as a % of total population	28.5	43.3
3. Economic development (paddy yield in quintal per hectare)	26.9	18
4. No. of civic associations[b] including self-help groups[c] per 1000 population	3.01	1.82
5. No. of civic associations excluding self-help groups per 1000 population	0.85	0.48
6. Votes polled by Left parties (%) in the local (i.e. *Panchayat*) elections	22.28	12.97

a Presence of these groups occupying the bottom strata of Indian society is often used as a proxy for poverty.
b These include registered clubs, voluntary associations, youth clubs, women's associations, libraries and labour unions. These data are for the Block level.
c These are groups of women who collectively save some money every month and receive loans from the government to engage in small business; they are also sometimes engaged in other self-empowering activities

SOURCE: BLOCK DEVELOPMENT OFFICE OF REMUNA AND CHASAKHANDA

A retired rural development officer said: 'One political party supports one group, another party supports another group. As a result difference in opinion (*manomalinya*) is created between brothers in a family, between neighbours'. This view was shared by an agricultural worker: 'The election system and the party feelings are a source of conflict in the village. Different people are attached to different parties. This creates conflict'. Even a mill owner echoed the view of the agricultural labourer: 'Political party system is even dividing family. Members of one family are with different parties hoping that they will get something from party leaders, a loan, a job'.

A Left politician explained in some details self-reflexively:

> Clubs and associations should enhance social relationships among people. But we politicians are not allowing that to happen. Because by dividing them we get votes ... If we unite them, it is possible that they will support us today en masse, but it is also possible that the whole group will support someone else. Their division ensures support for me from some people. ... Nowadays, you see 3–4 clubs in small villages. The reason for that is that people are divided. ... People do come together and do something such as cleaning of the road, etc. But that is rare.

It is easy for politicians to divide and weaken people because of the latter's economic weakness/vulnerability. As a government worker said: 'Workers are generally people in want. ... Political party leaders give them money, help them getting some benefits from the government. That's how they [workers] are getting divided'.

Politicians enjoy the power of the state, and this political power is a source of their money-power. The poor people, politically un-organized, have no power. The relations between politicians and the poor are vertical relations. The networks of vertical relations do not create (much) social capital and are not beneficial for the poor (although they benefit the network of politicians). Politicians are well connected among themselves (and to government officials). *Their* network is much more powerful than that of poor wage labourers. As DeFilippis, who is critical of Putnam's social capital, puts it, 'certain social networks are in greater positions of power than others' and they can therefore yield much more substantial returns to their members' (2001: 791).

5   From the Empirical to the Theoretical: Concluding Comments

Labouring families help one another in so many ways. Reciprocity extends to food, money and much more. These families are also involved in voluntary associations through which they are engaged in collective actions for mutual benefit. If social capital is 'the ability of individuals to secure benefits as a result of membership in social networks or other social structures' (Portes and Landolt 2000, 532), then the networks of reciprocity and voluntary associations among wage labour families are forms of social capital.

There is limited evidence that the practice of reciprocity – bonding social capital and even of bridging social capital – exists because of 'bounded solidarity' of the working *class*. This is the solidarity based on an emergent sentiment of we-ness among working-class people who face similar adverse situation (Portes and Sensenbrenner 1993, 1327–8; Callinicos 1988, 199–203). In contrast to Portes and others, I distinguish between two aspects of class relations: a) objective class positions; and b) their consequences which constitute the social crisis of the working class. These two aspects of class relations are associated with two forms of consciousness: consciousness of objective class positions, and consciousness of the consequences of class positions. Objective class position is indeed an important factor underlying reciprocity: some labourers are conscious of the fact that they are a class which owns little property and whose livelihood therefore depends on wage work. A part of what goes on in terms of reciprocity in the study areas *is* based on this consciousness. Then there are *consequences* of labourers' class position. One consequence is insecurity and another is poverty. No one knows that he/she will get some wage work tomorrow and have some food to eat. It is the combination of insecurity and poverty that underlies the defensive mechanism of norm/practice of reciprocity within working class communities. Indeed, Harvey (1985: 120) says, 'Reciprocity exhibited in working-class neighbourhoods is to a large degree a defensive device'. Workers' social-cultural associations also have a similar logic. As Cooke's work on labour geography in Wales shows, labourers' associations spring 'from the collective response of ordinary workers to the needs and suffering of their communities, as a means of improving the day-to-day conditions of life' (Cooke 1985: 237).[12] It is also the case the class of people that are

---

12   The study of working-class social capital in this chapter indirectly sheds some light on what Mike Savage (1996:68–69), one of the spatially minded sociologists, calls the 'socio-cultural class formation' of labourers. The latter involves, he says, 'the construction of dense ties which allows the forging of solidaristic and communal identities over time ... Here, classes can draw upon "community", face-to-face relationships [that characterize] dense neighbourhood networks' and so on. Class relations underlie working-class social capital, and the latter in turn has some impact on class formation. While I have shown the first aspect of this relationship, I have not shown how working-class social capital affects class formation, how, that is, workers' 'friendship ... , their clubs and associations [and so on] ... bring about a commonality of background and attitude which

dependent on wages is internally divided into higher and lower-income groups as well as higher and lower caste groups, and this inequality undermines reciprocity within the class.[13]

Given the general theoretical importance of class in social sciences, including human geography (Gibson and Graham 1992; Sheppard and Barnes, 1990; Smith 2000; Thrift and Williams 1987; Wood 1998) and in the light of specific connections that I had 'hypothesized' between class and social capital, I had expected that class would be a much stronger basis for the practice of reciprocity. This is not borne out empirically. The extent to which labourers are conscious of their objective class position – both in the sense that they have no access to the means of production, must rely on wage labour to live, and are thus exploited, and in the sense that they have the power to reduce and ultimately stop their exploitation through political action, is limited and spatially uneven. Labourers are more conscious of *the consequences* of their class position, especially poverty and insecurity as consequences of class position, than of their actual class position. Because of this, empirically speaking, poverty and insecurity are a stronger foundation for norms/practice of reciprocity rather than class position as such. This points to the fact that 'People ... come to realise the force of class in and through the immediate circumstances they can experience and understand directly' (Walker 1985: 187). Poverty, insecurity, etc. are some of these circumstances.

Two points should be noted here parenthetically. On the one hand, corresponding to common people's consciousness of the consequences of their class position is the trade unionist consciousness – the consciousness that the consequences of class position can be mitigated through people's struggles against the bosses and capitalist state bureaucrats/politicians for concessions. On the other hand, class consciousness proper exists when people are conscious of

---

crystallises a social class into a collectivity' (Scott in Thrift 1987, 26–7). This is worth investigating.

13   This is as much true about Odisha as elsewhere. But unfortunately the post-modernized Left has taken the fact of (working) class is heterogeneous to mean that it is not useful to talk about class with any seriousness (see Walker 1985, and Seddon 2002 for counter-arguments). What the critics of the concept of the working class forget is this: if the working class has many groups within it, there must be something common among them which makes all of them working class in the first place. The internal heterogeneity of an entity – in the natural and social worlds – does not mean that it does not exist, or that its existence is non-significant. A dialectical approach to the world allows for difference. But unity and relations, among both parts of an entity and among different entities, have ontological primacy over difference. This is indicated by the numerous workers' struggles that happen across the world almost every single day.

their objective class position as such (the fact that they have little or no control over property, that they are exploited in the workplace and that *their* interests and the interests of the capitalist bosses are fundamentally incompatible and therefore the socialist movement is the answer to their problems). Trade unionist consciousness is a lower form of class consciousness (Lenin, 1902). The difficult economic conditions such as poverty and insecurity which are consequences of class relations, and the consciousness of those conditions that serve as a stronger foundation for the practice of reciprocity than class relations, are also the reason for people's economic struggle which generally takes a trade unionist form. The latter is not exactly the same as class struggle proper, which is against the wage slavery itself and which is against the very existence of the state itself that defends wage-slavery.

Class positions and consequences of class positions are not the only factors that condition the production of social capital. To a large extent, norms of reciprocity and associational life exist because labourers live together in a locality. And neighbourliness- and class-based norms of reciprocity co-exist in particular places. Class and location co-influence social capital. In both the study areas, as in many other parts of India, labouring class people, and especially low-caste labourers, live in separate hamlets from high-caste property-owning families. Norms of reciprocity based on 'neighbourliness' – the consciousness behind proximity-based reciprocity – cannot be entirely explained by class and class-related consciousness. In reality, and in the minds of the labourers, labourers are more than labourers. They are also human beings who live in specific places in a spatial relationship, i.e. in spatial juxtaposition or 'happenstance arrangement in relation to each other' to use Doreen Massey's term (Massey, 1999: 283). And the fact that they live next to each other, that they are neighbours, and that they *perceive* themselves as such, partly underlies the norms of reciprocity among them. Neighbourliness is neither merely a proxy for class, nor is it an independent process unconnected to class.

The fact that neighbourliness or location underlies reciprocity speaks to a wider body of research in sociology, human geography, and other disciplines on the spatiality of class and other structures of social relations. Spatial structures reproduce-reinforce and undermine social processes. Consider place-based networks as spatial structures. As Gilbert (1998) says, these are both enabling and constraining. On the one hand: 'Spatial contiguity', expressed, for example, in terms of neighbourhood relations among working-class people, 'is a very important base' for (understanding) working-class experience (Walker 1985, 187). More specifically, place-based networks of mutual help in working-class neighbourhoods can be important to varying degrees in the day-to-day lives of working-class poor people. But on the other hand, place-based networks can be constraining because 'everyday interactions ... tend to be highly localised' (Gilbert 1998, 600). Norms and practice of reciprocity are spatially bounded.[14] People have access to resources of the place-based networks of which they are a part, but these resources are limited not only because of class, but also because these networks stretch across geographically limited areas.

Whether social capital is influenced by class, by consequences of class or indeed by the spatiality of class (i.e. the fact that working-class people are also neighbours, whose lives are embedded in spatially limited areas), the benefits of social capital for wage labour are very limited in both the localities under study. The reason for this that I have highlighted here is, broadly speaking, class. I have said that class is more constraining than enabling of social capital. This may need further explanation.

With respect to bonding social capital, two points can be made. Firstly, the working class is excluded from, and relatively deprived of, society's *material resources* (especially, means of production). Given this fact, which is indicative of their objective class position, workers have limited subsistence resources to share among themselves. And, without *resources* to share on a more or less continuous basis, informal *rules* of sharing in a place and over space are difficult to sustain for long and in a significant way. When poor people are small property owners, they can share their tools, information about market, etc., and thus social capital can play *some* role in the improvement of their material conditions. But when poor people are without property, whose main source of income is wage labour, and when they rarely have anything to share, the role of their social capital is very limited. Indeed, their major 'asset' is their labour power, the power of their body to perform labour. That is the major thing that they can potentially share. But (norms of) sharing labour power do not amount to much because labour power has to be applied to physical property such as land which they do not have. For example, my discussions with them indicated that they were very keen on being involved in fishery in village ponds on a collective basis. But ponds, generally, do not belong to them. In spite of norms of reciprocity which generate their willingness to use their labour power collectively, these norms are of little use because they do not own property. Norms of reciprocity – or the idea that 'the poor have each other' (Woolcock and Narayan 2000) – are not be much help in this sort of

---

14   If a person needs some food or has to be taken to hospital, she is more likely to need help, and get help, from her neighbours or villagers than from those living miles away. The spatiality of reciprocity within the working class is for the similar reason that, for example, the sale of labour power tends to occur in geographically circumscribed areas (Harvey, 1985; Cox and Mair, 1988).

context. Bebbington, perhaps the most enthusiastic social capitalist among geographers, says 'a social relationship is a resource that can facilitate access to other resources' (2002: 801). But, a social relationship is not necessarily/automatically a resource. To be a resource, it has to be a social relationship of a particular kind. Indeed, what kind of resource can a social relationship between two poor wage earners be and how useful can it be to alleviate their poverty? As DeFilippis, a geographer who is very critical of social capital, rightly says, ties that define social capital, or '[c]onnections ... do not, of themselves, make the people in any place rich or poor' (2001: 790). *Norms* of sharing things are not of much use without people having things to share, even if they are kinship groups or members of an association.[15]

Secondly, and very importantly, mutual help is based on an expectation of a certain degree of *security*: that when one is in difficulty, one expects that one's relations with others will act as a source of help. Yet, a fundamental aspect of the working-class life is *insecurity*, not just exclusion from material resources. Because the working class has been separated from the means of production, its access to the means of subsistence, generally, depends on securing wage work, which, however, is not guaranteed. One never knows how one is going to get through to the end of the week. There are many instances where people have a little bit of food or money to share but they are reluctant to share simply because they do not know whether they themselves are going to eat tomorrow. Further, the *insecurity* of the working class tends to undermine the conditions for the reproduction of norms of trust and reciprocity, which, however, presuppose a sense of *security*.[16] If a person borrows something from her neighbour promising to return it on a given day, and if she fails to keep her promise because she does not get any wage work, she loses the trust of her neighbour. This conclusion does not sit well with Putnam's idea that an effective norm of generalized reciprocity requires that people can be confident that 'trusting will be requited, not exploited' (1993: 172). For Putnam, if relations of trust are lacking, then it is because individuals are selfish. This amounts to explaining social norms in terms of psychology, disregarding the material constraints

---

15   Indeed, social capitalists see individuals/families as nodes and social capital as lines (which represent feelings of trust, relations of kinship, and association activity) connecting the nodes (Narayan and Pritchett, 1997). This idealization of kinship as benign and tension-free is not borne out by the findings of some anthropologists. Ethnographies written by the latter have documented extensively not merely the antagonism latent and/or realized in the kinship domain, but also that such conflict is invariably linked to access to, or control over, the means of production (and/or financial resources) in the context concerned.

16   This is the case unless there are strong countervailing forces (e.g. extra-local support).

under which people live. The material conditions under which people live fundamentally shape the ways in which they think about their lives. People do act against difficult conditions but not with a degree of freedom they would want to enjoy. Working-class people do practise mutual help and they do possess feelings of neighbourliness. But they do not do this under the conditions of their own choosing.

Now consider the constraining effects of class and politics on bridging social capital. For one thing, establishing and running socio-cultural associations require that people contribute free labour. But daily labourers are busy with their work. If they do not perform wage-labour, they do not get to eat. They have little time for associations. They are not 'middle-class' members of Putnam's bowling clubs! It is not at all clear to what degree the floral societies, which Putnam speaks favourably of as a site of the production of social capital, can help the poor. Apart from time, people also need money to run associations. And, money is something poor labourers do not have much of either. They start fighting over who will contribute how much money and/or labour to these associations. Also, lack of funds makes them vulnerable to the attempts of politicians to prey upon them and their associations. Indeed, civic organizations of poor wage labourers find it very difficult to sustain themselves without vertical relations of patronage vis-à-vis politicians. In other words, horizontal connections that Putnam associates with civic organizations tend not to characterize poor people's lives and their organizations. When wage labourers do form associations, political parties try to control these and create conflicts among members to pre-empt any potential counter-surveillant role these associations might play vis-à-vis corrupt politicians and local entrepreneurs. Politicians also seek to control these associations to get votes. For a given political party, a particular association is a potential vote bank *for* its opposition, so it tries to capture it (or at least some of its influential members).

As a part of my social capital research, with help from some of my research assistants, I helped a working class hamlet in one of the localities set up a labour association. One purpose was to see how it works. There was also a desire to see some real improvement in the lives of people. The association had a fund, which included some contribution from labouring families, a donation from my research fund (as a token gift to people for the time they spent during interviews) and some personal fund. If a household did not have money to buy food, the association immediately made available several hundred rupees which were returned when the borrower had the money. People were able to borrow from the association to travel to the nearest town to see a doctor and obtain medical treatment. Because many were construction workers, many were suffering from tuberculosis. The words about the labour association spread to far-away locations, so the labour contractors who used to cheat the workers became more 'careful'. By using the association's resources, working class families were able to check some corruption on the part of the local politicians. Relations of reciprocity improved a little. However, within 3–4 years, the association ceased to function. Local politicians contributed to its weakening (as expected): differing loyalties to political parties carefully culti-vated by politicians undermined the unity that the association had created. As well, some people borrowed money but did not return (in part because of their grinding poverty), so norms of trust and reciprocity weakened.

The main point I wish to stress is that objective class relations and conse-quences of class – or more generally, the economic-political conditions under which poor people live – are more constraining in the production of social capital than enabling. This conclusion is supported by some of the existing geographical and social science literature as well. For example, Meert says, if a person lacks sufficient purchasing power, it will be difficult for her to support and participate in associations, and be a part of a network of reciprocal help (2002, 328–9; also Meert et al. 1997). Meert's study of reciprocity in a village close to Brussels shows that:

> Given widespread poverty among most members of social networks, opportunities for the poor households of Houwaart to swap goods or ser-vices ... are rare. In fact, mutual exchange among these households effec-tively means the reciprocal swapping of poverty.
>
> 2002, 333

Indeed, recent research in advanced country contexts shows that work-related time constraints and poverty negatively influence civic engagement (Price 2002).

Moser's (1998) work on reciprocity in poor urban communities in four dif-ferent parts of the world reaches similar conclusions to mine, Meert's and others'. She found traditional credit arrangements in these places whereby the poor borrow on a short-term basis from neighbours, and nearby relatives, for daily consumption needs such as food, thus indicating the usefulness of social capital. But social capital can be quickly eroded due to adverse economic conditions.

> [W]here households have sufficient resources, reciprocity in cash and non-monetary exchanges has been sustained. ... [But] economic crisis has pushed some households beyond the point at which they can sustain such reciprocity.
>
> MOSER 1998, 13

My study clearly does not support the optimistic claims such as the one that social capital is the capital of the poor, especially if it is social capital in the Putnam sense. Like other geographers such as Mohan and Mohan, DeFilippis and others, I am therefore concerned about social capitalists' attempts to privilege social capital over material conditions and class-based social relations as primary determinants of people's lives. In short, it is impossible 'to separate social capital from material circumstances' (Mohan and Mohan 2002, 206), i.e. from people's class context. Along with similar studies such as those by Moser and Meert, my study is expected to contribute to the growing literature on the critique of social capital (Harriss 2002; Fine 2002). It is extremely problematic to treat the existing level of social capital as an independent variable and poverty (or social crisis, more generally) as a dependent variable, or to see social capital of the poor as a missing link in long-term development or in long-term resolution of the social crisis experienced by common people. This is not at all to say that social capital of the poor – their norms of reciprocity, and informal networks, etc. – is of no importance at all. Social capital can be a source of short-term and limited help in certain social-geographical milieu. It always has been (Harvey 1973; Polanyi 1944). In this sense there is nothing new about the social *practice* that the currently fashionable *concept* of social capital refers to.

References

Beall, J. (2000). Valuing social resources or capitalising on them: social action and limits to pro-poor urban governance Partnership and Poverty working paper 19, University of Birmingham.

Bebbington, A. (2002). Sharp knives and blunt instruments: social capital in development Studies. *Antipode, 34*: 800–803.

Bebbington, A., Woolcock, M., Guggenheim, S., & Olson, E. (2002). Grounding discourse in practice: Exploring social capital debates at the World Bank mimeo.

Biggart, N., & Castanias, R. (2001). Collaterized social relations: the social in economic Calculation. *American Journal of Economics and Sociology 60*: 471–500.

Buck, D. (2000). Growth, disintegration, and decentralization: the construction of Taiwan's industrial networks. *Environment and Planning A, 32*: 245–262.

Callinicos, A. (1988). *Making History: Agency, Structure and Change in Social Theory.* Ithaca: Cornell University Press.

Christerson, B., & Lever-Tracy, C. (1997). The third China? Emerging industrial districts in rural China. *International Journal of Urban and Regional Research, 21*: 569–588.

Cooke, P. (1985). Class practices as regional markers: a contribution to labour geography. In D. Gregory and J. Urry (Eds.), *Social Relations and Spatial Structures*. (Pp. 213–241). London: Macmillan.

Cox, K., & Mair, A. (1988). Locality and community in the politics of local economic Development. *Annals Association of American Geographers, 78*: 307–325.

Das, R. (2001). The spatiality of social relations: an Indian case-study. *Journal of Rural Studies, 17:* 347–362.

Das, R. (2004). Social Capital and Poverty of Wage Labourers: Problems with the Social Capital Theory. *Transactions of the Institute of British Geographers, 29*(1): 27–45.

Das, R. (2009). Class Relations, Material Conditions, and Spaces of Class Struggle in Rural India. *Human Geography: A New Radical Journal, 2*(3): 52–74.

de Haan, A. and Dubey, A. (2005). Poverty, Disparities, or the Development of Underdevelopment in Orissa, *Economic and Political Weekly*, 40: 22/23, pp. 2321–2329.

DeFilippis, J. (2001). The myth of social capital in community development. *Housing Policy Debate, 12*: 781–806.

DeFilippis, J. (2002). Symposium on social capital: An introduction. *Antipode, 34*: 790–795.

Fine, B. (2001). *Social Capital vs Social theory*. London: Routledge.

Fine, B. (2002). They f**k you up those social capitalists. Antipode, *34*: 796– 799.

Fine, B. (undated). *It ain't social, it ain't capital and it ain't Africa*. School of Oriental and African Studies. University of London mimeo.

Gertler, M. (1995). Being there – proximity, organization, and culture in the development and adoption of advanced manufacturing technologies. *Economic Geography, 71*: 1–26.

Gibson, K., & Graham, J. (1992). Rethinking class in industrial-geography – creating a space for an alternative politics of class. *Economic Geography, 68*: 109–127.

Giddens, A. (1987). *Social Theory and Modern Sociology*. Cambridge: Polity Press.

Gilbert, M. (1998) 'Race', space, and power: the survival strategies of working poor women. *Annals of the Association of American Geographers, 88*: 595–621.

Gittel, R., & Vidal, A. (1998). *Community organizing: Building Social Capital as a Development Strategy*. Thousand Oaks: Sage.

Harriss, J. (2002). *Depoliticising Development: The World Bank and Social Capital*. London: Anthem Press.

Harriss, J., & De Renzio, P. (1997). Missing link or analytically missing?: The concept of social Capital. *Journal of International Development, 9:* 919–937.

Harvey, D. (1973). *Social Justice and the City*. Baltimore: Johns Hopkins University Press.

Harvey, D. (1985). *The Urbanization of Capital*. Baltimore: John Hopkins University Press.

Holzmann, R., & Jorgensen, S. (1999). Social protection as social risk management Social Protection Discussion paper no 9901 The World Bank.

Kennedy, B., Kawachi, I., & Brainerd, E. (1998). The role of social capital in the Russian mortality crisis *World Development, 26*: 2029–2043.

Kozel,V., & Parker, B. (1998). Poverty in Rural India: The Contribution of Qualitative Research in Poverty Analysis. The World Bank mimeo.

Lenin, V. (1902). *What is to be done?* https://www.marxists.org/archive/lenin/works /download/what-itd.pdf.

Levi, M. (1996). Social and unsocial capital: a review essay of Robert Putnam's Making democracy work. *Politics and Society, 24*: 45–55.

Massey, D. (1999). Spaces of politics. In D. Massey, J. Allen and P. Sarre (Eds.), *Human Geography Today*. (Pp. 274–294). London: Polity Press.

McDade, B., & Malecki, E. (1997). Entrepreneurial networking: industrial estates in Ghana. *Tijdschrift voor Economische en Sociale Geografie, 88*: 262–272.

Meert, H. (2002). Rural community life and the importance of reciprocal survival Strategies. *Sociologia Ruralis, 40*: 319–338.

Meert, H., Mistiaen. P., & Kesteloot, C. (1997). The geography of survival: household strategies in urban settings. *Tijdschrift voor Economische en Sociale Geografie, 88*: 169–181.

Mohan, G., & Mohan, J. (2002). Placing social capital. *Progress in Human Geography, 26:* 191–210.

Mohanty, M. (1990). Class, caste and democracy in a backward state: Odisha. In F. Frankel and M. Rao (Eds.), *Dominance and State Power*. Delhi: Oxford University Press.

Molina-Morales, F., Lopez-Navarro, M., & Guia-Julve, J. (2002). The role of local institutions as intermediary agents in the industrial district. *European Urban and Regional Studies, 9:* 315–329.

Moser, C. (1998). The asset vulnerability framework: reassessing urban poverty reduction strategies. *World Development, 26*: 1–19.

Narayan, D., & Pritchett, L. (1999). Social capital: evidence and implications. In P. Dasgupta and I. Serageldin (Eds.), *Social Capital: A Multi-Faceted Perspective.* (Pp. 269–295). Washington: The World Bank.

Patnaik, U. (1999). *The Long Transition: Essays on Political Economy*. New Delhi: Tulika Press.

Pinch, S., & Henry, N. (1999). Discursive aspects of technological innovation: the case of the British motor sport industry. *Environment and Planning A, 31*: 665–682.

Polanyi, K. (1944). *The great transformation: The political and economic origins of our time*. New York: Farrar & Rinehart.

Portes, A., & Landolt, P. (2000). Social capital: promise and pitfalls of its role in development. *Journal of Latin American Studies, 32*: 529–547.

Portes, A., & Sensenbrenner, J. (1993). Embeddedness and immigration: notes on the social determinants of economic action. *American Journal of Sociology, 98*: 1320–1350.

Price, B. (2002). Social capital and factors affecting civic engagement as reported by leaders of voluntary associations. *Social Science Journal, 39*: 119–127.

Putnam, R. (1993). *Making Democracy Work.* Princeton (N.J.): Princeton University Press.

Putnam, R. (2000). *Bowling Along: The Collapse and Revival of American Community.* New York: Simon and Schuster.

Sahoo, P. and Paltasingh, K. (2019). Examining Growth–Inequality Nexus in Post-reform Odisha: A Sectoral Decomposition Analysis. *Journal of Development Policy and Practice. 4*(1): 12–34.

Savage, M. (1996). Space, networks and class formation. In N. Kirk (Ed.), *Social class and Marxism.* Aldershot: Scolar Press.

Sayer, A. (2000). *Realism and Social Science.* London: Sage.

Seddon, D. (2002). Popular protest and class struggle in Africa: a historical overview. In L. Zeilig (Ed.), *Class Struggle and Resistance in Africa.* (Pp. 24–45). Cheltenham: New Clarion Press.

Sheppard, E., & Barnea, T. (1990). *The Capitalist Space Economy: Geographical Analysis after Ricardo, Marx and Sraffa.* London: Unwin Hyman.

Smith, N. (2000). What happened to class? *Environment and Planning A, 32*: 1011–1032.

Thrift, N., & Olds, K. (1996). Refiguring the economic in economic geography. *Progress in Human Geography, 20*: 311–337.

Thrift, N., & Williams, P. (1987). The geography of class formation. In N. Thrift and P. Williams (Eds.), *Class and Space: The Making of Urban Society.* (Pp. 1–22). New York: Routledge.

Uphoff, N. (2006). Understanding social capital: learning from the analysis and experience of Participation. In P. Dasgupta and I. Serageldin (Eds.), *Social Capital: A Multi-faceted Perspective.* (Pp. 215–249). Washington: The World Bank.

Walker, R. (1985). Class, division of labour and employment. In D. Gregory and J. Urry (Eds.), *Social Relations and Spatial Structures.* (Pp. 164–189). London: Macmillan.

Wood, E. (Ed.). (1997). *In Defense of history: Marxism and the postmodern agenda.* New York: Monthly Review press.

Wood, E. (1998). *The Retreat from Class,* revised edition. London: Verso.

Woolcock, M. (1998). Social capital and economic development: toward a theoretical synthesis and policy framework. *Theory and Society, 27*: 151–208.

Woolcock, M. (2000). Social capital in theory and practice: where do we stand, chapter prepared for the 21st Annual Conference on Economic issues (http://www.worldbank.org.ezproxy.library.yorku.ca/poverty/scapital/index.htm).

Woolcock, M., & Narayan, D. (2000). Social capital: Implications for development theory, research, and policy. *World Bank Research Observer, 15:* 225–249.

World Bank. (2001). *World development report 2000/2001.* Washington: World Bank.

Wright, E. (Ed.). (1989). 'Rethinking, once again, the concept of class structure' in E. Wright ed. The debate on classes, Verso, London, 269–348.

CHAPTER 5

Social Capital at the Zone of Interaction between the State and Civil Society

Raju J. Das

I examine social capital in civil society in the last chapter.[1] My focus in this chapter is on social capital at the interface between civil society and the state. The now-extensive literature on social capital asserts that state–society synergy understood as the relations of trust and cooperation between state actors (officials and politicians) and common people, benefits the latter. This claim is examined on the basis of primary evidence from fieldwork conducted in Odisha, Eastern India (mentioned in the last chapter), and my theoretical critique of the social capital literature as well as my alternative class-theoretical approach to social capital.

Two questions are addressed. First, to what extent are there relations of trust and cooperation between state actors and poor wage-workers? Second, what are the factors that explain the observed level of trust and cooperation between state actors and poor people? Two arguments are made here, both of which have wider applicability beyond the study areas. Because of the unequal relations of power between state actors and the poor, the power that reflects the class character of both society and the state, the conditions for state–society synergy (the site of what is called linking social capital) in support of the interests of the poor, are undermined. By contrast, where there is a pro-poor political organization – a factor that usually falls outside the scope of social capital enquiry, given its neo-liberal underpinnings – there may be greater levels of state–society synergy with some limited benefits for the poor, limited because of the class character of the state and society.

The remainder of the chapter is divided into five sections. In section 1, expanding on the points made in Chapter 3, I briefly look at the literature on state–society synergy, as an aspect of social capital, and situate it within the on-going debates on development/peasant studies. In the next two sections, I analyse the empirical material from questionnaire surveys and qualitative interviews. In section two, I show that overall there is very limited amount of

---

1   This chapter is based on an earlier publication (Das, 2005).

trust and cooperation between officials and poor labourers in the study areas. I also explain why this is the case. In section three, I show that to the extent that there is some social capital, it varies between the places, and I discuss how the place-specific political mobilization of the poor might explain this. In the concluding section, I reflect critically on some general conceptual issues regarding the nature of the relationship between the state and society.

1   Synergy, Social Capital and the Old Rhetoric[2]

As discussed in the last two chapters, social capital refers to relations of trust and cooperation and networks and organizations which can promote co-operative actions (Putnam, 1993: 167; Woolcock, 2000). There are three types of social capital (World Bank, 2001). The first two types ('bonding' and 'bridging' social capital) inhere in civil society, and this has been discussed empirically in the previous chapter. In response to criticisms that this is an overly society-centric view of social capital, recent works have recognized that there is a third form of social capital. This partly inheres 'in an enduring set of relationships that span the public-private divide' (Evans, 1997: 184). According to the World Bank (2001) this is an aspect of what is known as linking social capital, which refers to the relations of trust and cooperation between poor people and people in positions of power in formal organizations such as the state.

The most important characteristic of the social relations that constitute the linking social capital is state–society synergy. The literature on state–society synergy is a very important part of a larger literature in development studies and other social sciences that deal with state–society relations (Alavi, 1992; Das, 2000; Evans, 1997; Jeffrey, 2000; Jessop, 2002; Migdal, 1994; Woolcock, 1998). Indeed, Evans (1997: 204) says that 'Better understanding of the nature of synergistic relations between the state and society and the conditions under which such relations can most easily be constructed should become a component of future theory of development'. But what exactly does state–society synergy mean? Synergy, following Evans and *pace* Woolcock, has two aspects: embeddedness and complementarity. Embeddedness refers to (face-to-face) ties between citizens and public officials, based on mutual trust relations (Evans, 1997). It is the form of direct involvement of public officials which is crucial in getting citizens' efforts organized and sustaining citizen

---

2   There will be some overlap between the discussion here and parts of the literature review in Chapter 3.

involvement. Examples of embeddedness include neighbourhood meetings where officials and communities participate to resolve conflicts.

Complementarity, on the other hand, refers to the fact that the state provides things that the communities do not or cannot have, but will complement what they have (Evans, 1997). The scale and bureaucratic organization of the state allow it to provide more effectively certain kinds of collective goods which complement inputs more efficiently delivered by private actors. These can be material goods such as physical infrastructure. The state also provides intangible collective goods such as the rule of law. To complement state provision of these goods, citizens contribute local knowledge, experience and sometimes free labour. State–society synergy is not automatic, however. It requires a number of conditions to be met for it to exist. These are: (1) a corporately coherently Weberian bureaucracy; (2) the decentralization of bureaucracy to allow inputs from below; (3) officials who identify themselves with the communities in which they work; (4) relative equality in civil society; (5) democratic political competition plus the rule of law (the rule of law is a complement to the efforts of less privileged groups to organize themselves); and (6) the presence of pro-poor officials or 'reformists' (Evans, 1997: 180; 195–200).

Several empirical studies have been conducted in many countries on state–society synergy and linking social capital. Ostrom (1996) outlines both how poor neighbourhoods in a Brazilian city had to rely mainly on the government to produce trunk sewer lines which they could not have provided on their own, and how they also collaborated in producing this infrastructure. Further, face-to-face interaction between them and officials facilitated the maintenance of the system. Bebbington and Perreault's (1999) study of Ecuador maintains that the state, specifically its workers with a bias towards indigenous Highland communities, helped the latter build local organizations and then linked these to higher-level ones. These organizations have in turn led to state policies benefiting rural communities in the Ecuadorian Highlands. In Brazil's Ceara State, the government invested in building relations of trust between officials and people who were earlier very suspicious of them; once established, these trust relations licensed increased interaction between both parties, the outcome being an improved performance of a public health campaign, thereby reducing infant mortality (Tendler, 1997).

Similar studies have been conducted in Asia. The joint forest management by local communities and state officials in several parts of India is said to have resulted in positive outcomes – for example, increased village incomes (Serageldin and Grootaert, 2000). Williams (1997) chronicles the mutual interpenetration of state and society in India's West Bengal State, and in particular how the rural population makes use of the local government for their own ends.

Wang (1997) argues that in China the state and the peasantry are engaged in a mutually empowering relationship, since by this, peasant demands are fed into state power through grassroots democracy and self-governing villager committees. A Taiwan study conducted by Lam (1996; 2001) argues that development success depends on interaction between highly bureaucratized government agencies and self-organized local communities. In his study of the way the irrigation system operated, he found that many of the concerned government staff concerned with it were born locally, they have lived locally, and also farmed in the communities they served as officials. In the event of their being corrupt, it was possible for villagers to censure them.[3] There is, in short, an enmeshing between them and locals that raises the effectiveness of the state at local level. Or, to put it in more general terms, the more the agent overlaps with local community members who might react in other dimensions of social interaction, the less likely the agent is to 'cheat' on any one dimension. In other words, local social capital, or local structures of accountability, can make a difference (Conning and Kavane, 2002: 382).

Thus relations of trust and cooperation are formed in the process of close interaction between people and state actors – that is, when the latter become a part of the communities in which they work (Evans, 1997: 178, 184). The state itself is seen as playing an important role in the production/ reproduction of state–society synergy (or, linking social capital). This, it is argued (Evans, 1997: 189, 192), consists of scaling up the social resources, structuring relations of trust and cooperation within communities – the social capital of civil society – so as to generate solidarity ties and social action that are politically and economically efficacious.

There are obvious difficulties with such arguments. Like the more society-centric view of social capital, many of these and similar studies tend to be rather too sanguine about linking social capital and the related conceptual apparatus. They tend to ignore or downplay the fact that society and communities are class-divided, that so-called ordinary citizens belong to particular classes and that state actors have a class character because of the class character of the state as a structure as such. Therefore, such studies also ignore or downplay the fact that the most important context structuring state–society synergy is one of class relations that enormously constrain the lives of common people.[4] In

---

3 There is an interesting parallel here with the findings of Thawnghmung (2003) in her study of peasant/state interaction in Burma/Myanmar.

4 It is surprising how far removed this literature is from the important discussions on the class character of the state in the peripheral capitalist countries (Alavi, 1982; Ougaard, 1983; for a more recent discussion, see Das, 2022: Ch. 11; Das, 2020: Ch. 7).

order to examine the synergy between the state and society, and understand its implications for common people, we need to understand class power as well as state power (as revealed in the power of state actors), so we need to examine how state actors with enormous power (which is at least partly derived from the nature of the state as a class organization) (Clarke, 1991) interact with, and dominate, the lower classes of society, and how the latter in turn respond. For this reason, of particular interest is the embeddedness aspect of state–society synergy – that is to say, its social context. I view the latter as codetermined by two processes, i.e. class relations, and the administrative power of state actors, from a standpoint which recognizes a very limited degree of autonomy of state actors but which also sees the state 'as a part of society divided into classes' (Jessop, 1990: 25).

There is a need to examine the class character of state-society synergy that social capitalists talk about in order to overcome the specific problems that stem from their class-blindness. On the one hand, therefore, and with particular reference to class, the focus is on poor daily wage labourers and the socio-economic inequality that separates them from state actors (officials and politicians). On the other, and with particular reference to administrative power, the focus is on the power of state actors, which is partly associated with the class character of the state. State–society synergy is itself a function of these two structural elements. Events cannot be entirely and satisfactorily explained in terms of structures. So, of interest will also be the ways in which the political mobilization of these labourers influences state–society synergy, and especially counters the structural effects of their weakness vis-a`-vis the state. Because political mobilization of the poor is place-specific, the nature of state–society synergy will also be so.

The specific questions addressed here are as follows. To what extent are there relations of trust between state actors and poor people/labourers? That is, do common people believe that officialdom does its duty in line with the law, and that consequently they will not be unfairly treated by the state? For their part, to what extent do state officials participate in the daily lives of the poor, sharing the same social space, and to what extent does this in turn enhance the trust the poor may repose in these officials? Linked to this is to what degree are trust and cooperation, and – more generally – the nature of interaction between officials and citizens, place-specific? What factors explain the observed level of state–society synergy? In particular, what role might the economic situation of agricultural wage labourers plus the extent of their political mobilization have in the production of state–society synergy, in countering the economic and political power of state actors with whom they deal? Answers to all these questions are made with reference to a specific context where fieldwork was conducted in early 2000s in the State of Odisha in eastern India. (The details about the fieldwork have been provided in the previous chapter).

2   The Relative Absence of Linking Social Capital

Instances of state officials in Odisha having cordial relations on an informal basis with agricultural labourers are, as one would expect, few in number. Some government officials are, however, remembered as having been helpful, a term which covers acts such as the provision either of information about government policies or an application form for government benefits. Although the relationship between officialdom and the poor is usually fraught with antagonism (as will be shown below), the fact of this relationship is not wholly immaterial and irrelevant to agricultural labourers. It is interesting to note that close to 90 per cent of questionnaire respondents in both study areas said that, without government help, their economic situation would be worse, there being no difference on this issue between the two localities under study. Of course, whether this is an evidence of state–society synergy is debatable. Typically, however, the interaction between state officials and the poor has specific features, all of which are inimical to the operation of state– society synergy in the interest of those in the subordinate category. These are: selectivity, lack of trust and the absence of cooperation. Selectivity refers to the fact that government officials are seen as interacting with selected groups of individuals. Even within the ranks of agricultural labourers, some (for example, those with political connections) are favoured at the expense of others. If we consider civil society as a whole, and not just workers, government officials are also more inclined to interact with some people than with others. As one person said:

> They interact with people who are like them, who are of their category (meaning educated, relatively well-off people). They never interact with other people ... Those officials who sympathise with poor people are those who don't have much power, the lower level officials.

This was confirmed by another who said:

> If they deal with contractors (who are politicians themselves or are their friends/relatives) they will get something in return. What will they get from ordinary people?

One specific category with which officials frequently interact is, of course, the propertied classes, including rich contractors who carry out state-funded infrastructural projects aimed at creating employment for poor labourers. Another category is politicians, many of whom belong to the well-off, property-owning class. As the interviewee last quoted went on to say:

> Officials interact with politicians. They belong to one group. They don't interact much with ordinary people. ... They don't pass on information about government policies to ordinary people.

Politicians act as middlemen between officials and labourers. As an ex-Chairman of Remuna Block (an elected politician) said, the interaction between local-level government employees and labourers is limited because the middlemen's role is increasing.[5] 'Poor people', he commented, 'trust the middleman more than they trust government employees'. Another person agreed completely with this when he suggested that: 'A poor person cannot get his work done directly in an office. He has to go through some middleman. He has to pay (a bribe). The bribe is shared among the politicians, the middlemen, and the officers'.

Officials, of course, defend themselves against the charge that their interaction is limited to politicians/middlemen and/or the members of the rich, non-labouring class. As one official said:

> There are no government policies for the rich. All policies are for the poor. We always deal with poor people. We don't have any linkage with the rich people. Not at all. ... This Bulu Babu (referring to a rich politician who happened to be present during the interview) is a rich man. But he is here as a representative (actually his sister-in-law is the elected representative, and Bulu Babu is working on her behalf). ... He is giving us some advice. ... We don't have any relation with them as rich people. Only as representatives. (Note the stress on 'as representatives', not 'as rich people': RJD). Wherever we go, we deal with sugar and kerosene and poor people.

The relation between officials and agricultural labourers is characterized not just by selectivity, but also by a lack of trust. Asked whether people trust Block

---

5 There are several village clusters (organized as Panchayats or village council) under one Block (or Development Block). Several Blocks make one District.

(i.e. local level) government officials, one respondent said emphatically: 'No, No, No. Trust them?! They won't do anything without taking money'.

This and numerous quotes below reinforce the fieldwork findings about trust, itself an important indicator of state–society synergy. In terms of trust, respondents were asked whether officials deliver what they promise to, or are required by law or tradition to deliver.[6] The responses to the questionnaire survey reveal that a large percentage of people in the study areas have no trust at all in government officials, and on the other hand, only about a fifth have a great deal of trust (Table 1). This is especially interesting in view of the fact that the level of generalized trust is very high: 76 per cent of respondents said that they would generally trust most people. What this means is that, while people are disposed generally to be trusting, it is particular groups – that is, officials (and politicians) – that they do not trust.

If trust is lacking, the relationship is as a result unlikely to be one of cooperation and help. Officials are seen as unconcerned about the welfare of the poor. As one interviewee said:

> I have never seen Block officials in the village asking them [ordinary people] about their welfare. From my young days to my old days, I have not seen Block officials enquiring whether people got a loan or peasants got seeds. You are doing this survey and asking us about all this. Why are these Block officials not doing this? Why are they not enquiring whether people are getting work, getting food or whether government benefits are reaching them?

Information about government policies is a great help to the poor who are illiterate or semi-literate, and officials are supposed to provide this. But only a third of the respondents said that officials are one of the sources of information about government policies. Not only are officials seen as uncooperative, but along with politicians, they are also seen as exploitative. Indeed, government officials are widely perceived as corrupt and demanding bribes.

Their interaction is often limited to those who can pay. This is especially but not exclusively the case in one area, Chasakhanda, where several people commented critically on corrupt officials and politicians.

> Earlier landlords used to compel people to do forced labour. Now that thing has come to the political sphere and to politicians. Landlordism has

---

6   For this definition of trust, see Rothstein (2000).

gone. Now there is a new form of landlordism. Those who rule the country are making good plans for the poor but the poor are not benefiting.

Officials and politicians ... are eying us for our little bit of property ... They are all exploiters. ... The MLA (Member of the Legislative Assembly) comes and talks to village leaders only. She will go by what these leaders say. She will not listen to what ordinary poor people have to say. ... When government officials' work finishes, politicians' begin.

Officials are our number one exploiters. Politicians are second. ... Officials become rich quickly. Once you become rich, will you look back?

Indeed, in both the areas combined, 35.6 per cent of respondents said that government officials were responsible for their poor economic condition. About 60 per cent complained that government officials usually/sometimes demand a bribe (with much spatial variation though, as will be discussed below).

Why is there so much ill-feeling and distrust – the opposite of what would constitute linking social capital and state–society synergy – between officials and common people who are in the main poor labourers? There are many possible reasons, of which two will be considered here: first, the structure of the state – the ways the state works (at the local level), including the structural conditions under which officials work and the power they exercise; and second, the class structure (social-economic inequalities between officials and labourers) in which this interaction takes place.

In terms of the structure of the state itself, some staff members (and especially of those at lower levels) themselves face problems of overwork, understaffing, irregular payment and job insecurity, all of which contribute towards an absence of staff motivation to cultivate cooperative relationships with the poor.[7] About this situation a government official, who I, along with one of my research assistants, visited rather earlier in the day at his official residence, observed that:

There is no scope for labourers to interact with us. We are busy in our office from ten to five. We also go on tour. We have to attend meetings. Also understaffing is a problem. ... We don't have time. You see, I am an

---

7   Irregular salary payment and job insecurity are problems faced especially by employees at the lower levels in the administrative hierarchy. To the extent that there is any support from the state for the poor in terms of the actual delivery of material resources, this is more likely to come from these employees.

Odia Hindu. I will spend some time to worship god. My food has been served but I can't eat. Piles of records are already there for me to handle. Where shall we get an opportunity to interact with the poor people? There should be enough staff. They should specialize in one or two things and they should go to people and explain them about the policies. ... (but) we can't specialize.

This was confirmed by another, similar comment: 'Officials do not have time to interact with people. ... There is a huge amount of workload on them. There is a reduction in staff. Vacant posts are not filled'.

The issue of understaffing and 'overloaded bureaucracy' (see Beall et al., 2000) relates in turn to broader issues of the role and size of the state under neoliberalism, which will not be considered here. There are two additional issues of importance: first, the political conditions under which officials work, and second, the power they exert over agricultural wage labourers, both of which are about state–society interpenetration. That political conditions under which officials work in the localities are indeed a barrier to state–society synergy in the interest of the poor is clear from the following observations:

When officials go to the village, there will be party feelings, political conflicts. ... When officials come to the village, they will first interact with elected representatives. A representative can only get those people who have voted for him to come (to the meetings with officials) and to interact and sit together. He will not keep relations with those who did not vote for him. If he does, he will get beaten up. ... This is all because of party feelings.

An official makes the following comment:

Officials are stopped, bribed, threatened not to come (to village meetings). Officials' mouth is shut by politicians. Politicians are saying to them 'you don't go. We will do our pallee sabha' (village meeting where distribution of government benefits is decided). Politicians call their own supporters, have meetings and take decisions.

This means, as noted earlier, that officials tend to interact with a limited section of civil society, a narrowness reinforced by the additional fact that such interaction is itself filtered through politicians. From the viewpoint of the officials themselves, this is the reason why they are unable to generate a positive linkage with those at the local scale. That is, a lack of direct interaction tends to undermine conditions for trust and cooperation between officials and common people.

Seen from the standpoint of local-level interaction between the state and civil society, however, such a lack of direct interaction has a less benign explanation. Officials are perceived as having an enormous amount of power, in part because they occupy positions within the hierarchy of the state, which is an institution of domination, the main objective of which is to control and suppress the exploited masses. This power enables them corruptly to extract money from the poor. On this subject one respondent remarked perceptively:

> Labourers generally [see] officials with suspicion. The reason is that they demand bribe from labourers. To expedite work, labourers are forced to bribe. ... Officials and politicians, these two groups, are changing the condition of the society. ... There is a politician-bureaucracy karasadi (conspiracy). Because of this, labourers and people in general have less trust in government institutions. This is surely happening.

Similarly, a political leader-cum-journalist said:

> To get a fund of Rs.22,000 (this is a loan for construction of houses for the poor), a person may have to meet these officials fifty times in two years. On top of it, he has to pay from this amount, Rs.3, 000 at the office, Rs.2,000 to the Sarpanch, and some more to the Junior Engineer as bribe money. So, what attitude will the poor have towards these officials! A person earning Rs.50 per day may have to stop work for 4– 5 days in a month to meet the Sarpanch [the local level elected representative], the block officials, the bank people, with just the hope of getting the loan. How much loss is he suffering! What relationship will this person have with the Block level officials!

In a discussion with a group of labourers in a hamlet of Chasakhanda, one labourer had a similar tale to tell:

> There's hardly any interaction (between government employees and the poor). ... They don't discuss anything with us because they fear that by being familiar with us, their doings will come to the open. They won't be able to 'get the cream'.

Social and economic inequality between agricultural labourers and officials – an inequality which rests on the prefiguring disadvantage of the position occupied by the worker within the class hierarchy – cannot but impede cooperative interaction between them. This is unavoidably so, given that any exchanges between them are informed by the powerful position that officials occupy by virtue of their being a part of the state. The lives led by agricultural labourers are insecure – they do not know if they will obtain paid work tomorrow, and thus get something to eat. They are rather obviously poor people, the median monthly household income in the two areas combined being Rs.1,200.[8] The average inhabitant in each area has had little if any schooling (only 40 per cent of respondents have had some school or college education). Asked why poor people do not directly interact with officials and go through politicians, one respondent said:

> We cannot talk to BDO (Block Development officer, the chief bureaucrat in the local administration). When I cannot talk to you properly, how shall I talk to BDO? People do not know how to write an application to BDO. (Because ordinary people are not literate), politicians get an opportunity to make money.

Agricultural labourers see themselves as being doubly disadvantaged in their dealings with those better positioned in the class hierarchy. Not only in terms of impoverished material conditions, therefore, but also in the very form taken by the interaction itself, an effect of their lack of education. An official explained: 'Labourers are busy working. Suppose we have gone to a village, they don't have time to interact with us. If they spend time with us, they can't work'.

A participant in a group discussion in Chasakhanda noted:

> In our schedule caste [lowest caste group] settlement, all are daily wage earners, we get to eat only if we work. The leaders and the Block officials promise us one thing but do the opposite. We can achieve something if someone takes our leadership, sacrificing his self-interest. ... [O]ur present leaders will be able to go to the Block for a day and if they go the second day, they will have to remain hungry. That's why they can't go often.

Similarly, the fact that officials are perceived by agricultural labourers and poor peasants as being socially superior also stands in the way of cooperative interaction. One person asked: 'Will rich people (officials) like the poor people?' He himself provided the following answer: 'No one will do anything for the poor

---

8   This was equivalent to about US$26 at the time of the interviews (early 2000s).

people. Everyone is for the rich people and their relatives'. One woman from the ranks of the rural poor demonstrated the depth of her bitterness about the officials by saying:

> Please do not mention them ... it is better to maintain a distance from the government employees. They feel they are different from us as they are government employees.

A wage labourer in a group discussion in Chasakhanda expressed a similar level of bitterness:

> The government employees ... want to get richer and richer. They want to build double-storied buildings. They want their children and grandchildren to live happily. They don't pay any attention to us.

Some officials agree. When asked why there is not much interaction between officials and labourers, an official from the politically conscious Remuna said:

> Officials think they are born with a difference, they are a separate class from the common people. We are forgetting that we are being paid out of the taxes people pay. ... People think of us as corrupt, as making money out of our positions, that these officials will not empathise with us. They have been observing for a long time that the officials come to villages and write something down about us but do not help us, the data remain on paper only.

Another official echoed this view that describes the actuality of 'development on paper': 'there is a problem of attitude between the employees and the labourers. There is a feeling among the employees that they belong to a higher status as they are government employees and that the others are mere labourers'.

What this shows is that officials are economically better-off than the labouring poor, but – as importantly – they are not only seen by the latter as such. That this economic difference – which is a consequence of class relations – translates into an insuperable political and ideological barrier. It is this which generates animosity and ill-feeling at the local scale, and thus militates against state–society synergy. This rather obvious point about the prefiguring significance of class is one to which the ardent advocates of social capital seem to be oblivious.

The extent to which class 'intrudes' on and shapes interactions between officialdom and common people – often local-level state officials and the people they 'serve' belong to the same locality – is evident from the direct form this occasionally takes. In some cases, therefore, conflicts of interests between a local official and common people may result from the fact that the latter are employed by the former, and may be working for them as wage labourers or tenants. Hence the following observation:

> If I get a loan from the government, I will not work for you (for the officials). So you will make sure that I do not get the loan. ... If my economic situation improves due to government help, I will not respect you, I will be your equal. One [person] wants another [person] to be poorer. This happens everywhere.

Conflicts of interest are not purely economic. Upper castes demand respect from poorer people. But the former fear that if the economic conditions of the poor improve through government programmes, they may cease to show the respect that they do currently. The ideology of caste relations, which is functional to the reproduction of class relations in India (and which are indeed reproduced within the state hierarchy), can also act as barriers to trust and synergy, as the following observation confirms:

> We have a Zamindar (landlord) who works in the tehsil office (subdistrict government). He hates Harijans (ex-untouchables). He thinks Harijans will be brazen when their living standard improves a little.

The two statements below, about officials from two informants in Rangas hamlet of Chasakhanda, tell us a similar story:

> They want us to remain as pet dogs. They don't familiarize with us or cooperate with us for the fear of compromising their vanity. They always guard their position. They want to keep us schedule caste people under them.

> In reality, the whole community of government employees does not like people belonging to the scheduled caste.

Thus socio-economic inequality between officials and the poor is a fundamental obstacle to the existence of relations of trust and cooperation. The situation is particularly bad when multiple identities overlap. That is, when officials are richer, property-owning, powerful and high caste but those with whom they interact are day-labourers, poor, low-caste, illiterate with little political power. In such circumstances, there is very little chance of state–society synergy happening in the interest of the poor.

3   Inter-locality Differences, Local-Scale Mobilization and State–
        Society Synergy

Trust and its 'other', mistrust, are founded on a twofold process: first, a positive expectation that in the eyes of those who have it is reasonable and thus realizable; and second, a negative perception generated as a result of the unfulfilled expectation, or the transformation of trust into mistrust.[9] It is easy to understand why common people hold this negative perception of officialdom, while the affluent sections adhere to a contrasting (= positive) view. Broadly speaking, therefore, in their dealings with representatives of the state, the poor will frequently be asked – if at all[10] – in what way their situation can be improved, what problems remain unresolved, and what in their opinion needs changing. They respond to such questions from bureaucrats and extension officers by pointing out what needs to be done, and why, in order to rectify and/or improve their situation. Unsurprisingly, when nothing happens as a result of this exchange of information, trust in the efficacy of state– society synergy diminishes, or – more usually – vanishes altogether.

When they deal with public officials, by contrast, the better-off elements at the local scale, more often than not, find that their expectations are fulfilled. This may be due to a combination of factors: either because of their superior bargaining power, their capacity to influence the planning or decision-making process directly or indirectly, their ability to bribe officialdom, or because they and the officials concerned share a common class, or economic, position. For this reason, the better-off components of society – unlike their poorer counterparts – tend to regard such transactions in a more positive light, a perception that is reflected in a greater trust extended towards officials with whom they come into contact. The general picture of trust and state–society synergy that emerges, therefore, is one of two variants: either there is an absolute lack of

---

9   This non-fulfilment of an expectation regarded by those at the local scale as reasonable is, of course, the definition informing the concept 'moral economy' associated with the work of E.P. Thompson (1991). To some degree, it also fits the concept of 'patronage' as seen by a client.

10   Note that the complaint made by several respondents from among the poor was that officials hardly ever visited them to enquire about their situation.

trust in state officials, and consequently a complete absence of state–society synergy; or both the latter and its accompanying element of trust operate only on behalf of the rich. Evidence from fieldwork location in Odisha, however, suggests the presence of a third variant: while the pattern outlined above is indeed applicable to Chasakhanda which is a politically conservative place, this is not the case in Remuna which is a left-leaning place.

In exploring the state–society synergy, therefore the starting point is trust. The literature on trust suggests that richer people, 'the winners' in society, tend to be a little more trusting than poorer people (Newton, 2001). Therefore, one can say that poorer citizens, 'the losers', will tend to be less trusting in the officials than their richer counterparts. The qualitative interviews conducted in Odisha confirm this, and suggest that the poor with fewer connections or little power do indeed have a limited amount of trust in officials (and politicians). On this point, the questionnaire findings are revealing.

There appears to be a statistical association between income and the degree of trust in government officials, this trust being an important indicator of state–society synergy, although the strength of the association might vary between the localities. Respondents' income was divided into two categories: everyone whose monthly household income was less than the median monthly income for the combined sample for the two localities (Rupees 1,200) was considered low income; the rest were classified as high income. Trust in Block officials was categorized in three ways: as 'a great deal of trust', 'a little trust' and 'no trust at all'.

In Chasakhanda, 67 per cent of inhabitants defined as low-income do not trust government officials at all. Only 7 per cent have a great deal of trust. By contrast, only 28 per cent of richer people have no trust in officials, while close to 12 per cent have a great deal of trust. Poorer people tend to be more distrustful of government officials than the higher-income ones. This is confirmed by the qualitative interviews with poor people, especially from Chasakhanda.

The findings from the other fieldwork location in Odisha, however, are interestingly different from those of Chasakhanda. In Remuna, while 48 per cent of poorer people have no trust or a little trust in officials, 86 per cent of richer people have no or a little trust. And, more importantly, while 52 per cent of poorer inhabitants have a great deal of trust, the figure for richer people is a paltry 14 per cent. One can see that there indeed seems to be a negative association between the level of trust (see Table 5.1) and income: in Remuna poorer inhabitants tend to trust the officials more than richer ones. This is not what the literature leads one to expect, and Remuna seems to be a very different place. Even if the element of poverty is excluded from consideration, Remuna is still different. It is simply the case that in Remuna representatives of the state, including officials, are perceived as being more trustworthy than those

TABLE 5.1   Level of trust between officials and people in the study areas combined

Percentage of respondents who have no trust at all (A) or have a great deal of trust (B) in:

	A	B
Block-level officials	30.89	22.80
Village politicians	54.10	9.60

in Chasakhanda. It is not just in terms of trust but also other aspects of state–society synergy that Remuna is different from Chasakhanda. Where people's perceptions about officials demanding bribes and being responsible for their poverty are concerned, Remuna is better than Chasakhanda in this regard (see Table 5.2).[11]

To explain why Remuna is different from Chasakhanda in terms of state–society synergy, including trust, one needs to look at the political specificity of Remuna. Located just to the south of one of India's communist bastions (West Bengal State), Remuna is one of the few localities in Odisha State where leftists have some influence. The local member of the State legislature is a communist, and Remuna has a history and culture of radical mobilization against the propertied class and officials. The Left party [the CPI(M)] has scores of politicians who are either elected representatives occupying positions in the local administrative apparatus of the state, or are closely interacting with officials and the poor on a day-to-day basis, producing what is recognizably state–society synergy.

Left politicians are (seen as) more pro-poor and less corrupt than other politicians. They are perceived as being more trustworthy than politicians from other parties: a greater proportion of respondents have more trust in – and correspondingly less mistrust of – Left parties in this particular location than is the case in Chasakhanda, showing the influence of the Left over the political landscape there (Table 5.3a, Table 5.3b). Whereas in Remuna people tend to trust left parties more than they do other political parties, the opposite is the case in Chasakhanda. Accordingly, Remuna is a left-wing bastion, while

---

11   On the other hand, some better-off elements – for example, landowners and mill owners – are not happy with the communists. A large percentage of the rich do not have much trust in the officials in Remuna. This is unsurprising: it has become difficult for these elements to deploy officials entirely for their own ends, because of the presence of communists at the local scale.

TABLE 5.2   Economic power relations between officials and people

	Remuna	Chasakhanda
Percentage of respondents saying that government officials:		
Are (among others) responsible for		
their economic plight	26.0	56.0
Usually demand bribes	39.5	79.6
Never demand bribes	54.7	12.2

TABLE 5.3A   The level of trust in left and other parties

	Remuna	Chasakhanda
Percentage of respondents who have no trust in:		
Left Parties	28.9	60.0
Other Parties	31.9	26.0

TABLE 5.3B   The level of trust in left and other parties

	Remuna	Chasakhanda
Percentage of respondents who have a great deal of trust in:		
Left Parties	42.3	24.0
Other Parties	16.3	50.0

Chasakhanda can be taken as an example of the reverse, if trust in leftist parties relative to non-left parties is an indicator.

Remuna being a place where the Left is strong makes some difference to the nature of state–society synergy. Because the CPI(M) is a cadre-based party, its workers are relatively well organized. Given this, (petty) politicians from mainstream parties are less likely to be able to prevent officials interacting directly with the poor, a problem in Chasakhanda and indeed wherever the poor do not have a political organization of their own. Left politicians have some control over the Block level officials. If the latter refuse to listen to them, left politicians quickly arrange a gherao (a sit-in), a form of 'from below' pressure identified in the course of group discussion with CPI(M) workers and interviews with officials. One of the latter [not particularly sympathetic to the CPI(M)] based in Remuna said: When labourers are conscious of their rights and are aware of what is coming for them from the government, the officials are getting slightly scared.

Officials, like others, generally see communist politicians as less corrupt and more pro-poor, and therefore less pliable; in short, the kind of politicians with whom it will be a little difficult to share a bribe extorted from the poor. Thus the fact that left politicians both enjoy popular support at the local scale, and have gained certain degree of trust from less well-off people, does affect the way officials treat the latter. Partly because of this, and partly because of a fear of grassroots agency (protests and sit-ins), government officials interact with lower-income people in ways that benefit 'those below' a little more than elsewhere. The outcome is that such interaction is reciprocated, and the poor in Remuna have more trust in officials than is the case in Chasakhanda.

When asked if the level of interaction between government officials and the poor is greater in Remuna, it being a CPI(M) area, than elsewhere, a CPI(M) worker participating in a group discussion there said:

> Yes, definitely it is more. When we select the genuine cases (for government benefits in village meetings), we involve the bureaucracy in the process, along with us. In this way, there is a co-operation, an interaction between the two. Due to our leadership, it is a success although partially.

Many others concur. One person said:

> When I was the sarpanch I did not allow the middlemen to mediate between the poor beneficiaries and government officials. ... We have done this in all panchayats where we are in power. ... We get the work done ourselves by going to the officials with the poor people. We are using the CPI(M) party structure as a mediation between the poor and the government to check the use of money.
> Stress added

Another person said:

> The party is demanding that what the labourers ... are entitled to get (they) must get. Even if they are not in power, if you go and complain before them, they will exercise their power [influence] to ensure that you get your entitlement from the officials.

Even a rich person from Remuna, a tractor owner, believed that:

> This [better interaction between officials and citizens because of the presence of CPI(M)] is definitely happening. Officials do fear CPM [CPI(M)] workers, so a little more work is done here than in other places. There is a lot of exploitation happening in other places.

In many cases, communist politicians are said to be facilitating and even demanding officials' interaction with the poor. Indeed, 58 per cent of questionnaire respondents in Remuna said that the presence of a Communist Party there contributes to the better interaction than in other areas between on the one hand government officials and on the other poor peasants and workers. As a government official of Remuna noted, the implementation of government policies such as the distribution of rice and sugar happens through communists cooperating with government officials.

4   State–Society Synergy, and Gender

That there is greater degree of state–society synergy in Remuna is also evident from the way female self-help groups are working there, but not in Chasakhanda. Self-help groups (SHGs) are small-savings groups who invest their savings in income-generating activities, but who are also involved in wider social activities. These are very popular in India (Shurmer-Smith, 2000: 85) and in other less-developed countries, where they are organized by government and NGOs. In Srikrishnapur, a hamlet in Remuna, the SHG is organized by an NGO called Reeds. When women from lower-income backgrounds from Srikrishnapur visited a local exhibition on SHGs conducted by Reeds, they liked the idea and wanted to form one. They contacted the Chairman of Reeds who helped them by providing the group training in SHG management. At the time of the fieldwork interview, this SHG had 19 members. Every month it manages to save Rs.60 per member, and already had some Rs.7,000 in the bank. That this financial resource is being used for the state-society synergy can be shown by its successful attempt to improve water supply in the village. As in many parts of the less-developed world, so in this area it is the responsibility of women to carry water. Since water had to be brought from a distance, they decided to establish a piped water supply in their hamlet. The group members along with some other people – some 30–35 people in all – contacted the local MLA (Member of the Legislative Assembly) and requested the installation of the piped water supply. The MLA agreed, and using government money, he supplied both the pipe and piped water. But there were no government funds for the construction of drainage, so the SHG itself provided the finance.

Since the formation of the group in the hamlet of Srikrishnapur, its members observe, mutual relations among them have improved. They help each other out in times of need. As an informant said: the SHG worked for the mutual benefit of the members and in the larger interest of the village. The way the SHG represents 'developmentally efficacious state–society synergy' can be shown by its successful attempt to improve water supply in the village. One informant said:

> There was not much interaction among us ... there were not very good relations earlier ... but after the formation of the SHG, there is better interaction. We help each other in times of need.

It is not just the social relations of trust and cooperation among women that have been enabled by the SHG, but also those between women and men. The formation of women's SHGs and group activities are time-consuming activities. In a patriarchal society, however, husbands have a large degree of control over their wives' time. As members of the SHG said, their husbands do not want them to 'waste away' their time on the SHG. But now that their wives have 'done something' for the village, their husbands' initial response has changed. Because the women-led SHG has been able to achieve results – resolve conflicts in the village, building links with the government, improve the hamlet's infrastructure, and so on – gender relations have to some extent been transformed. As one participant in a group discussion with the SHG observed:

> Men were opposed to us forming a group. We tried to make them understand. They were saying, 'why do you join the group, you can't finish household work?' ... But now they have understood (the importance of the SHG) ... that these women have done something for the village.

Male consumption of alcohol is a big problem in Remuna (as in many other parts of India) giving rising to the complaint that men waste money on drink, thereby depriving poor households of much needed resources. Members of an SHG in the Salabani hamlet of Remuna, which has been formed with the help of a female government official, have been fighting successfully against alcohol sales in their village, in the face of resistance from men. Women attribute their success to the strong support they have received from the district level state officials, but more importantly from the village level female official who helped them form the group. Indeed, one member of this SHG said: 'She strengthened our fist which increased our courage'.

These two brief case studies shed light on social relations of cooperation ('social capital') and on synergistic relations between the state and society. In social capital language, the 'bonding social capital' that there was – relations of trust based on neighbourhood, kin and gender – has been transformed into 'bridging social capital'; that is, relations of trust across the different social-demographic groups (of women in SHGs). This bridging social capital in turn was the basis for 'linking social capital', the social capital that links the poor to those in power. And one form of linking social capital creates another form. Although the government also organizes self-help groups, the women of Srikrishnapur decided not to get help from the government because they thought that the officialdom did not do a good job to help (they did not provide training, for example). So they took the initiative of contacting an NGO which could help them form an SHG. And once they did so – once they were linked with the NGO, creating thereby 'linking social capital' – that helped the group link up with government [in this case the local MLA who belonged to CPI(M)] which produced some success. In Salabani, a hamlet of indigenous people (called *Adivasis* or Scheduled Tribes), it was the female government official who took the initiative: she mobilized poorer women to form the group, and they in turn co-operated with her.

5   Concluding Comments

While state officials are in day-to-day interaction with civil society, such inter-action does not necessarily produce state–society synergy – or linking social capital – in the interests of the poor. The beneficial interaction of state officials is often limited to local politicians and proprietary classes (private contractors, rich landowners). Their relations with the less well-off in society, or those who belong to the wage labouring class, are typically characterized by a lack of trust and therefore by lack of mutual cooperation. As Porta et al. (1997: 311) note: 'Trust should be more essential for ensuring cooperation between strangers, or people who encounter each other infrequently, than for supporting coop-eration among people who interact frequently and repeatedly'. Without trust between officials and the poor who meet each other infrequently, there is little scope for cooperation.

It is easy to interpret the unequal relations between state officials and the poor – and especially officials' oppressive behaviour – as evidence for an unrestrained autonomous power. The state is indeed a relatively autonomous structure of power relations, but this is more a surface reality than the underlying truth. Here the word 'relatively' is crucial in the sense that the autonomy is rather very limited and temporary, for as I have argued elsewhere, 'The bureaucratic, and therefore undemocratic, nature of the state-form, is a necessary feature of capitalism. This type of state-form, unlike the Paris Commune type [Marx in (Lenin, 1977: 43–44)], ... insulates the state from popular influence on, and surveillance over, the state, and thus facilitates the appropriation of state rents (e.g. bribe), power, etc. by officials' (Das, 1996: 50).[12] Accordingly, the oppressive behaviour by state actors, and thus the corresponding absence of state– society synergy (that advocates of social capital and state–society synergy think will benefit the poor), is a part of the structural condition (i.e. the class character of the state), whether it is the metropolitan or the peripheral state. The class character of the structure of the state places inherent and significant limits on the relations of trust and reciprocity (or, state-society synergy) between actors of the state and the masses. This also means that social capital and its cognate concepts need to be placed in their proper political and economic – that is, class – context, as emphasized in the last two chapters.

The findings that have been presented here are consistent with a few other studies that show limited trust in government officials, in both poor and rich national contexts (Brewer and Sigelman, 2002; Gran, 2002; Hirschmann, 1999; Levi and Stoker, 2000). Evidence of state–society synergy that Evans and others enthusiastically talk about) is – and must be – very limited. The results from the two fieldwork areas in Odisha are also not inconsistent with results at the national level in India. According to a national survey, the percentage of respondents who have a great deal of trust in government officials varies from 5.6 to 35.1 per cent across major States, both these figures being extremely low (see Table 5.4). The national survey also points in the direction of limited interaction between citizens and officials, a finding that the qualitative interviews from my study villages confirms.

However, the state – even at the local level – is not a monolithic entity, because the state is organized territorially (it exists at multiple scales, including the local). We should therefore expect that state–society relations will vary between localities (and regions and provinces, etc.). There are indeed place-specific instances of state–society synergy enabled by the intervention of civil society organizations such as NGOs and by state actors who are honest and development-oriented and who take up the cause of the oppressed sections of

---

12   See Das (2022) for a detailed elaboration of the state autonomy thesis and why much of
      what is said about it by Marxists is mistaken.

TABLE 5.4   Interaction between government officials and common people at national, provincial and local levels

Percentage of respondents who trust government officials a great deal have ever contacted any government official for any need or problem

All-India average	18.00	17.75
Odisha	34.30	16.10
Study villages[a]	23.00	n.a.

a   Refers to the villages in this study.
SOURCE OF DATA ON INDIA AND ODISHA: NATIONAL ELECTION STUDY, 1996, CENTRE FOR DEVELOPING SOCIETIES, DELHI, QUOTED IN SERRA (1999).

society. This shows that reinforcing pre-existing kin and friendship ties with a benign political input from the state (in the Remuna case, the ties among the women members of the SHGs) may indeed help transform traditional ties into what Evans (1997) calls developmentally efficacious social capital. However, it must be stressed that such cases are few in number, and are anyway not easy to replicate, as Evans himself acknowledges. For these reasons, they cannot be considered a development model.

It is important, however, to stress that, in terms of a specifically material achievement, the outcome of the limited state–society synergy encountered in certain parts of Remuna is not spectacular. That on occasion the poor organize on their own behalf should not, therefore, lead to the erroneous conclusion that this is the direction that local economic development should take in future. The difficulties with the latter view are twofold.

Firstly, such a conclusion is precisely that drawn by neo-liberals, who maintain that all economic development ought to adopt this problem-solving strategy: that is, by undertaking small-scale local initiatives designed specifically to solve local needs.[13] Not only does this kind of solution require no state funding (and thus obviates further taxation, a particular beˆte noir of neo-liberals)

---

13   This is the view of, for example, of the influential analyses of the informal sector by de Soto (1989) and Hart (2000). They advance two claims on behalf of small-scale self-help initiatives which circumvent regulation by the state. First, that they are the 'natural' forms of economic organization in so-called Third World countries. And second, that such informal sector enterprise empowers those at the local scale. For an incisive critique of these views, see Overton (2001).

but – more importantly – it leaves intact both the market and private own-ership/control of the means of production (the sine qua non of neo-liberal economics).

To some extent, there is a parallel between what is argued by social capital-ists (i.e. their localist perspective on social-economic development) and the Stalinist idea of socialism in one country promoted since 1924 against Trotsky's entirely valid criticisms (Trotsky, 1996). Just as capitalism, driven by its law of value, transcends localities and nations to become a truly global process, simi-larly, socialism can only be a global process, which means that socialism in one country is a regressive and mistaken concept. If socialism is not possible at the national scale, let alone at the local scale, isolated from the global processes, significant and durable progressive social-economic development also is not possible at the local scale.

There is indeed an interesting local–global dialectic here. Neo-liberalism has both global and local aspects to it. An important pre-requisite for the free operation of capitalist markets at the global scale is neo-liberalism, and espe-cially the withdrawal of the state from support given to the lower classes and smaller local businesses earlier. Indeed, since the neo-liberal project started, Remuna has faced the impact of de-industrialization: neighbouring factories have started closing down, due to global competition and the withdrawal of state support. On the other hand, encouraging local initiatives, including self-help ones – favoured by post-Marxists and other sections of the 'left' – is also a part of the same neo-liberal project. As Petras (1997) has suggested, these kinds of micro-scale initiatives, in spite of their leftist connotations, are indeed the 'bottom-up' aspects of neo-liberalism. In this local–global dialectic, the global moment (i.e. the capitalist imperative) constrains the local-level state-society synergy in support of the working masses. In one of the hamlets in Remuna populated by indigenous people, there is a very strong organization based on tribal identity and social relationships. The group leaders contacted the district administration several times to ask for the provision of an irrigation facility, only to be told the government has no money. This is unsurprising, since the State of Odisha has been engaged in the privatization of irrigation provision on a large scale, with 'assistance' from global institutions such as DFID (Department of International Development of the British state), all in the name of encouraging local farmer-supported irrigation provision, the so-called water panchayat (vil-lage council).[14] The fact that in spite of a strong social organization (and plenty

14   DFID's 'development' interventions have been widely critiqued. Odisha's prominent pro-gressive journalist, Sudhir Pattnaik, says: 'We call it [Odisha] a DFID colony. The common saying is that the DFID is into everything that concerns the governance of the [State]....

of 'bonding' and 'bridging' social capital), state–society synergy has proved to be an impossibility in the face of neo-liberalism underlines the limits to such localist development strategy.

And secondly, the idea that state-society synergy can be the direction that local economic development process should take fails to address the systemic roots of impoverishment and why the latter persists despite some local-level state–society synergy that does exist. The fact that existing large-scale commercial enterprises and agribusiness corporations are able to continue to exercise their economic dominance unhindered has long-term consequences for small-scale economic self-help schemes involving the poor.[15] For this reason, those in the latter category need to be able to exercise political power at the national and global levels (as distinct from only the local level).

A related theme, involving trust and cooperation between the state and citizens as important and desirable aspects of state–society synergy, is the issue of political mobilization by the poor. The fact that the latter process varies contextually has an impact on state–society synergy. In Remuna, where the poor (mainly day labourers) are relatively well organized, and where a left-wing political infrastructure as a part of a strong civil society keeps an eye on state actors, poor peasants and agricultural workers tend to trust officials to an extent not found in Chasakhanda. In the latter context, by contrast, the poor are disorganized and split along political party lines, all competing for limited government aid.[16] Officials do not keep their promises. They make the poor run to them for their entitlements. They are authoritarian. The findings from my Odisha fieldwork villages bear out those from the classic comparative study by Kohli (1987) of the relation between political organization and regime type (whether social democratic or clientelist), and the success of state-led poverty-alleviation strategies. Indeed, Remuna's 'rare conjuncture' of left party activity among the poor creates a situation where officials are trusted more, and which contributes accordingly to better local-scale interaction between the citizens and the bureaucracy. In such contexts, therefore, state–society synergy works to a certain extent.

      In every sector you will find the presence of the DFID. "this comes from the DFID" is the standard response you get from bureaucrats. [One of them used to say that]... at the beginning of every week he gets a memo saying the DFID wants this or that' (quoted in Corporate Watch, 2010).

15   These consequences include a gradual cessation of state regulation that was promulgated and implemented at the national level favouring the poor, who accordingly remain at the mercy of the market and their richer neighbours.

16   This confirms the state theory of Poulantzas (and others) who argue that the state plays an important role in *disorganizing* the lower classes (Poulantzas, 1968: 190–91).

However, to overemphasize the role of (local-level) political organization, and that too, one that is electoralist and social-democratic, would be unjustifiable, since even in Remuna a large number of the poor do not trust their officials (and politicians, including left politicians). Nor is it the case that SHG success is a dominant trend. So Remuna, Odisha's bastion of local-scale left politics, is no paragon of pro-poor state–society synergy. This is due in part to the fact that left-wing organization has not as yet reached all the poor. Furthermore, it cannot be said with certainty that all left-wing politicians in Remuna are wholly untainted by connections with officials who exploit the poor. Indeed, the fact that the CPI(M) organization is always monitoring its own politicians (including those who are a part of the local administration) through regular meetings [the CPI(M) members stressed this] – that is, the fact that this sort of surveillance was necessary – suggests that there are some actual/potential dishonest politicians within the ranks of the left.

A general point is that the state and society interact with one another, a theme also emphasized in the neo-Weberian approach to the state [see Migdal (1994)], but whether this interaction will produce state–society synergy and therefore social capital for the poor on a sustainable basis is, however, contingent. It depends, in short, on factors such as the (local-scale) organization of the poor.

It may be noted here that the notion of 'complementarity', signified by that of synergy, when applied to relations involving the bureaucratic/administrative cadres of the state and ordinary people, the difficulties are twofold. First, the officialdom is wrongly regarded as an undifferentiated group, to be counter-posed as such to a similarly homogeneous common people or the peasantry, etc. While junior officials are clearly at an advantage when dealing with poorer people, this is not the case when they deal with rich peasants, merchants and/or large commercial farmers. The latter are capable of engineering the transfer or even the removal from post of a junior official who opposes their interests. This, too, has to be seen as an effect of class power. Even when they wished to do so, therefore, junior officials have been unable to prevent well-off peasants in, for example, agrarian co-operatives from appropriating co-owned resources (land, technical inputs) and employing poor peasants as hired workers. And second, it adheres to the central tenet of bourgeois (=neo-classical) economic theory: namely, that the state is a benign and disinterested institution, a law-giving/enforcing arbiter of disputes in which it has no interest. According to this theory, the origin, existence and effect of the state are all neutral, and its role is simply to see that the law – whatever this might be, and similarly without a history or reflecting an interest – is obeyed. The capitalist state must, more or less, reproduce capitalist private property relations and capitalist logic of accumulation, *at the expense of* the masses.

Woolcock and Narayan (2000), two prominent advocates of the social capital framework who are also associated with World Bank, express the hope that 'a state that opens up and explicitly builds bridges to excluded groups' – thus producing linking social capital for the poor – increases 'the likelihood that the poor will be able to gain access to the resources and services to which they are entitled' (Woolcock and Narayan, 2000: 237–8). By contrast, it is argued here that this will not happen automatically. Political mobilization of the masses vis-a`-vis state officials (and the propertied elements with whom they ally themselves) is one of the ways in which *some* state-society synergy can be achieved. While state actors usually interact very well with the richer and more powerful sections of civil society and serve their needs, non-political civic organizations (e.g. floral societies[17] and the type that Putnam talks about) are pleasantly populated by the relatively well-off elements and are unlikely to be able to significantly help the masses in controlling state actors' power and to promote welfare. To believe that that is possible is indeed to depoliticize development issues. At best the role of such organizations will be limited, and in this respect they represent a stark contrast with the effectiveness of radical political mobilization by the lower classes. It is the latter, above all, that, to some extent, can compel state actors to keep their promises and to act according to the nominal laws of the state.[18] In short, the radical political mobilization by the lower classes dissuades state actors operating at the local level from using the state as a personal fiefdom for exercising what Mann (1984) calls 'despotic power'.

The fact that people in Remuna have a greater degree of trust in left politicians and that left politicians were able to democratize, to some extent, the relations between state officials and the common people points to a larger question: what can left do, within all the limits of the capitalist society, to contribute to people's lives and in the process mobilize them politically. The Left-led mobilization can aim to do at least four things.[19] These are to: 1) win concessions from employers, traders, bankers and landowners on the basis of strikes and protests by common people (workers and small-scale producers); 2) win concessions from the government at all levels (national, provincial, local levels), in the form of progressive policies to meet common people's needs,

---

17 'Floral societies' represent informal non-political civil society associations that typical middle-class Americans are involved in.

18 This will produce a form of state–society engagement in the interests of the lower classes in Kerala (Heller, 1997). Borras (2001) argues that redistributive land reform policy in the Philippines had some success because action of state reformists 'from above' positively interacted with social mobilizations 'from below'.

19 For more details, see Das (2020: 480–483).

including the policies which reflect their needs, whether or not the system says it can meet them (these are transitional demands to which I return below)[20]; 3) defend democratic rights, including of the groups oppressed based on their gender, racial, religious, racial and other identities; 4) ensure that the policies introduced under the pressure of the Left are actually implemented, and reach the masses in a transparent, non-divisive, and non-corrupt way. And, the Left can and must impart political education to the masses to develop classed solidarity among them and to stop them from falling for false promises made by the political representatives of the ruling class, and especially, the reactionary elements.[21]

Political mobilization of common people by Left forces is important in terms of state-society synergy. Yet, it is precisely such political mobilization that the advocates of linking social capital, and indeed, many of those who place great faith in state– society synergy, do not want to talk about.[22] Linking social capital – relations of trust between people with less power and those with more power – is supposed to be a critical input into the development process (Woolcock, 1998), but – as has been suggested here – the production and reproduction of linking social capital is itself a problematic process. The power of the state actors existing by virtue of the class character of the state and the fact of socio-economic inequality separating them from the common people who constantly experience social crisis including grinding poverty (this is a fact that reflects the class relations in society) undermine the conditions for the relations of trust between state actors and common people. In principle, it is possible to accept the arguments made by exponents of social capital and (especially) state–society synergy – that the state is not all bad; that reformist, pro-poor state officials can help the poor; and that the embeddedness of officials in communities and relations of trust and cooperation between them

---

20   These include: food security; secure employment; inflation-adjusted living wages; better prices for petty producers and protection from unfair dispossession from their small-scale property; freedom from debt; reduction in working hours without loss of wages; pension; and universal access to state provided high-quality health-care, education, housing, transportation and culture.

21   False promises amount to lies, the aim of which is to merely distract and deceive the masses. Fascistic regimes in particular, specialize in promising to deliver good things for the poor people. Of course, they do not mean to do anything or much. But in the process of making false promises and fuelling fake pride in the nation or majority religion, etc., they recruit sections of the masses into, and gain support for, the fascist mass movement. They cannot deliver what they promise because doing so will hurt the basic interests of capital which they are servile supporters of.

22   The work of Heller (1997) is an exception.

and those they are supposed to assist may contribute to state–society synergy. But this is rather like saying good things will create good things. Indeed, if we see the conditions mentioned by Evans as being necessary for state–society synergy to exist, the list of 'good things' is very long.

In spite of the critique advanced here of state/society relationships, the findings do not – it must be emphasized – support the neo-liberal call for 'getting the state right', which in reality means deregulation in the interests of the better-off (= 'getting the state off the backs of the people') and the reduction in the responsibility of the state towards the welfare of common people. Much rather, the opposite is true: within capitalism, the state can be crucially important. The can provide nonmarket material inputs (e.g. free or heavily subsidized education, healthcare and nutrition) to meet the subsistence needs common people. The state can, to a certain extent, regulate the market (including its law of value) and the functioning of the big businesses, in the interests of common people. After all, reproducing a healthy educated well-fed working class is in the interest of the capitalist class.[23] But the state does not, and will not, do all this automatically, just as capitalists will not automatically pay higher wages than the prevailing wages even if they *can* do so. To the extent that there can be state-society synergy in support of the material interests of the common people, the process must not be in the form of philanthropic assistance from the top. Common people must make transitional demands on the state, at all geographical scales, including the local.[24] They must demand that everyone enjoys secure employment with a legislated living wage that rises with inflation in the cost of subsistence goods and services, and that there be no discrimination in the labour market based on gender, religion, ethnicity, caste, etc. They must demand the democratization of the relations between state actors and common people, and that state actors do

---

23 Within limits, the state can also encourage self-help activities, especially, at the local scale (for example, it can help workers set up a cooperative). See Wallis and Dollery (2002), and also Thomas (1992) for critical views on this. In any case, the solution is not a lean state but the demand for 'radical democratization' of the state at different scales, thereby enabling the lower classes to have a significant degree of control over the modus operandi of its different apparatuses, even within the limits of the structure of the state. This is an agenda that is opposed to the neo-liberal one, of which the social capital discourse is an ideological prop.

24 Transitional demands stem 'from today's conditions and from today's consciousness of wide layers of the working class and unalterably leading to one final conclusion: the conquest of power by the proletariat' (Trotsky, 1931). These demands link the immediate or minimal demands to the task of seizing power but these demands themselves are not a call for revolution.

not behave like modern-day aristocrats. If certain trustworthy state actors can support people's transitional demands, then that will prove the effectivity of the state-society synergy that social capitalists talk about! The concept of transitional demands in relation to the state implies that: common people cannot look upon the state as a potentially benevolent structure or agency any more than they can rely on corporate social responsibility where big companies are expected to be compassionate towards, and conscious of, common people's interests and to spend a small part of their profit to help them (for example, by building roads or schools).[25] Instead of expecting moral responsibility from state actors, common people must make demands on them, the demands that reflect their actual needs. Marx says that workers must make demands on the capitalists, 'without any appeal to [their] heart' even if they 'may be a model citizen', because 'the thing that [the capitalists] represent ... has no heart in its breast' (Marx, 1867: 163). If this principle applies to the capitalists, then this should apply to state actors too

Of course, such demands will be refused by the state and the ruling class. This would not be necessarily because of the absence of linking social capital (i.e. absence of trust and reciprocity between state actors and masses) but because of the very class character of the state and of the 'civil society' dominated by the logic of capital. Rather than expecting relations of trust and benevolence with those who manage the affairs of the capitalist state, common people must fight for what they need, and in this process, they must, ultimately, aim to *replace* the capitalist state itself and to establish a transitional state that is democratically controlled by them and that operates in a society where the logic of capital ceases to operate. Only in such a context can there be true state-society synergy.

References

Alavi, H., (1982). State and Class under Peripheral Capitalism. In H. Alavi and T. Shanin (Eds.), *Introduction to the Sociology of 'Developing Societies'*. London: Macmillan.

Azadian, A., Masciangelo, M., Mendly-Zambo, Z, Taman, A., & Raphel, D. (2022). Corporate and business domination of food banks and food diversion schemes in Canada. *Capital and class*. 0(0). https://doi.org/10.1177/03098168221092649.

---

25   With close affinity with the social capital thinking is the growing literature on corporate citizenship or corporate social responsibility: see Azadian, *et al.*, 2022; Blowfield, 2005; Carroll, 1999; Gjølberg, 2009; Oglesby, 2004; Postel and Richard, 2019; and Preuss, *et al.* 2015.

Beall, J., Crankshaw, O., & Parnwell, S. (2000). Local Government, Poverty Reduction and Inequality in Johannesburg. *Environment and Urbanization*, *12*(1). 107–122.

Bebbington, A., & Perreault, T. (1999). Social capital, Development, and Access to Resources in Highland Ecuador. *Economic Geography*, *75*(4). 395–418.

Blowfield, M. (2005). Corporate Social Responsibility: reinventing the meaning of development? *International Affairs*, *81*(3): 515–524.

Borras, S. (2001). State–society Relations in Land Reform Implementation in the Philippines. *Development and Change*, *32*(3). 545–575.

Brewer, P., & Sigelman, L. (2002). Trust in Government: Personal Ties that Bind? *Social Science Quarterly*, *83*(2).

Carroll, A. (1999). Corporate social responsibility. Evolution of a definitional construct. *Business and Society*, *38*(3): 268–295.

Clarke, S. (1991). The State Debate. In S. Clarke (Ed.), *The State Debate*. New York: St Martin's Press.

Conning, J., & M. Kavane, (2002). Community-based Targeting Mechanisms for Social Safety Nets: A Critical Review. *World Development*, *30*(3).

Corporate Watch. (2010). Dodgy development iv: 'a DFID colony'. *Corporate Watch*. Retrieved from: https://corporatewatch.org/dodgy-development-iv-a-dfid-colony/.

Das, R. (1996). State Theories: A Critical Analysis. *Science and Society*, *60*(1). 27–57.

Das, R. (2000). State–society Relations: The Case of an Anti-poverty Policy. *Environment and Planning C: Government and Policy*, *18*(6). 631–650.

Das, R. (2005). Rural Society, the State and Social Capital in Eastern India: A Critical Investigation. *Journal of Peasant Studies*, *32*(1): 48–87.

Das, R. (2020). *Critical Reflections on Economy and Politics in India: A Class Theory Perspective*. Leiden: Brill.

Das, R. (2022). Marx's Capital, Capitalism and Limits to the State: Theoretical Considerations. London: Taylor and Francis.

de Soto, H. (1989). *The Other Path: The Invisible Revolution in the Third World*. London: I.B. Tauris.

Evans, P. (1997). Government Action, Social Capital, and Development. In P. Evans (Ed.), *State–society Synergy*. Berkeley: University of California Press.

Fine, B. (2001). *Social Capital vs Social Theory*. London: Routledge.

Gjølberg, M. (2009). The origin of corporate social responsibility: Global forces or national legacies? *Socio-Economic Review, 7:* 605–637.

Gran, T. (2002). Trust and Power in Land Politics in South Africa. *International Review of Administrative Sciences, 86*(3).

Hart, K. (2000). *The Memory Bank: Money in an Unequal World*. London: Profile Books.

Harriss, J. (2002). *Depoliticisng Development: The World Bank and Social Capital*, London: Anthem Press.

Heller, P. (1997). Social Capital as a Product of Class Mobilization and State Intervention: Industrial Workers in Kerala, India. In P. Evans (Ed.).

Hirschmann, D. (1999). Development Management versus Third World Bureaucracies: A Brief History of Conflicting Interests. *Development and Change, 30*(2). 287–305.

Jeffrey, C. (2000). Democratisation without Representation? The Power and Political Strategies of a Rural Elite in North India. *Political Geography, 19*(8). 1013–1036.

Jessop, B. (1990). *State Theory: Putting the Capitalist State in its Place*. Cambridge: Polity.

Jessop, B. (2002). *The Future of the Capitalist State*. Cambridge: Polity.

Kohli, A. (1987). *The State and Poverty in India: The Politics of Reform*, Cambridge: Cambridge University Press.

La Porta, R., Lopez-de-Silanes, F., Shleifer, A., & Vishny, R. (1997). Trust in Large Organizations. *American Economic review, 87*(2). 333–338.

Lam, W. (1996). Institutional Design of Public Agencies and Co-production: A Study of Irrigation Associations in Taiwan. *World Development, 24*(6). 1039–1054.

Lam, W. (2001). Coping with Change: A Study of Local Irrigation Institutions in Taiwan. *World Development, 29*(9). 1569–1592.

Lenin, V. (1917). The Tasks of the Proletariat in the Present Revolution. *Marxists.org*. Retrieved from: https://www.marxists.org/archive/lenin/works/1917/apr/04.htm.

Lenin, V. (1977). *The State and Revolution*. Moscow: Progress Publishers.

Levi, M., & Stoker, L. (2000). Political Trust and Trustworthiness. *Annual Review of Political Science, 3*. 474–507.

Mann, M. (1984). The Autonomous Power of the State: Its Origins, Mechanisms and Results. *Arc. Europ. Sociol., 25*. 185–213.

Marx, K. (1867). *Capital volume 1*. https://www.marxists.org/archive/marx/works /download/pdf/Capital-Volume-I.pdf.

Migdal, J., Kohli, A., & Shue, V. (Eds.). (1994). *State Power and Social Forces: Domination and Transformation in the Third World*. Cambridge: Cambridge University Press.

Newton, K. (2001). Trust, Social Capital, Civil Society, and Democracy. *International Science Review, 22*. 201–214.

Oglesby, E. (2004). 'Corporate citizenship? Elites, labor, and the geographies of work in Guatemala', *Environment and Planning D-Society & Space 22*(4): 553–572.

Ostrom, E. (1996). Crossing the great divide: Coproduction, synergy, and development, World Development, *24*(6): 1073–1087.

Ougaard, M. (1983). Some Remarks concerning Peripheral Capitalism and the Peripheral State. *Science and Society, 46*(4): 385–404.

Overton, J. (2001). Peasants on the Internet? Informalization in a Global Economy. *The Journal of Peasant Studies, 28*(4): 149–170.

Petras, J. (1997). Imperialism and NGOs in Latin America. *Monthly Review, 49*(7).

Postel, N., & Richard, S. (2019). Corporate social responsibility (CSR): an institutionalist Polanyian analysis. *Society and Business Review, 14*(4): 381–400.

Preuss, L., Gold, M., & Rees, C. (Eds.). (2015). *Corporate Social Responsibility and Trade Unions Perspectives across Europe*. London: Routledge.

Poulantzas, N. (1968). *Political Power and Social Classes*. London: New Left Books.

Putnam, R. (1993). *Making Democracy Work*. Princeton (N.J.): Princeton University Press.

Rothstein, B. (2000). Trust, Social Dilemmas and Collective Memories. *Journal of Theoretical Politics*, 12. 477–501.

Sayer, A. (1992). *Method in Social Science*. London: Routledge.

Sayer, A. (1997). The Dialectic of Culture and Economy. In R. Lee and J. Wills (Eds.), *Geographies of Economies*. London: Arnold.

Schneider, A. (2020). Bound to Fail? Exploring the Systemic Pathologies of CSR and Their Implications for CSR Research. *Business & Society*, 59(7): 1303–1338.

Serageldin, I., & Grootaert, C. (2000). Defining social capital: an integrating view. In P. Dasgupta and I. Serageldin (Eds.).

Serra, R. (1999). "Putnam in India": Is Social Capital a Meaningful and Measurable Concept at Indian State Level. *IDS Working paper*, No.92.

Shurmer-Smith, P. (2000). *India: Globalization and Change*. London: Arnold.

Tendler, J. (1997). *Good Government in the Tropics*. Baltimore: The Johns Hopkins University Press.

Thawnghmung, A. (2003) Rural Perceptions of State Legitimacy in Burma/Myanmar. *The Journal of Peasant Studies*, 30(2). 1–40.

Thomas, A. (1992). Non-Governmental Organizations and the Limits to Empowerment. In M. Wuyts et al. (Eds.), *Development Policies and Public Action*. Oxford: Oxford University Press.

Thompson, E.P. (1991). *Customs in Common*. London: The Merlin Press.

Trotsky, L. (1931). The Transitional Programme. *Marxists.org*. Retrieved from: https://www.marxists.org/archive/trotsky/1938/tp/tp-text.htm.

Trotsky, L. (1996). *The Third International after Lenin*. Atlanta: Pathfinder Press.

Wallis, J., & Dollery, B. (2002). Social Capital and Local Government Capacity. *Australian Journal of Public Administration*, 61(3). 76–85.

Wang, X. (1997). Mutual Empowerment of State and Peasantry: Grassroots Democracy in Rural China. *World Development*, 25(9). 1431–1442.

Williams, G. (1997). State, Discourse, and Development in India: The Case of West Bengal's Panchayati Raj. *Environment and Planning A*, 29(12). 2099–2112.

Woolcock, M. (1998). Social Capital and Economic Development: Toward a Theoretical Synthesis and Policy Framework. *Theory and Society*, 27(2). 151–208.

Woolcock, M. (2000). Social Capital in Theory and Practice: Where do We Stand?. Chapter prepared for the 21st Annual Conference on Economic issues [World Bank social capital website].

Woolcock, M., & Narayan, D. (2000). Social Capital: Implications for Development Theory, Research, and Policy. *The World Bank Research Observer*, 15(2). 225–249.

World Bank (2001). *World Development Report 2000/2001*. Washington, D.C.: World Bank.

CHAPTER 6

The Social Economy and Socialist Strategy

Aram Eisenschitz and Jamie Gough

Neoliberalism has seen the growth in many developed countries of the 'social economy', not-for-profit enterprises frequently producing socially useful and environmentally responsible goods and services (see Chapter 2).[1] The expansion of this sector has been particularly noticeable in the US and Britain, in contrast to other European countries with stronger traditions of cooperative organisation (Amin et al., 2002: 9–11). In the former countries, new social enterprises have particularly been in evidence in poor neighbourhoods (Oatley, 1999). Forms of enterprise include cooperatives owned by their labour force and community businesses owned by trusts. Other social enterprises are non-production: community development banks, micro-credit ventures and credit unions; housing cooperatives; Community Development Trusts for redeveloping neighbourhoods; while Local Exchange and Trading Schemes organise mutual production through an alternative currency. These developments are part of what we have called the 'bootstraps' strategy, that attempts to counter the powerlessness of disadvantaged localities in a global economy through bottom-up strategies (Eisenschitz and Gough, 1993). The social economy has been particularly popular during the recessions that have punctuated global economic stagnation since the 1970s. For the Right and Centre, community enterprise promises stabilisation of class relations, while for the Left it promises jobs and services in the face of capitalist abandonment.

The defining characteristics of the social economy include having a 'social purpose', being run democratically, not distributing profits to individuals, and holding assets in trust for a defined community to whom they are accountable (Pearce, 2003: 31ff). But the social economy is diverse. Pearce lists nine criteria with which to describe the sector, each of which involves a spectrum rather than a simple duality. In size they span the micro-level to the very large enterprise; they may be located anywhere in the formal or informal economy; and they may or may not make profits. They may be staffed by any combination of volunteers and paid labour, and they may be anywhere from wholly independent to wholly dependent on state subsidy (Hudson, 2009).

---

1   This chapter is based on an earlier publication, Eisenschitz and Gough (2011).

The social economy is also a *political* chameleon, posing difficult dilemmas for socialists (Gough and Eisenschitz, 2006: 157–61; Hudson, 2009: 506–9). Many of these initiatives have been sponsored and supported by the right (Reisman, 1991) and bear its imprint – fragmentation of labour, an extension of the informal economy, under-funded self-help; some social enterprises originate as privatisations of state services, using un-unionised low paid or unpaid labour. The social economy gives moral legitimacy to enterprise and hence neoliberalism, because it directly addresses the latter's obvious deficiencies (Dart, 2004). In Britain, the Conservative prime minister in 2010–5, David Cameron, was an enthusiast of this strategy, which he dubbed the 'Big Society' in counterposition to the 'Big State'. The social economy was also strongly supported by the 1997–2010 Labour government as part of its programmes for poor neighbourhoods and for 'social inclusion'. It fitted perfectly the tenets of Labour's 'Third Way' strategy, charting a course that avoids the hazards of both state- and market-led development (Caterall et al., 1996; Imrie and Raco, 2003; HMSO, 2007). For socialists, on the other hand, the social economy promises to meet immediate needs for jobs and services for the poor, does so in ways which embody considerable direct democracy and participation, and on this basis is genuinely popular (Moulaert and Ailenei, 2005); it may even pre-figure alternatives to capitalism. This draws on a two-hundred year history of cooperative and community enterprise (Yeo, 1988), including utopian socialist communities (Harvey, 2000). With the conversion of the major post-capitalist societies (USSR, China) to capitalism and defeats of the trade union movement, the social economy appears as a site for a new left politics.

In this chapter we analyse these contradictory roots of the social economy. Our aim is not primarily to consider the tensions between social enterprises' 'social aims' and their economic survival within capitalism, a subject well-aired in the literature (e.g. Amin et al., 2002; Amin, 2009; Hudson, 2009) and which we discussed in Chapter 2; rather, it is to consider how the social economy might fit within a wider strategy for socialism *beyond* capitalism.

In recent years there has been considerable discussion of the social economy by left geographers and urbanists. A number of authors have embraced the social economy enthusiastically as both practical measures against poverty and as an empowering alternative to, or radical variant of, capitalism (Gunn and Gunn, 1991; Gibson-Graham, 1996, 2006; Lee 1999; Haughton, 1998; Gittell and Vidal, 1998; Amin, 2009). In this viewpoint, the *formal* difference of the social economy from both private firms and the state underlies the assertion that it is 'radical'. Other authors have been more pessimistic. Fuller and Jonas (2003), for example, detect and deplore a tendency for credit unions in Britain to move away from their small-scale, voluntary, neighbourhood-based origins towards larger scale, professionally-run businesses, partly under pressure from the state, thus losing their foundation in trust and their potential to empower. Pearce (2009) sees a similar trend across the whole British social economy. Amin, Cameron and Hudson (2002; 2003), on the basis of their survey of the social economy in four British localities, diagnose a systematic tension between seeking profitability and financial autonomy, on the one hand, and the meeting of social needs and involvement of ordinary people on the other. Indeed, they argue that the social economy is often an 'iniquitous' (2003: 28) practice, trapping the poor into economically unsustainable enterprises. They conclude (2002: 122–5) that the social economy cannot feasibly provide jobs and welfare on a substantial scale, but that it can, and should, offer modest, small-scale *symbols* of a better society (see also Hudson, 2009).

In this chapter we argue that the actually-existing social economy is indeed riven with tensions which academic enthusiasts and Third Way policy makers tend to ignore. But we also argue that a socialist strategy for the social economy, one centred on empowerment, the building of cooperative social relations, and links to the organised labour movement, can be more ambitious than 'the pessimists' imply: it can aim to go beyond exemplary, isolated, small-scale, enterprises of the poor.

The most elaborate, and best-known, academic theorisation of the social economy has been that of Gibson-Graham (1996; 2006) and collaborators (see also Chapter 2). Adopting an institutionalist approach cast in post-structuralist language, they argue that many different forms of enterprise are possible within capitalism, a continuum of many hybrid forms. Social enterprises can thus potentially flourish within a capitalist 'environment', and in this way the sector can aim to grow indefinitely. They see this as a more realistic strategy for empowerment than trade union struggles with a perspective of a socialist economy. In our view, this treats capitalism as merely 'markets' and ignore its specific dynamics – the indefinite accumulation of capital by exploitation of wage labour, hence its endless expansion into new fields of production and consumption. Amin (2009) follows this approach, systemically conflating capital with 'markets'. Correspondingly, Gibson-Graham ignores the specific dynamics of social enterprises – their paucity of capital and their inhibitions in accumulating it. They accordingly downplay the systematic undermining of the social economy by capitalism (see Chapter 2, section 5). We therefore regard the gradual conversion of capitalism to the social economy as utopian; the 'old' 'fundamentalist' struggle for workers' and citizens' control of the mainstream economy is still necessary. Our discussion in this paper considers how the social economy can fit with the latter aim, rather than being a complete strategy in itself.

We first consider the socialist promise of the social economy. We argue that it is one manifestation of the need for socialisation of production and reproduction within capitalist society, contradicting capitalism's foundations in private property and private decision making. The social economy has arisen in particular historical circumstances. The strong, institutionalised types of socialisation created during the Keynesian era have been undermined by neo-liberalism in order to allow greater freedoms and power for capital (Chapter 2). But the need to address socialisation has remained, and indeed has in some ways intensified: the effects of neoliberalism have pushed both capital and labour into developing new forms of socialisation, including the social economy. These, however, have generally been developed in modes compatible with, and even supporting, neo-liberalism. Nevertheless, the contradictory origins of the social economy mean that it can potentially be developed in a variety of political directions. In particular, with leadership and strategy from the left it can show the potential for increasingly radical and far-reaching forms of socialisation and worker and citizen involvement, and can thus provide an important site for furthering the struggle for socialism.

1   The Promise: Overcoming the Splits in Capitalist Society

The promise of the social economy for socialists is that it can embody ideas of self-determination and radical democracy in both the economic and social spheres. It does so by promising to overcome the particular fragmentation and dualisms that characterise capitalist society. The hierarchies found in both social and economic life are underpinned by a set of dualities: the splits between work and leisure, manual and mental labour, employment and unemployment, work and home, and public and private. Through them we internalise class relations and the separation of exchange and use value. All anti-systemic political movements have had to oppose these dualisms in order to make progress in any sphere: for example, radical changes in the home require measures in waged work and vice versa. Anti-capitalist politics thus tends to strengthen the unity of daily life (Gough and Eisenschitz, 2010).

How could the social economy achieve these kinds of aim? Forms of enterprise such as the cooperative can overcome divisions between management and labour through job rotation and training. Being worker-owned they offer the potential to overcome the alienation of workers from the labour process and the means of production and to some extent from the product and consumers. Community economic initiatives can produce much-needed goods and services, so that workers produce directly for themselves and their neighbours, in control of their product and how it is produced; thus use value considerations predominate over exchange value. Democratic control over the enterprise can ensure that surpluses are retained within the area, creating more local jobs. If the enterprises can reproduce their fixed and working capital, or receive a state subsidy, labour can avoid the pressures resulting from enterprises paying dividends. Instead of regeneration imposed by state and private sector professionals and shareholders, the locality's development is able to grow out of its population's needs and capabilities. This makes it possible for workers, consumers and citizens to combine a degree of autonomy with reduced alienation (Bowring, 1998), particularly if projects are able to create a social and political infrastructure for community control over the social enterprises (Wiewel and Gills, 1995).

In this way, the social economy could begin to unify the fragmented world of capitalism. Mental work is integrated with manual work; skills are opened to all rather than used by employers to set groups of workers against each other. The 'unskilled' unemployed can use and develop their capacities without stigma. Welfare can be directly produced by local people instead of being organised by a state in ways which reproduce class and patriarchal discipline (Bowles and Gintis, 1976; Wilson, 1977). To the extent that the social economy replaces production for exchange with production for use, relations of appropriation no longer need to dominate production. Community agriculture, for example, can develop alternative social relations whereby food is locally produced with community ownership; the irrationality of capitalist social relations is exposed since this farming is less ecologically damaging, produces more nutritious food, is more productive and cheaper than the commercial sector, and can reach the most deprived since they are able to work for their share (Williamson et al., 2002: 254ff). Enterprises are therefore free to experiment with non-hierarchical social relations, while new relations can be forged between production and consumption. LETS, for example, not only bypass the market but can be a means of redefining needs and developing a culture of reciprocity (Lee, 1996; Williams et al., 2003). Where production is community controlled, it can *incorporate* social aims from the beginning instead of the state attempting to mop up the problems caused by private ownership. In this vision, as we construct the social economy we also transform ourselves, overcoming the fragmentation and dualisms we have internalised. The movement thus potentially develops democracy as self-determination, returning economic, social and political power to exploited and oppressed groups, not only the most disadvantaged. This corresponds to the central meaning of democracy (Arblaster, 1987: 8; Fotopoulos, 1997: Ch.5); it is a socialist vision with roots stretching back to the Enlightenment.

## 2	Capitalism and Socialisation: Some Contradictions

But can the social economy actually be realised in this socialist mode, with such a liberatory dynamic? To begin to explore this question we need to consider the impulses within capitalist society which have been realised by the social economy.

There is a paradox at the core of capitalist society: its class relations threaten the viability of capitalism itself by disrupting the conditions for continued accumulation (Meszaros, 1995: Ch.2). If private capitals are allowed free rein, class relations tend to take an overtly authoritarian form in order to extract the maximum surplus value. Each capital pursues its individual interests irrespective of their impact on the social conditions of profitable production. Collective action is then required to create (minimum) coherence of the system as a whole (Gough and Eisenschitz, 1996).

Class relations damage accumulation in a number of ways. Private ownership and unrestricted individualism cannot adequately reproduce the bases of production in such areas as the social and physical infrastructure, the environment, food safety, or the capacities and attitudes of labour. Labour relations which are simply repressive may seriously inhibit production: marginalisation of oppressed groups may deprive firms of skills, while demarcation between white and blue collar labour may inhibit the initiative and cooperation of workers (de Brunhoff, 1978). Moreover, the social realm – home, family, environment, community, city – has major (and increasing) impacts on labour power and production (Gough, 2001). The accumulation of capital itself therefore produces pressure for greater cooperation and coordination in many aspects of society (Cox, 1998; Gundogdu, 2020).

Failure to address socialisation can result not only in large direct costs to capital but also in political conflict which imposes further costs on it. If, for instance, environmental issues are not addressed, not only can production and profits be directly affected, but popular political pressure can force capital into costly solutions. Similarly, if healthcare is not addressed collectively, the profits for medical capital are likely to be outweighed by adverse impacts upon productivity, industrial conflict and upward pressure upon wages. In Britain, the price of the weakening of the unions achieved in the last two decades has been growing exclusion of sections of the working class and increasing social disorder (Young, 1999; Gough and Eisenschitz, 2006: Part II). The creation of disordered inner cities in which the unemployed fail to constitute an effective reserve army is hardly in capital's interests. Trying to get by without addressing socialisation therefore tends to lead to social and political conflict, and these to economic penalties for capital.

While the state can act in the collective interests of capital to overcome some of these tensions, such attempts at socialisation always have to deal with the rights of private firms against each other and their rights over workers. Thus although neglect of socialisation leads to political conflicts, so too do collective solutions. Coordination requires an authoritative institution able to articulate capitalist rationality through collective action for the survival of the logic of accumulation (Roweis, 1981); able, for instance, to exert power over those fractions of capital which disrupt the conditions for investment, syphon profits from productive uses, or obstruct new lines of investment.

These problems tend to be particularly acute in countries such as the US and Britain with liberal political traditions emphasising the priority of private interests. In these countries policies for collective capital tend to be opposed by interests directly affected, and are thus weak, or are highjacked by sectional interests, or deflected by disciplinary class relations. Intervention into housing in Britain, for example, has seldom been geared to improving productivity, but rather has attempted to reproduce disciplinary relations by instilling morality into the working class and separating off the 'respectable' layers physically and culturally (Jones 1971: 193ff); this has contributed to the difficulties for capital of obtaining good quality labour power. Thus although socialisation is of central importance to accumulation, capital is unwilling to allow the state much freedom in organising it for fear of political conflicts.

Another instance in Britain of these contradictions has been the failure to develop industrial democracy. Pressure for formal worker involvement in enterprises has come not only from workers but also from some employers who have recognised that cooperation could boost innovation and productivity improvement. But successive moves to introduce workers' representation in large enterprises – in state-owned industries, after the 1977 Bullock Report recommendations, or under pressure from the EC/EU – have come to nothing because of the excessive demands they might encourage, given the organisational strength of the unions in Britain and their 'distance' from management born out of their exclusion from decision making. Symptomatic was the treatment of the workers'- plan in the 1970s at Lucas Aerospace, an ailing British armaments manufacturer (Wainwright and Elliott, 1982). The plan demonstrated how the firm'-s surplus labour and plant could be used both to develop socially-useful products and to compensate for its declining profitability. But this was turned down by the firm because of the influence it promised to workers, and the suggestion that the state take a more socially responsible role in its procurement decisions. For exactly the same reasons, the Labour government in 2008 refused the demand of occupying workers that it buy (for almost nothing) a modern plant making wind turbines shut by its owners, despite the paucity of such manufacturing capacity in Britain and the government's green commitments. These stories point to the fine line between a role for workers which helps capital and one which develops into opposition.

The deepening of economic internationalisation has sharpened these contradictions. The increasing intensity of competition and widening geographical scale of capital mobility paradoxically require stronger production bases and hence more effective and comprehensive planning (Swyngedouw, 1989). Reproduction of both productive capital and of labour power involves longer time horizons. Yet the turnover time of many sections of capital is decreasing, and apparent global opportunities make business restless and unwilling to commit itself to territorially-based socialisation.

As we shall see shortly, the social economy promises a way of handling the simultaneous conflicts *and interdependencies* between private interests and public coordination, between cooperation and conflict of capital and labour, and between mobile capital and effective socialisation.

3   The Death and the Ghost of Keynesianism

The depth of these contradictions can be seen in the demise of post-war Keynesianism (see also Chapter 2, section 1). Keynesian regulation of the macro economy, state industrial policy and the welfare state tried to create a class settlement to safeguard key aspects of society from the anarchy of accumulation. But in the 1960s and 1970s this resulted in ever-increasing demands being made on capital by the working class, and on the state itself by both classes; state policies which responded to these pressures tended to create further antagonisms; the organisation of socialisation became increasingly politicised (Offe, 1984; Bowles et al., 1990). Capital concluded that such intervention can snowball once the working class see the achievements of collective action; in the crisis of the late 1960s and early 1970s in Western Europe and the US, capital saw a dangerous dynamic towards self-determination.

Neo-liberalism responded to these dangers by retreating from socialisation and reimposing the disciplines of the market onto both firms and workers. Capital was freed from linkages and obligations to particular workforces, sectors and territories. The new freedoms were expressed in a new prominence of banking and property capital, of speculation, and of one-off sources of profit like asset-stripping. But this freedom for capital has come at a price. The working class has been increasingly exposed to economic and social instability, and institutions which legitimated the social order have been eroded. Neo-liberalism has endangered both political stability and economic efficiency.

These problems have been addressed through increasing repression of workers and trade unionists by employers, of blacks and youth by the police, of the poor by the welfare agencies. But this repression can be fragile, as Thatcher found to her cost.

Urban planning illustrates these tensions and political oscillations. Capitalist ownership of land and buildings inhibits rational production, and hinders the reproduction of labour as rentier capital profits out of subsistence (Roweis, 1981). Keynesian urban planning attempted to socialise land allocation by taking these costs and problems into account. But it was impossible to prevent the intrusion of private property (I.Gough,1979). Each issue demonstrated that spatial issues were at heart class issues, and that optimum solutions for production, such as the public ownership of development rights, constituted a potential threat to capital's power. Neo-liberalism consequently weakened state regulation of property development – but at the same time damaged those aspects of urban planning most important for capitalist reproduction (Thornley, 1991; Bowie, 2008).

4   The Social Economy for Capital: Socialisation without Political
       Conflict

The neglect of socialisation by neo-liberalism has thus posed problems for capital, of which its more far-sighted representatives are aware (Hutton, 1995). The contemporary promise of the social economy *for capital* is that it can organise socialisation in ways which avoid the political conflicts which earlier Keynesian programmes ran into (Noya and Clarence, 2007). The dominant practice of community economic initiatives in Britain since the 1980s has been to assist in the reproduction of labour power and the ideological integration of the working class which neo-liberalism has undermined, and more generally to modify the class relations which damage reproduction and stifle growth (Gough and Eisenschitz, 1996; Amin et al., 1999; Gough, 2002). These are potentially relevant not only in poor neighbourhoods but also in the mainstream economy. There are a number of aspects to this project of capital. (In this section we focus on the British case.)

First, the social economy is able to intervene in the organisation and provision of subsistence consumption and in particular tackle the problems that its commodification has given rise to. Initiatives span a wide range of reproduction goods from social housing, banking, environmental improvement, food and recycled furniture among others. However, this provision may be directly linked to capitalist order; the Community Development Corporations in the

US, for example, tend to provide housing in a way which reinforces social discipline, recapitulating the housing initiatives of the Victorian ruling class (Stoecker, 1997).

Second, there can be significant impacts on the attitudes of workers and on industrial relations. Economic democracy encourages self-improvement by giving self-confidence and helping individuals into the mainstream labour market. Alternative forms of enterprise encourage self-help, educate workers in 'market realities', and absorb economically and politically marginalised groups into the culture of work via intermediate labour markets. The socialisation of responsibility, control and profits through new forms of industrial democracy and co-ownership may reduce anomie and restore motivation (Lincoln, 2003). By diffusing the ownership of capital, cooperatives reduce opposition to profit both ideologically and materially, and increase capital's share in national income (Britten, 1984). Thus cooperative values are fostered, in contrast to the authoritarian management of neoliberalism, enabling an economy in which labour actively contributes to production (Hodgson, 1984; Cooke and Morgan, 1998). These values are particularly important in planning the networks of private and social capital required for new waves of investment. The social economy could potentially provide a model for such relationships (Maddock, 1991). It is this promise to renew the bases of accumulation in the capital-labour relation that makes the social economy attractive to sections of capital.

Third, the social economy is presented apolitically. It has distanced itself from its roots in the community activism of the 1960s (Mollenkopf, 1983; Lees and Mayo, 1985). The ethos of the contemporary social economy is that poor areas are weak markets that need reinvestment rather than political mobilisation. Community economic development aspires to replace the conflict that used to characterise the inner cities with pragmatism and consensus (Fuller and Jonas, 2003).

Fourth, within the social economy welfare ceases to be a right. Welfare is to be based on enterprise; the social economy fails to challenge the notion that welfare derives ultimately from the private sector (HMSO, 2007) . On the one hand it has to be bargained for through the emerging institutional consensus – in the US and Britain particularly through the business-dominated local partnerships. On the other, welfare needs are to be met through self-help. The social economy promotes values of 'enterprise' to replace 'a culture of dependency', thus further eroding the legitimacy of local government. Through these arrangements, different disadvantaged groups and different neighbourhoods come to compete for funds, thereby fragmenting class solidarity. Universalist discourses of welfare are replaced with post-modern difference: decentralisation, fragmentation, and 'a continuum between market and state' (for a critique see Taylor-Gooby, 1994). In these ways, the popularity of the social economy reflects the temper of the times.

Fifth, within the social economy the locality is to be strengthened and individuals are to be empowered, but in ways which are consistent with improving competitiveness and capital accumulation, hence fitting with neo-liberal ideas. Neo-liberalism is represented not by the aggressive small firm but by cosy community-based enterprises which popularise capitalism with their softer values, their flatter hierarchies and their less disciplinary workplace environment.

Sixth, the social economy is decreasingly managed directly by its workers or participants. Institutionalist commentators increasingly see the key to competitiveness of social enterprises as being the same as for mainstream ones, that is, the professional manager, engineer or designer linked into geographically-wide networks (Florida, 2002). Thus Amin et al. (2002: Ch.5) have argued that many of the most durable social enterprises owe their success to such leadership, and that, in consequence, the social economy is more dynamic in localities in which there is a large professional or entrepreneurial middle class, and weaker in old industrial areas (see also Hudson, 2009). A new profession has been created for this purpose, the 'social entrepreneur'; the Labour government sought to bring business people 'with a conscience' into the Third Sector through, *inter alia*, the Ambassadors programme.

Seventh, the social economy transforms national pressure for greater democracy into the fragmented democracy of the local project. Neoliberalism has curtailed democracy in the economy and local government, but ostensibly re-introduced it at the community level (Duffy and Hutchinson, 1997). As part of Labour's shift from government to 'governance', its reforms of local government emphasised community participation. By implementing 'democracy' within an unsupportive institutional framework, non-profit enterprises are pushed into behaving like small firms. The sector could resist these forces and assume some political power if it were coordinated as a network, politically organised and motivated and well-supported by the local state. But support from the state and business is forthcoming precisely to the extent that the sector is organised as fragmented individual enterprises and projects. In consequence, democracy is equated with the right of access to markets and with equal rights within the market's atomistic social relations. It fosters self-help rather than mutuality, individualism rather than collectivity. Community development trades on these inherent ambiguities in the notions of 'democracy'- and 'empowerment'-. To workers these are attractive notions in the face of neo-liberal authoritarianism. But in practice they often amount to no more than formal decentralisation and token participation.

Finally, business has become interested in the sector as a means of providing social reproduction outside the politicised sphere of the local state. This field is often difficult to commodify and is politically sensitive; business has always had difficulties in getting involved with social reproduction. Distancing this function from the state through social enterprises gives business better leverage over its organisation. Thus Business in the Community, an organisation made up of the largest firms, has been involved in initiatives around all aspects of reproduction, where it acts as a broker between the private sector and the social economy. Indeed, the majority of social enterprises in the old industrial cities of Glasgow and Middlesborough are services previously provided by local government but now contracted out (Amin et al., 2002, Ch.4). However, this process may be resisted by residents suspicious that the state is washing its hands of public services, as when tenants in Tower Hamlets vetoed further transfers of housing stock to a social enterprise (*ibid*.: 110–1).

These attributes of the social economy movement have meant that, on the whole, the initiatives have been able to address socialisation without stimulating 'excessive' working class demands. Indeed, they have fostered not only economic integration but a set of values which are compatible with capitalism even in its neoliberal form: self-reliance, earning of welfare, competition between localities and between sections of the working class. Community and cooperation have been configured in reactionary senses, as modes of social integration and class stabilisation.

The social economy has developed in this conservative fashion partly through conscious actions of capital and the state. Where the growth of social enterprises brings them into competition with mainstream firms, the latter have sometimes taken measures to keep them within the ghetto of the disadvantaged; in the US the banks mounted a successful legal challenge to the credit unions (Gunn, 1997). Moreover, the formal autonomy of alternative enterprises hides the arms-length control exerted by their suppliers of capital and by firms up and downstream from them. Non-profit enterprises can generate substantial profits through their higher intensity and quality of work, but these are often appropriated at other points in the production chain. Thus some social enterprises exist to provide cheap accommodation and services to conventional SMEs but without affecting the latters' social relations (Amin et al., 2002: 66–72, 78, 107–8). Where worker- or community-control is weak, social enterprise executives may appropriate profit as enormous salaries (£250,000 p.a. in one case), or make themselves owners. Local partnerships between the state and business have politically moulded the social economy. The national government, too, has taken measures to prevent initiatives developing in the direction of self-determination. It has repeatedly forbidden

alternative enterprises to engage in political debate if they are to receive funding. It has taken steps to distance social enterprises from their local roots, for
example in the loosening of the 'community bond' for credit unions (Fuller
and Jonas 2003). The Housing Corporation has squeezed the self-run housing cooperatives, preferring the professionalised Housing Associations. Social
security regulations tend to restrict the social economy; LETS, for example,
have limited relevance to the unemployed because local-currency earnings
may be treated as income-in-kind which prevents them claiming benefits. All
these interventions have served to push the social economy in a conservative
direction.

5   How Can the Social Economy Be Developed in a Socialist Direction?

We argued at the beginning of this article that the social economy has potential for socialists; how can this be developed? Three actually-existing examples
show both possibilities and some difficulties. A dynamic social economy with
active involvement of the trade unions has been developed within Quebec;
by 2002 this claimed to comprise 160,000-odd jobs (Mendell, 2009). The long
term regime of Quebec was important to this: social democratic and nationalist, strong corporatism of the provincial state, capital and unions, high union
membership, and a long tradition of cooperatives. In 1983 a trade union federation set up a fund for the social economy based on its members' voluntary
contributions. In 1996 a tripartite conference on economic strategy led to a
Coordination (Chantier) of the Social Economy, which has now become a
fourth pillar of Quebec corporatism; its board is independent of the state, and
includes the two trade union federations as well as social economy bodies and
local development centres. In 2001 a special office for the social economy was
established within the provincial state. In 2007 the Chantier set up a long term
investment bank funded by state and unions, which actively seeks out and
helps to construct investments. This framework has been vital for the growth
of the Quebec social economy. However, it has not guaranteed good working
conditions within it. Nor does it appear to have linked into militant democratic
politics in the private and state sectors, presumably because of the 'social partnership' under which it has developed.

The potential of the social economy to stimulate workers' self-organisation
and struggle against capital is better demonstrated the Dudley Street
Neighbourhood Initiative in Boston's South End. This has been based on mobilisation involving nearly the whole local population, starting with simple issues

like litter (Medoff and Sklar, 1994). In developing welfare services it has hired experts strictly under community control rather than allowing domination by 'the suits'. It managed to obtain unique powers of eminent domain, originally devised to allow hotel development to take place on low-value land; this allowed the community, with finance from the Riley and Ford Foundations, to take into custodianship their local slum landlords, and then to develop new housing vested in the community in perpetuity. The radicalness of these new social relations of reproduction is indicated by the Initiative's Declaration of Community Rights, which include the right to good health, public transport, housing, education, environment and land. The Initiative has not, however, taken the next step of setting up alternative *production* enterprises. Similarly, Community Land Trusts in the US and Britain have developed alternative social relations to resist gentrification and promote house price stability, but this approach has not extended into production and other fields (Williamson et al., 2002: 250ff).

The city of Bologna in the 1970s shows what can be achieved where social economy initiatives are situated within *socialist* regional and local political traditions (Jaggi et al., 1977). Since the struggle against fascism, Bologna and its surrounding region of the Third Italy had had a strong Communist Party tradition, spanning trade unions, local government and even small and medium employers (Brusco, 1982); they have a strong history of cooperatives. At a national level the serious defeats of the unions had yet to come. Many of the social economy initiatives were similar to those in contemporary Britain for collective self-help and empowerment: the difference lies in the support given by the local state and the unions. Those powerful and democratic institutions were able to support a degree of collective empowerment unthinkable in contemporary Britain and the US, against strenuous opposition. First, they created appropriate economic-legal spaces. They constructed a legal planning framework that, for example, allowed a cooperative to develop a covered shopping centre that would keep out the chains and favour local shops. They compelled the employers to contribute a percentage of their wage bill for social infrastructure such as public transport and childcare – a social wage. Secondly, the unions and local authorities were aware of the class struggle across its many forms and the impact of all of these on working class residents, and so sought to create policy linkages between different aspects of life. Distributional policy was linked to production in order that the entire chain from producer to consumer stayed in the cooperative sector and provided improvements in both job quality and prices. This required a politicised planning policy which aimed to prevent land speculation and enable residents in the inner city to reclaim their neighbourhoods and for working class people to reclaim the city centre. Social policy became more holistic. Speech therapy, for instance, was provided in order to prevent social discrimination that could affect children's life chances. To ensure the elderly were socially included required action over housing markets and the politics and structure of the health profession. Thirdly, the impact of these initiatives led to widespread awareness of their benefits – enhanced quality of life, lower subsistence costs, greater job security, reduced stress and improved services. Cooperatively-built flats, for instance, were a third cheaper than those in the private sector, as was food from the cooperative sector. There was wide understanding that those benefits needed *continuing* strong participation in both unions and local government since this social economy would otherwise be under threat from central government and capital. Thus not only did the social economy benefit from the support of labour movement organisations, it reciprocally helped to maintain popular support for them. Fourthly, direct democracy was implemented through neighbourhood committees that involved large numbers of people and which scrutinised all decisions, again only possible because their decisions were supported by the local state and the unions. As a result, the social economy offered substantial power to ordinary people.

These examples suggest that, despite the pressures on it, there is potential to take the social economy in a socialist direction. We have seen that capital has deep dilemmas around socialisation – requiring it for productive efficiency yet unable to organise it due to its own internal competition, its mobility and its political fears. These contradictions are reflected in profound ambivalences of capital and the state towards the social economy and lack of decisive strategies towards it; these hesitations create opportunities which socialists can exploit, pushing beyond liberal reforms towards fundamental social change. Moreover, the depredations of neo-liberalism have produced profound longings within the working class for more stable jobs, for work of less tyrannical intensity, for reproductive services which are not only affordable but sensitive to people's varied needs, and for better local environments; social enterprises which pursue these aims without concession to capital are therefore potentially very popular. Where such aggressive initiatives can be built, they can gradually and iteratively build people'-s confidence in their own collective organisation, and re-legitimate notions of working class control over economies and reproduction (Wiewel and Gills, 1995) – notions which neoliberalism has all but erased from public discourse. The potential for this trajectory obviously depends on the state of class struggle more widely; but the social economy can be a significant site of that struggle.

To unleash these liberatory dynamics, conscious strategies are needed. As in Quebec and Bologna, initiatives for popular control need to extend to all spheres of life, so that people become aware of the workings of capitalism and how apparently discrete areas of society are connected (see further Chapter 7). Even as they use state support they need to subvert its capitalist and authoritarian logics. And as they seek support from unions and social movements, social enterprises can help to radicalise them. In other words, a radical social economy can have a *dynamic, two-way relation with mainstream labour and popular movements.*

We can suggest a number of strategies which could further these aims. First, we have seen that the fragmentation of alternative initiatives qualitatively weakens them. We should push for the strongest possible linkages between projects, so that initiatives in housing, the environment, transport, child care, training, job creation, credit and so on not only support each other but also pose new demands on each other; this point has been particularly stressed by theorists of the 'solidarity economy' (e.g. Mance, 2010). In this way they can not only meet some immediate employment and reproduction needs, but can open windows into radical forms of socialisation for labour (O'Gorman, 1995).

Second, following the Quebec example, the social economy should refuse to take over services provided by the state (Mendell, 2009). Rather, they can develop new types of service with cooperative relations between workers and 'clients', and demand that these be funded by the state. In Britain and the US this has been done on a small scale by the women's, gay and black movements, for example in counselling services and women's refuges, while green housing initiatives have suggested better methods for building social housing. Conversely, we should push for the more caring and cooperative social relations sometimes achieved within social enterprises to be adopted by state-run services. But this is only possible through – and can thus stimulate – radical democratisation of the state sector. To this end the social economy needs to link up with trade unions within the welfare state, and with community groups which put demands on it.

Third, a radical social economy movement should demand legislative and regulatory support from the state, for example through fiscal incentives, purchasing from the social economy instead of from capitalist firms, and powers of compulsory purchase of land. Given their low capital base and the frequent absence of a community bank, social enterprises often need state investment, as in Bologna and Quebec. Here, the state should avoid creating excess capacity in particular types of social enterprise, and should check the democracy and probity of the community organisations involved. However, as social economy becomes stronger, it needs to combat conservative pressures which may come from dependence on the state.

Fourth, workers in social enterprises should be unionised, linking to campaigns for unions to accept the unemployed as members. Unions should protect the conditions of workers in social enterprises, and combat the constant
tendency to self-exploitation. Moreover, links to unions are relevant to the
management and direction of social enterprises. We have noted that the most
dynamic social enterprises are largely run by professionals, and that working
class people (conventionally defined) play little role. Contrary to Amin et al.
(2002: 117, 120–2) this as due not mainly to an absence of social capital or community organisation within poor areas – there is a lot (e.g. Forrest and Kearns
2001). Rather, the poor have been demoralised and disempowered by neoliberalism, including by the state's 'community' and small-area initiatives themselves, so that they feel that participation in economic governance will make
no headway (Gough and Eisenschitz 2006: 200–1, 205, 219–20). Links to the
potentially-powerful unions can help to overcome this demoralisation, provide funding, and also broker union members and officers to provide technical
expertise and advice in management to social enterprise cooperators. Social
enterprises need, however, to ensure that the often-conservative politics of
trade unions, particularly their ambivalence to cooperatives and worker directors, do not block their strategies. Reciprocally, the social economy can also
have a beneficial impact on the union movement. The experience of cooperative forms of working could inspire workers in capitalist firms and the state
to demand greater control over labour processes and products and erosion
of managerial prerogatives. Unionists in social enterprises could play a particularly useful role in campaigns of 'community unionism' (Wills and Simms
2004): the latter tend to operate at the same neighbourhood scale as social
enterprises, and aim at unionising mostly small workplaces for which social
enterprises could be exemplary.

In these ways, building the social economy does not remain in a ghetto. The
social economy can become more than conservative communitarianism or a
social democratic panacea for poverty. With a socialist strategy it can influence
labour and community organisations in the mainstream society, and receive
support from them. It can thus expand outwards into larger fields of social and
economic life (O'Gorman, 1995). The progressive role of the social economy
then goes beyond the purely ideological one which pessimistic commentators
envisage, since it is *practical* links between a radical social economy and popular collective organisations in the mainstream that are crucial. With this orien-
tation, the social economy could play a modest but significant role in renewing
the struggle for socialism.

References

Amin, A. (2009). Locating the social economy. In A. Amin. (Ed.), *The Social Economy.* (Pp. 3–21). London: Zed Books.

Amin, A., Cameron, A., & Hudson, R. (1999). Welfare as work? The potential of the UK social economy. *Environment and Planning A 31*: 2033–2051.

Amin, A., Cameron, A., & Hudson, R. (2002). *Placing the Social Economy.* London: Routledge.

Amin, A., Cameron, A., & Hudson, R. (2003). The alterity of the social economy. In A. Leyshon, R. Lee, and C. Williams (Eds.), *Alternative Economic Spaces.* (Pp. 27–54). London: Sage.

Arblaster, A. (1987). *Democracy.* Milton Keynes: Open University Press.

Bowring, F. (1998). LETS: an eco-socialist initiative? *New Left Review 232*: 91–111.

Bowie, D. (2008). *Housing and the Credit Crunch*, London: Compass.

Bowles, S., & Gintis, H. (1976). *Schooling in Capitalist America.* New York: Basic Books.

Bowles, S., Gordon, D., & Weisskopf, T. (1990). *After the Wasteland.* New York: Sharpe.

Britten, S. (1984). *Jobs, Pay, Unions and the Ownership of Capital.* London: Financial Times.

Brusco, S. (1982) The Emilian model: productive decentralisation and social integration, *Cambridge Journal of Ecoomics,* 6, 167–84.

Caterall, B., Lipietz, A., Hutton, W., & Girardet, H. (1996). The Third Sector, urban regeneration and the stakeholder. *City,* 5–6: 86–97.

Cooke, P., & Morgan, K. (1998). *The Associational Economy.* Oxford: Oxford University Press.

Cox, K. (1998). Spaces of dependence, spaces of engagement and the politics of scale; or, looking for local politics. *Political Geography, 17*(1): 1–24.

Craig, G., & Mayo, M. (Eds.). (1995). *Community Empowerment.* London: Zed Books.

Dart, R. (2004). The legitimacy of social enterprise. *Nonprofit Management and Leadership, 14*(4): 411–424.

de Brunhof, S. (1978). *The State, Capital and Economic Policy.* London: Pluto Press.

Duffy, K., & Hutchinson, J. (1997). Urban policy and the turn to the community. *Town Planning Review, 68*(3): 347–362.

Eisenschitz, A. and Gough, J. (1993). *The Politics of Local Economic Policy.* Basingstoke: Macmillan.

Eisenschitz, A. and Gough, J. (2011). Socialism and the 'social economy', *Human Geography* 4(2) 1–15.

Florida, R. (2002). *The Rise of the Creative Class.* New York: Basic Books.

Forrest, R., & Kearns, A. (2001). Social cohesion, social capital and the neighbourhood. *Urban Studies, 38*(12): 2125–2143.

Fotopolous, T. (1997). *Towards an Inclusive Democracy*. London: Cassell.

Fuller, D., & Jonas, A. (2003). Alternative financial spaces. In A. Leyshon, R. Lee, and C. Williams (Eds.), *Alternate Economic Spaces*. (Pp. 55–73). London: Sage.

Gibson-Graham, J. K. (1996). *The End of Capitalism (As We Know It)*. Cambridge, Mass.: Blackwell.

Gibson-Graham, J. K. (2006). *A Postcapitalist Politics*. Minneapolis: University of Minnesota Press.

Gittell, R., & Vidal, A. (1998). *Community Organizing*. Thousand Oaks, CA: Sage.

Gough, I. (1979). *The Political Economy of the Welfare State*. Basingstoke: Macmillan.

Gough, J. (2001). Work, class and social life. In R. Pain, M. Barke, D. Fuller, J. Gough, R. MacFarlane, and G. Mowl (Eds.), *Introducing Social Geographies*. London: Arnold.

Gough, J. (2002). Neoliberalism and socialisation in the contemporary city: opposites, complements and instabilities. *Antipode, 34*(3): 405–426.

Gough, J., & Eisenschitz, A. (1996). The construction of mainstream local economic initiatives: mobility, socialization and class relations. *Economic Geography, 72*(2): 178–195.

Gough, J., & Eisenschitz, A. (2006). *Spaces of Social Exclusion*. Abingdon: Routledge.

Gough, J., & Eisenschitz, A. (2010). Local left strategy now. In A. Pike, A. Rodriguez-Pose, and J. Tomaney (Eds.), *A Handbook of Local and Regional Development*. Abingdon: Routledge.

Gundogdu, I. (2020). Space, particularity and the socialisation of production. *Cambridge Journal of Regions, Economy and Society, 13*: 543–558.

Gunn, C. (1997). The nonprofit sector: radical potential? *Review of Radical Political Economics, 29*(3): 92–102.

Gunn, C., & Gunn, H. (1991). *Reclaiming Capital*. London: Cornell University Press.

Harvey, D. (2000). *Spaces of Hope*, Edinburgh: Edinburgh University Press.

Haughton, G. (1998). Principles and practice of community economic development. *Regional Studies, 32*(9): 872–7.

HMSO. (2007). *Making Assets Work: The Quirk Review of Community Management and Ownership of Public Assets*. London: HMSO.

Hodgson G. (1984). *The Democratic Economy*. Harmondsworth: Penguin.

Hudson, R. (2009). Life on the edge: navigating the competitive tensions between the 'social' and the 'economic' in the social economy and in its relations to the mainstream. *Journal of Economic Geography 9*: 493–510.

Hutton, W. (1995). *The State We're In*. London: Cape.

Imrie, M., & Raco, M. (2003). *Urban Renaissance?* Bristol: Policy Press.

Jaggi, M., Muller, R., & Schmid, S. (1977). *Red Bologna*. London: Writers and Readers Publishing Cooperative.

Jones, G. S. (1971). *Outcast London*. Oxford: Oxford University Press.

Lee, R. (1996). Moral money? LETS and the social construction of local economic geographies in Southeast England. *Environment and Planning A 28*: 1377–1394.

Lee, R. (1999). Local money: Geographies of autonomy and resistance? In R. Martin (Ed.), *Money and the Space Economy*. Chichester: Wiley.

Lees, R., & Mayo, M. (1985). *Community Action for Change*. London: RKP.

Lincoln, A. (2003). Alternative work spaces. In A. Leyshon, R. Lee, and C. Williams (Eds.), *Alternate Economic Spaces*. (Pp. 107–127). London: Sage.

Maddock, S. (1991). *New Values in Business, a Necessity Not a Luxury: Community Enterprise in the Small Business Sector*. Blackpool: 14th UK Small Firms Conference.

Mance, E. (2010). Solidarity economics. *Turbulance*. Retrieved from: http://turbulence.org.uk/turbulence-1/solidarity-economics (accessed 23 July 2010).

Medoff, P., & Sklar, H. (1994). *Streets of Hope*. Boston: South End Press.

Mendell, M. (2009). Financing the social economy in Quebec, *Makingwaves 20*(3): 46–50.

Meszaros, I. (1995). *Beyond Capital*. London: Merlin.

Mollenkopf, J. (1983). *The Contested City*. Princeton: Princeton University Press.

Moulaert F and Ailenei A (2005) Social economy, third sector and solidarity relations: a conceptual synthesis from history to present. *Urban Studies 42*(11): 2037–2053.

Noya, A., & Clarence, E. (Eds.). (2007). *The Social Economy*. Paris: OECD.

Oatley, N. (1999). Developing the Social Economy. *Local Economy 13*(4): 339–345.

Offe, C. (1984). *Contradictions of the Welfare State*. London: Hutchinson.

O'Gorman, F. (1995). Brazilian community development. In G. Craig and M. Mayo (Eds.), *Community Empowerment a Reader in Participation and Development*. (Pp. 206–217). London: Zed.

Pearce, J. (2003). *Social Enterprise in Anytown*. London: Gulbenkian Foundation.

Pearce, J. (2009). Social economy: engaging as a third system? In A. Amin. (Ed.) *The Social Economy*. (Pp. 22–36). London: Zed Books.

Reisman, D. (1991). *Conservative Capitalism: The Social Economy*. London: Palgrave.

Roweis, S. (1981). Urban planning in early and late capitalist societies: Outline of a theoretical perspective. In M. Dear and A. Scott (Eds.), *Urbanization and Urban Planning in Capitalist Society*. (Pp. 159–178). London: Methuen.

Stoecker, R. (1997). The CDC model of urban redevelopment: a critique and alternative. *Journal of Urban Affairs, 19*(1): 1–44.

Swyngedouw, E. (1989). The heart of place: the resurrection of locality in an age of hyperspace. *Geographiska Annaler 7(B)*(1): 31–42.

Taylor-Gooby, P. (1994). Postmodernism and social policy. *Journal of Social Policy, 23*(3): 385–404.

Thornley, A. (1991). *Urban Planning under Thatcherism*. London: Routledge.

Wainwright, H., & Elliott, D. (1982). *The Lucas Plan*. London: Allison and Busby.

Wiewel, W., & Gills, D. (1995). Community development, organizational capacity and US urban policy: lessons from the Chicago experience 1983–93. In G. Craig and M. Mayo (Eds.), *Community Empowerment a Reader in Participation and Development.* (Pp. 127–139). London: Zed.

Williams, C., Aldridge, T., & Tooke, J. (2003). Alternative exchange spaces. In A. Leyshon, R. Lee, and C. Williams (Eds.), *Alternate Economic Spaces.* (Pp. 151–167). London: Sage.

Williamson T, Imbroscio, D., & Alperovitz, G. (2002). *Making a Place for Community.* New York: Routledge.

Wills, J., & Simms, M. (2004). Building reciprocal community unionism in the UK. *Capital and Class, 82:* 59–84.

Wilson, E. (1977). *Women and the Welfare State.* London: Tavistock.

Yeo, S. (Ed.). (1988). *New Views of Co-operation.* London: Routledge.

Young, J. (1999). *The Exclusive Society: Social Exclusion, Crime and Social Difference in Modern Society.* London: Sage.

CHAPTER 7

Rooting Working Class Struggle in Locality, and Taking It Beyond

Jamie Gough and Aram Eisenschitz

Leftwing local initiatives often develop out of a capitalist crisis – Germany in the 1920s, Italy in the 1970s, Britain in the 1980s, the US in the 1990s, Latin America in recent decades.[1] When living standards fall, when the proportion of those in unemployed or in poverty rises, when nation states either choose not to or are powerless to intervene, then a radical local politics *may* emerge. This politics may go beyond quantitative amelioration of economic conditions to develop qualitatively new social relations and genuinely liberatory politics. Crises do not always, however, lead to such local politics: the strategies adopted by the left can be crucial, and these are the subject of this chapter. We put forward our own views on left strategy, but include others' through critique. We consider High Income Countries and urban areas in Medium Income Countries, where the majority of the population depend directly or indirectly on waged labour.

Since the industrial revolution, the left, with the partial exceptions of anarchism, syndicalism and utopian socialism, has tended to see the national and international scales as strategically the most important. Key flows of capital and commodities are at these scales, and nation states have greater powers and resources than local and regional government; accordingly, the focus of the left has been to influence these economic flows and the nation state. But we shall argue in this chapter that the 'local' scale, stretching from home and workplace to region, is an essential scale for left politics, and indeed has specific strengths for the left. It is true that the place of the local within wider economic flows and higher-scale state structures makes left local strategy problematic and replete with tensions and pitfalls: localism has often been a trap for the left. The purpose of this chapter is to shed light on some of these difficulties and dilemmas, in the present context of neoliberalism and its ongoing crises. Such a discussion is particularly important in the present period due to the burgeoning of local economic initiatives and urban programmes, most of which

---

1   This chapter is based on an earlier publication, Gough and Eisenschitz (2010).

do not advance left politics and many of which militate against it. We therefore seek here to develop ideas for a distinctively left approach to local development which prioritises the interests of the working class and a perspective of socialism.

We first consider the dependence of left local politics on its national and international political setting by using the example of left initiatives in Britain since the late 1960s. We then consider the present difficult – but not hopeless – situation internationally for the left after 50 years of neoliberalism. Section 4 considers some strategic issues for a left local politics that can begin to overcome working class fragmentation and depoliticisation. Section 5 considers how these principles might be carried through in particular kinds of local initiative.

1   The Rise and Fall of the Local Left in Britain

In Britain from the late 1960s until the defeat of the miners' strike in 1985 there was an open political crisis, generated by unprecedentedly low profit rates of British capital, moves to austerity by capital and the state, and militant resistance to the latter by trade unions, social movements and residents' organisations (Glyn and Harrison 1980). While some of this resistance was nationally-organised, much of it arose from local organisations. Regarding employment, previously non-militant groups of workers such as British Asians and women in Ford, Imperial Typewriters and Grunwick, as well as previously well-organised workers such as dockers, printers and car workers, undertook long disputes; workers occupied closed factories; even the two crucial national miners' strikes of 1973 and 1984–5 were strongly rooted in the mining communities. A well-organised national network of shop stewards was sometimes able to link strong workplace organisation to solidarity within and beyond the industry. Resistance around council house rents and squatting was also highly localised and differentiated, as were many of the actions of the women's and black movements. Responding to grassroots resistance, the 1970s and early 1980s also saw radical initiatives issuing from some left Labour councils – sometimes rather grandly dubbed 'municipal socialism'. Their main foci were the maintenance of their services and the tax revenue to fund them, and initiatives to sustain and improve local jobs and further equal opportunities (Boddy and Fudge 1984; Eisenschitz and Gough 1993: 75–86; GLC 1985; 1986; Gyford 1985). The latter local economic initiatives were inspired by the dominant strategy adopted by the trade union and Labour left nationally, the Alternative Economic Strategy (Brown 1975; Coventry et al. Trades Councils 1980; London

CSE 1980). This strategy envisaged public investment in the private economy, with the state exerting increasing control, to improve innovativeness and productivity, widen and deepen skills, give workers greater say in their industries, and overcome social disadvantages within work; conversion to socially-useful and eco products was also proposed. These ideas made a brief appearance in the manifesto and first year of the 1974 Labour government; but otherwise local authorities had to carve out their left policies within tight legal and financial constraints, in opposition to national governments; after the decisive defeat of the miners and the government's 1986 abolition of the Metropolitan County Councils, these efforts collapsed.

The subsequent 35 years in Britain have seen very few localised struggles, notable exceptions being the local-national revolt against the poll tax in 1990 and some site-based ecological protests; the few workplace-based strikes have generally remained isolated and been defeated. Neoliberal discipline was imposed in Britain more heavily and successfully than in other developed countries except the US, through maintaining a high value of sterling (deflating manufacturing in particular), imposing anti-trade-union laws, use of agency labour, and privatising much of the previously well-unionised public sector. The strongly credit-based expansions of 1992–9 and 2001–7 gave the appearance that neoliberalism had regenerated the British economy, even though economic inequality increased. Local public services increasingly excluded both clients and workers from influence. Local politics became dominated by a consensual, apparently apolitical 'partnership' between councils, business and community organisations which implemented 'pro-business' policies (Cochrane 2007). Trade unionists, especially at the workplace level, were largely shut out of local politics, including from Labour Party decision making. Where residential communities were formally drawn in to urban programmes, as they increasingly were from the 1990s, they found that the key decisions were made elsewhere and that the militant community politics of the 1970s was ruled out (Atkinson 1999; Gough and Eisenschitz 2006: 148–56, 200–2). Deregulation and privatisation of housing and public transport effectively separated them from working class political influence. From 2010, using the excuse of the government debt incurred in bailing out the banks after the 2008 crisis, Conservative governments have cut national funding to local government by 50%, forcing closure of non-statutory services and cuts in others; but the Labour opposition has offered no resistance to this process, and there has been minimal opposition at the local level. Since the EU referendum in 2016, the government has used 'getting Brexit done' and then the pandemic to smother national working class opposition whether trade union or parliamentary. But at a local level there has been rising resistance. Localised union activity has taken off in sectors with the very worst conditions – cleaning, deliveries and warehousing. Worsening conditions and rising rents in the ever-expanding private rented sector have elicited much local tenant organising, though so far without national effect.

Because they promised a boost to production, some of the policies developed by left councils in the 1980s have come into the mainstream, but in forms compatible with, and even reinforcing, neoliberalism. Supporting old and new industrial districts was pioneered by the 1980s Local Enterprise Boards; under the 1997–2010 Labour government, fostering 'clusters' was the central strategy of the English Regional Development Agencies, shorn of considerations of job quality, equalities or workers' influence (Balls and Ealey 2000; Gough 2003). Promotion of the social economy, seen in the 1980s as opening to workers' self-management, under Labour became a central part of national and local anti-poverty policy, in the form of semi-private self-help and quasi-privatisation of public services (see Chapters 2 and 6). Training for oppressed groups has shifted from skilled waged work to self-employment and entrepreneurship. The comprehensive redevelopments for retail and offices coordinated by local authorities in the 1960s have been recapitulated in reactionary form by local councils in recent years investing in commercial property, usually outside their area, in order to bring in revenue to compensate for cuts in national grant, in some cases resulting in bankruptcy of the council. Even the 'new municipal left' authorities have indulged in switching purchasing to local firms in a zero-sum game. Thus lack of pressure from popular organisations has suppressed the radical potential of the earlier initiatives.

This history suggests some general points. Firstly, left advance at any spatial scale is critically dependent on militant struggles by popular collective organisations; left policies of government are a response to pressure from them. Secondly, the left may be able to take initiatives in particular localities against the flow of national politics; but these initiatives are limited and fragile unless there is a revival of the left at a national level. Thirdly, a given policy may be used in *politically* very different ways (Eisenschitz and Gough 1993: Ch.2; Gough and Eisenschitz 2006: Ch.8). In particular, for policies of the state and the voluntary and community sector to be implemented with empowering dynamics requires particular strategies and continuous pressure from popular organisations. We expand on these points below.

2   The Legacy of Neoliberalism

Since the 1980s neoliberalism has defeated, or inhibited the emergence of, left local initiatives not only in Britain but worldwide. Offensives by firms to raise their profitability have increased job insecurity and weakened union organisation, exacerbated by cuts and privatisation in state employment. Increased mobilities of productive and money capital and commodities have undermined the old centres of union strength and the working class community organisation that often went with that (Silver and Arrigi 2000). At the same time, an enormous reserve of labour has been opened up in the Majority World through industrialisation of agriculture and explosive growth of cities, resulting in an urban working class of two billion people, of which half are either un- or under-employed and a large proportion work in the informal economy (Petras and Veltmeyer 2001; Davis 2004). An increasing part of the urban working class globally makes its living through crime, particularly the illegal drugs industry which has been created by criminalisation, and crime organisation disorganises and sometimes directly attacks progressive collectivities (Ramonet, 2002).

Capital's demands and its mobility have weakened taxation, public spending and state regulation of business. Austerity has encouraged competition for welfare services and jobs within the working class, resulting in a steep rise in ethnic or religious identification and xenophobia throughout the world (Panitch and Leys 2002). Insecurity of personal and household income, widening of individual and household incomes, erosion of welfare services, and weakening of established community ties by enforced migration, have weakened cultures of collectivity and mutuality and encouraged anomie and possessive individualism (Vail, Wheelock and Hill 1999; Sennett 1998; Beck 2001). In the developed countries particularly, workers, even the poor, come to blame *themselves* for their problems (Galbraith 1992). The disavowal of responsibility for economic and social wellbeing by neoliberal states has further inhibited working class political involvement. Socio-economic weakening of open, formal popular organisation, and states' and capital's repression, have meant that much collective organisation is (semi-) illegal, hidden within sub-cultures (Scott, 2005).

Thus neoliberalism has had major success in its central objectives – to atomise and individualise the world working class, weaken collective organisations in both production and social spheres, and depoliticise the population by imposing 'the rule of markets'.

Since the 1990s, however, there has been a certain revival of both militant unionism and urban struggles (Moody 1997; R. Cox 1999; Merrifield 2002; Leitner et al. 2007). This process has been highly uneven between countries due to in part to differences in the severity of the attacks on living standards, in the effective fragmentation of the working class, and in direct repression. Resistance has also varied with territorially-specific political-economic traditions which can be durable over many decades and to some extent survive changes in global regulation such as neoliberalism; even among the HICs there are enormous variations in 'national regimes' (Coates 2000). Thus in the US, Britain, Canada, Australia and Japan since the 1980s, and the former Eastern Block countries since 1989, collective resistance has been weak. By contrast, in many EU countries since the 1990s there have been militant struggles around jobs, pensions, unemployment and racism. In these countries local and regional governments have in some cases been able to maintain or innovate some top-down, mildly social democratic policies, partially shielding their populations from neoliberalism; in the US, the weakness of social democracy has meant that this role has in some places been played by innovative community development initiatives (Williamson et al. 2002). Countries in the Majority World which have achieved strong long term growth have nevertheless experienced accumulation and/or financial crises which have elicited much militant, even explosive, collective action, even in the face of brutal repression; this has tended to remain localised because of repression of national popular networks (Sanyal 2008). In those parts of the Majority World with low or negative growth, the economic weakness of the working class has mostly enabled dictatorial regimes to prevent collective action for economic and social aims, or to channel it into inter-ethnic conflict; this is true of most of the Middle East and Africa, and to some extent India. In many of the poorest countries, regions are controlled by warlords and the big cities by criminal gangs; in this hyper-neoliberalism, there is no question of progressive politics by workers and residents. It is in Latin America that popular resistance to neoliberalism has been strongest, including movements of the rural poor, struggles by unionised and unemployed workers and by *indigenos,* often organised at the neighbourhood level, mostly against the state; these have led to the formation of left or social democratic governments (Panizza 2005). Overlaid on these national differences are, in many nations, large differences in the strength of the left between regions and localities (Jonas 1996; Agnew 1997; K. Cox 1998). The possibilities for building left initiatives at a local level, then, start from very different positions in different continents, countries and localities.

3   **Strategic Ideas for Left Local Politics**

3.1   *Class, Collectivity and the Local*
In these circumstances, how can left initiatives be built against neoliberal disempowerment using the local scale? Basic principles should be to combat neoliberal individualism and anomie by building wide, varied and comprehensive collective *organisations* of ordinary people, developing collective *control* over

the economy, enhancing collective *social reproduction,* and thus extending *democracy* through all aspects of society. Empowerment must be collective to combat the market-fatalism that social atomisation has created, to provide force of numbers against capital and (often) the state, and to begin to plan production and reproduction according to genuinely social criteria. This implies that a social democratic strategy limited to progressive policies carried out top-down by the local state (for example Allmendinger 2003) is inadequate. But equally, a libertarian/anarchist strategy limited to building islands of progressive practice such as individual social enterprises (Gibson-Graham 1996) or Foucauldian heterotopias (Genocchio 1995; MacCannell 2008) is inadequate in that it organises only a small elite, does not confront capital, and does not offer solutions for the majority of the population; it therefore cannot develop broad, strong organisations and action.

A strategy of collective organisation needs to be rooted in, though not limited to, the local scale. This scale facilitates the involvement of increasing numbers of people through the immediacy and visibility of local problems of economic, social and cultural life. Collective organisation can draw on existing bonds of friendship, acquaintance and trust. The sharp constraints of money and time that most people have for participation in politics are easiest to overcome with local organisation. In some cases, longstanding local traditions of solidarity can be drawn on (Wills, 1998). Thus Sklair (1998) argues that, even to confront the major *global* institutions and practices of power, local action is the essential starting point – even though this needs to be multiplied and linked at higher spatial scales. The local scale is thus essential to a strategy of collective organisation and action. It is then possible to build 'a sense of local community' and 'local social capital', not as reinforcement of local hierarchy and competition with other localities, but in a progressive way which can contest power (Cowley et al. 1977; Massey 1993; Craig and Mayo 1995).

Collective working-class organisations are, in the first place, *oppositional* to capital and the state rather than 'constructive', since by definition they do not have control over the major social resources. Trade unions form and develop through defence against employers. Residents' organisations make demands on the local state and on property, infrastructural and service capital. This organisation around immediate, daily needs can involve large numbers of people in organisation and activity. The practical-oppositional nature of working class organisation is neglected by some 'Gramscian' strategists who see the *central* task of a progressive movement as being the construction of an alternative hegemonic ideology (Laclau and Mouffe 1985; Hall and Jacques 1989); this privileges the activity of left intellectuals and marginalises all others, and dodges addressing the immediate material needs of the majority. It is also glossed over by theorists who deny or downplay the existence of 'power over' (Allen, 2003) and who propose alternatives based on Deleuzian networks (Amin and Thrift 2002; Swyngedouw 2008); it is at best unclear how such networks can confront the major forms of power in contemporary society (Slair 1998; Chapter 2, section 1). Similarly, the oppositional nature of working class organisation is neglected by those, including all the major global institutions, who propose the building of *generic* 'social capital' in working class, especially poor, communities (World Bank 2000; Social Exclusion Unit 2001). This approach occludes how social capital and civil society are profoundly shaped by capital and the state (R.Cox 1999), and that local relations between people are *specific* to particular social projects and thus particular political strategies (Chapter 3; Fine 2001).

The crucial organisations here are not only those of the poor – the target group for so many mainstream local economic initiatives – but those of the whole working class, including the salaried middle class. Throughout industrial capitalism the non-poor have had had better formal organisation than the poor because of their stronger position in production and greater resources for organising; and in recent decades the poor have tended further to loose organisational capacity through economic and social atomisation and the drugs industry. A symptom of this problem is that in recent years the poor and deracinated have found expression for their anger in fruitless rioting, inter-ethnic fights, and battles with the police which lead nowhere, as instanced in South Los Angeles in 1992, British cities in 1981 and 1991, the Paris *banlieux* in 2004, and Greece in winter 2008–9. While some romantic anarchists have praised rioting (e.g. Zizek 2008), its only achievement is to legitimate intensified state repression, including of long standing working class organisations. Besides, in the last 30 years the non-poor have acquired increasing reasons for self-organisation and militancy. Job loss, insecurity, deskilling, loss of autonomy within work, and erosion of pensions and welfare services started with unskilled workers but have moved upwards through middle layers to professionals. Thus during the crisis of 2001–3 in Argentina, the middle class played a substantial role in local mobilisations (Ozarow 2007). The struggle specifically against extreme poverty therefore needs to link collective action of the poor to mainstream working class organisations; the latter have an interest in this since poverty is essentially a distillation and concentration of oppressions experienced by all the working class. If this link is made, then the poor will have more effective means of organisation than the riot (Gough and Eisenschitz, 2006: Ch.12). Left local strategy, then, can and should encompass organisation of the great majority of the population, from the poor to the middle class.

3.2   The Local State, Capital and Social Enterprises

While workers' organisations are in the first place oppositional, a left strategy cannot be *simply* in opposition to the local state. In all but the poorest countries, the local state has substantial powers and resources which the left needs to use and develop. Basic services such as education, health, social housing and environmental services cannot be adequately provided for without the taxation and borrowing powers of the state, and the socialisation of the economy cannot proceed without the powers and funds of the state. The left therefore needs to resist cuts in spending on useful services and restriction of local governments' abilities to tax and borrow, and defend direct state delivery of services against fragmentation into cost centres, contracting out, quangoisation and outright privatisation (Whitfield 2006). It needs to defend, or push for, egalitarian delivery of services which empower users and build their sociability, as for example in the revolutionary education practices of Reggio Emilia in Italy (Dahlberg and Moss 2006).

The left also needs to defend the existing powers of the local state to regulate investment, for example in the built environment, and to run trading enterprises. More ambitiously, it needs to push the local state to intervene into the local economy on the side of workers (Greater London Council 1985; Cumbers and Whittam 2007). The local economy is centrally important not just because most people's incomes depend on it, but also because it determines workers' autonomy, quality of labour and ability to organise within the working day. Local production politics has, however, to recognise that it may not be possible, in the medium term, to gain the necessary powers or funding.

'Support for state action' does not, though, mean allowing elected representatives and state officers a free hand. On the contrary, collective organisations in civil society need to impose continuous pressure on the local state, open up its processes of decision-making to inspection, and become an integral part of that decision-making – in short, a real and popular democracy. For example, any state policies involving employment and production need to be made in association with the relevant trade unions, and pupils, parents and teachers' organisations need to direct schools. Such possibility of real influence also encourages wider and more active participation in those collective organisations, which is the best insurance against their bureaucratisation, capture by 'leaders', or corruption (which are chronic problems everywhere). The Argentinian *piqueteros* negotiated for the neighbourhood in the street in order to put pressure on the state representatives and to prevent clientalist corruption (Starr 2005). Since the local state is formally controlled by political parties, left trajectories for the local state are also furthered by the development of left parties genuinely responsive to their membership and committed to working class interests. Politicians from such parties who control local government can both 'take the local state outwards' through supporting popular organisations and actions, and take these organisations 'into the local state' by making it more open and responsive to them (Wainwright 1994: Ch.7).

A corollary is that the oldest and still most popular aim of the left, extending democracy, is not achieved simply or mainly by extending formal methods of participation in local government: 'participation' needs to be of a form which achieves radical results. Collective organisations need to achieve real control and design of state services, investments and regulation of private interests (Eisenschitz, 2008). If this does not happen, participation simply results in demoralisation of people and bureaucratisation of their organisations. In particular, decentralisation of state powers and spending from nation to region to locality to neighbourhood in the name of increasing participation – a current consensus from right to left – is meaningless unless the smaller scale facilitates greater popular control over resources and powers. Moreover, for the left 'extending democracy' should not concern merely the state but private capital and indeed social enterprises: for socialists, the disempowerment of working people within production is central to their social, political and cultural disempowerment. If production is, then, to be subjected to greater democratic control, this must be partly through the direct actions of local collective organisations. Given these caveats, extensions of democracy into the state and economy can form virtuous circles, whereby ordinary people come to understand social mechanisms better, feel greater ability to change them, and thus propose more radical solutions.

These considerations raise important dilemmas concerning the contracting out of local state services to not-for-profit enterprises and the voluntary sector. This type of contracting out has been a major aspect of reform of local government in, for example, Britain; the Labour government has argued that 'the Third Sector' is more plural, democratic, responsive and innovative compared with the 'bureaucratic' and 'inflexible' state (Paxton and Pearce 2005). Some centre-left commentators of a post-modern or associationist bent have supported this process on the grounds that it empowers civil society, democratises the services, and weakens the overbearing state (Amin and Thrift 2002). It is true that non-state organisation have sometimes delivered essential services in ways which are more visionary and innovative than departments of the local state. For brief periods of crisis, community enterprises may form something of an alternative that may be a means of reshaping the state. In the city of Mosconi in Argentina, for instance, there were 300 projects built by well-organised grassroots organisations that effectively developed a parallel local state (Starr 2005). But the left needs to be cautious before calling for wholesale hand-over to the Third Sector. In the first place, these services remain dependent on state funding; the projects in Mosconi, for instance, relied on local and national state funding, World Bank-backed workfare schemes, and the goodwill of local oil firms (Schaumberg 2008: 378). Contracting out to the voluntary and community sector is taking place for the same, neoliberal reasons as contracting out to private firms: to lower wages and conditions, and to depoliticise services by passing the buck for ensuring their quality. This has fragmented service delivery, created greater unevenness across localities, and made it more difficult for the local state to pursue pro-working class policies (Chapter 2, section 4.2; Mayer 2007). A strong, continuing role for the local state in delivery of services is in our view essential in order to ensure their universality, equity and quality, and in order that they can be democratically planned across the locality. But, as we have just argued, these very roles of the local state need to be opened up to much greater control by residents, clients and service workers. The left needs to ensure that social enterprises funded to provide essential services do not under-cut public sector employment conditions, are genuinely democratically accountable, are efficient, and are not corrupt. Under these conditions, their innovativeness can help to make the services directly run by the state more innovative. With this kind of approach, many different concrete articulations of the local state, community organisations, and collective social groups are possible in delivering essential services.

A related debate concerns the role of social enterprises and worker cooperatives in producing marketed commodities. Some associationist (Cooke and Morgan 1998; Gibson-Graham 1996) and market-socialist (Nove 1983; Sayer 1995) authors argue that a *comprehensive system* of such enterprises, relating through markets, is a potential, feasible alternative to capitalist production. They argue that it is a desirable one since it allows workers much greater autonomy and control within their enterprises, increases innovativeness and productivity, and spatially decentralises decision-making. If this were so, then the left has a simple, comprehensive alternative to both state and market (Catterall et al. 1996); Mance (2009) speaks of social enterprises as 'the material base of post capitalist societies'. In the last decades there have indeed been many local left initiatives to support such enterprises (Pearce 2003). However, once again, we think that the left should not pursue producer cooperatives operating in free markets as the *only* strategy for production of commodities (Gough and Eisenschitz 1997; 2006: 216–21). Cooperatives tend to be under-capitalised and thus find it hard to out-compete the private sector. They often rely for survival on self-exploitation of the workforce. They typically need the state for both funding and coordination, so that they cannot so easily escape the state's 'dead hand' (see Chapter 2, section 4). We therefore need strategies for local state production and left strategies within-and-against the existing private sector. And since left strategy for social enterprise, in both state-funded services and commodity production, is far from straightforward, as we discuss further in section 5.

3.3   Connecting Different Aspects of Local Life

Left local strategies need to address all aspects of the locality *holistically*, in particular combating the characteristic splits in capitalist society between production and reproduction, the public sphere and the home, economy, social life and culture, and society and nature (Meszaros 1995: 464ff). Left strategy should refuse the division between 'economic', 'social', 'environmental' and 'cultural' policy-making. For example, democratisation of privately-controlled production means not only pushing for more skilled and autonomous work (Hales 1980; Cooley 1987) but also changing its goods and services towards basic human needs (Mackintosh and Wainwright 1987: Ch.7; Elson 1988). While reproduction of people under capitalism is centred on private domestic work and private use of commodities purchased, these are in fact strongly *socially* constructed, particularly by capital; left strategy should aim to make this socialisation conscious and democratic, whether it be food and nutrition, the geography of retailing, the design of housing, or public transport versus the car. In each of these areas there can be collaboration between workers in the service and residents consuming it, redesigning the service for the benefit of both groups (Lavelette and Mooney 2000; on housing see Arkitektkontor AB 1974; on public transport see GLC, 1985: Ch.20). Moreover, safeguarding of ecosystems through local action nearly always involves decisions which span the spheres of production and social life. Such actions across the two spheres are the best way of developing a culture of *care* for both humans and nature, by posing the question of the *aims* of production (use values versus private profit) and the nature of human and ecosystem *needs*. Such actions can expose the alienated nature of both production and consumption under capitalism (Pepper 1993).

Moreover, they imply collaboration between popular organisations in the respective spheres – trade unions, residents groups and social movements – and hence their mutual support. These alliances can be very powerful: for example, in Glasgow during the First World War and in Turin in 1969–70, strong and militant union organisation inspired revolts in the social sphere – rent strikes for rent controls in the former case, mass squatting of housing and free public transport in the second. These collaborations are not always easy, however: there are likely to be tensions between local groups due to their different preoccupations and foci: for example, workers in polluting industries may clash with local residents' groups; male workers may not see the point of expanding nursery provision; users of cars may be unwilling to see their use restricted. But the *local* level is the ideal scale at which to thrash out these disagreements and negotiate practical ways forward, since the different groups can meet face-to-face and also directly inspect the concrete local facts.

3.4   The Problem of Spatial Scale

While the locality is a necessary and potentially powerful scale for left action, this always needs to be linked into higher spatial scales. The world is constructed through the relations between territories, but by the same token each locality is constructed by its relations to others. The key task considered in this chapter, of constructing solidarity and collectivity *within* localities, is thus inseparable from constructing them at wider spatial scales (Swyngedouw 2000; Gough 2010). In modern society, social actors within any locality have powerful impacts on society and nature outside it. Conversely, progressive actions within localities can easily be undermined by markets in land, production, commodities and money operating at larger scales, by firms based outside the locality, and by spatially-higher levels of the state (Obi 2005). The latter problem is worse the smaller the 'locality' (another reason why spatial decentralisation of state decision-making can be counter-productive). The limitations of the local are *less* the more broad and inclusive are the local collective organisations (so that higher scale pressures do not so easily create divisions), and the more holistic are the initiatives being taken (so that the democratic forms of social and economic life in the locality have greater resilience). But the scale problem cannot be avoided. In consequence, local collective organisation always needs to seek the greatest solidarity and cooperation with similar organisations elsewhere. This solidarity is especially necessary when localities are linked by capital's investments: gains by workers in one workplace or locality can be easily undermined by capital (and workers) elsewhere in the same industry unless workers cooperate across space (Hudson and Sadler 1986; Gough 2004: Ch.13; Gough 2010). To the extent that a local civil society begins to direct local government in progressive ways, it needs to prevent undermining by both other local governments and the nation state. Thus left organisation, strategy and transformation at higher spatial scales are essential to any left local advance that is to last more than a year or two. To change the hallowed slogan, 'think *and* act locally *and* globally'.

Such cooperation across localities and nations cannot rely on the state nor even on national and international bureaucracies of popular organisations such as trade unions: it has to be built from the bottom up. Thus on employment, in recent years a new National Shop Stewards Network has been constructed in Britain, and many international campaigning organisations have been built from the grass-roots (Moody 1997) – an early pioneer was the Transnational Information Exchange (Chapkis and Enloe 1983). In the last fifteen years or so a loosely organised movement against neoliberal globalisation (or 'alter-globalisation movement') has emerged linking national, and to a lesser extent local, unions, community organisations and progressive NGOs. So far, this movement has not organised any large scale actions, but has yielded many bilateral cooperations (Amoore 2005; Routledge and Cumbers 2009).

Through this kind of overall strategy, the depoliticisation wrought by neoliberalism can start to be reversed, as the social nature of daily life becomes increasingly evident and it begins to be more strongly subject to collective political debate and action. These processes are path dependent; in particular, existing consciousness and socio-economic practices may mean that apparently modest reforms can have radical dynamics. We have noted the very different degrees of collective organisation and militancy between countries and localities, and these will affect how bold initiatives can be. Moreover, left tactics need to vary over time: in Britain for example, rather than simply resisting privatisation, we need to bring services back into public ownership. Tactics are important for the local left.

4   Fields of Action

4.1   *Struggles around Jobs*

The workplace is the most essential scale for trade union organisation and contestation: larger scale workers' organisation has no base and no purchase without it. The daily interactions between workers within the workplace, and the recognition of their common situation there, are the basis for collective organisation. At the workplace scale workers can act rapidly, and in ways that provide a spectacle of resistance in walk-outs, pickets and occupations, helping to win support from other workers *and* residents in the locality (Hudson and Sadler 1986; Jonas, 1998).

If the workplace is profitable, then it can be possible for workers to gain concessions from management through action restricted to that workplace; this was often done, for example, in large manufacturing plants in Britain in the 1960s, and this developed a strongly decentralised union movement. But when profitability is low or there is overcapacity in the industry, purely local action is insufficient: management can threaten to close the workplace if workers resist restructuring or wage cuts; and if workers are successful in keeping *their* plant open, this will tend to cause job loss elsewhere in the industry or multi-plant firm (Herod 1997; Harvey 1996: Ch.1). The spatial divisions and competition between workers orchestrated by management can be combatted only by cooperation between workers in different workplaces within the industry. The logic of such cooperation is then for unions to begin to monitor patterns of investment and disinvestment across the industry, at scales from the locality to the globe depending on the sector, and then begin to make demands on that investment: the germs of socialist planning (Gough 2004: 269–83; Gough 2010).

Where there is a locally-centred industrial district or dense local subcontracting linkages between workplaces, unions can gain strength from organising within the industry across workplaces, sometimes using blockage of contracting linkages for bargaining (GLC 1985: Ch.15; Castree et al. 2004: 162–5); powerful *local* solidarity can thus be developed. This approach can sometimes be used in industrial districts where workers and employers belong to the same minority ethnicity. The employers often use ethnicity to subordinate their workforce (Kakios and van der Velden 1984); but workers may use community bonds to organise *their* solidarity, as have the Turkish and Kurdish workers in the London clothing industry.

The local scale is also an essential one for organising the worst-organised workers. The extreme exploitation of most homeworkers can be addressed through community-based campaigns (Allen and Wolkowitz 1987). A large proportion of the workforce in HICs now works in small, non-unionised workplaces of diverse sectors within each locality. These have been addressed by 'community unionism' targeted on industrial neighbourhoods and using those spaces to develop solidarity (Wills 2001). 'Living wage' campaigns based in particular cities or neighbourhoods have successfully organised to improve wages of low paid, often casualised, sometimes illegal-immigrant, service workers, including those that work in small work units such as caretakers and cleaners (Savage 1998; Figart 2004). Thus London Citizens, based in residential-community, minority-ethnic and church organisations, has worked with unions to secure a living wage well above the national minimum wage for groups of low paid workers, something the unions alone had not achieved (Holgate and Wills 2007). In globally-traded goods, such local campaigns can be further strengthened through international networks of solidarity (Ross 1997). The recent successful unionisation drives among delivery (Deliveroo), taxi (Uber), warehouse (Amazon) and restaurant (Starbucks) workers have originated in local organisation, though sometimes successfully generalised to the national firm. Finally, the local scale is an essential one for organising the unemployed since they are outside (larger scale) production-related networks. In recent years local organisation has been the basis for regional and national marches and actions of the unemployed in some European countries, reconnecting them with employed workers and residents (Mathers 2007).

In times of acute crisis, workers' collective actions of different types can catalyse each other across a locality. Thus in the crisis of the early 2000s in Argentina militant neighbourhood assemblies and local organisations of the unemployed posed an alternative power to capital and state. With this support, workers in many localities tried to seize the means of production, despite more than half of workers being in the informal sector (Schaumberg 2008); some 170 cooperatives were formed as workers took control of (mostly small) closed factories (Dinerstein 2007).

Altogether, then, localities remain essential, though not sufficient, sites for workers' collective resistance to capital.

4.2   The Organisation of Production and Investment

Despite the very limited resources and powers of local and regional government around production (albeit with big variation between countries), there are progressive policies which they may be able to implement or at least push for. First, the local state may be able to invest in and run trading enterprises. The local authority in Glasgow, USA, for instance, provided a local telecommunications network giving a cheaper and better internet connection for residents and attracting strong inward investment (Williamson et al. 2002: 152). Such investments or plans for them can be used to put in question the efficiency and social impacts of private production (on building work see Direct Labour Collective 1978; on telecoms see GLC 1985: Ch.16).

Secondly, there is powerful legitimacy for the local state to bring into use underused resources, be they unemployed workers or unused land and buildings. The political point is further reinforced if these resources are used for innovative forms of production, for example worker cooperatives, skilled and autonomous forms of work, or socially-useful products.

Thirdly, investment money may be channelled into the locality by using political pressure on the major holders of savings, the pension funds and insurance companies; the latter are vulnerable to this pressure because they hold working people's savings. In social democratic countries such as Sweden trade unions have long had a say in how their industry's pension fund is invested; in other countries, unions and local governments can apply pressure for the same ends (Minns 1980; Blackburn 2003). Again, the point should be to democratise and politicise the process of investment and the choices it involves, for example to prioritise high unemployment areas or green production.

Fourthly, it is possible to take local initiatives in money circulation which put into question its capitalist forms. Local money (Monbiot 2009) can increase circulation and, if it stimulates corresponding production, is non-inflationary. Thus the city government of Curitiba in Brazil paid its own workforce partly in local money which it had organised for local municipal and private services to accept, leading to rapid local economic growth. In Argentina there was a massive growth in local voucher schemes from 1995 in response to economic collapse; the number of these *Trueques* peaked at 4700 in the 2002 crisis; the vouchers were exchangeable between schemes, creating an effective second national currency. The schemes enabled the unemployed, particularly women, to market their labour power, micro-enterprises and a few larger worker cooperatives to be set up, abandoned buildings and land to be used, unsold production from local factories to be exchanged, and local services to gain adequate custom. Half of surveyed local households made over half their income through the schemes, and many subsistence goods could be purchased with vouchers (Gomez and Helmsing 2008). Local Exchange and Trading Schemes (LETS) organise direct exchange of individuals' labour time, enabling production and consumption of useful services, albeit limited to those without substantial fixed capital or economies of scale (Walker and Goldsmith 2001). Cooperatively-owned credit unions or local government-owned peoples' banks can provide much better terms for savings and borrowing than the private sector (Fuller and Jonas 2003). All these forms of money make the link between production and consumption more direct and transparent, and thus encourage a *social* view of the local economy.

4.3   The Social Economy

The 'Third Sector', not-for-profit enterprises or the 'social economy' can play an important role in left strategy, by demonstrating the possibilities for workers' or residents' control of the enterprise, social innovation, production directly to meet social needs, and efficient production without capitalist direction. South Central Farm in Los Angeles, for example, improved food quality and security, preserved traditions of a peasant community recently uprooted to the city, and enabled members to develop as individuals and as a collective; the potentially militant dynamic of such initiatives is shown by the strong fight waged to take the land into community ownership (Irazabal, and Punja 2009: 11). However, social enterprises can equally well serve rightwing politics: they may survive through self-exploitation, with wages, hours and conditions inferior to the industry average; they may be used to habituate people to poor employment; they may be under-resourced self-help, an inferior substitute for formal welfare services; and the state may contract out to them in order to cut wages and conditions; in short, they may teach 'standing on your own two feet' rather than working class cooperation (Eick 2007). In Britain at present, for example, the social economy inclines more to the rightwing than the leftwing model (Amin et al. 2002; Fuller and Jonas 2003).

To lead the social economy in a leftwards direction strategy is therefore vital (Chapter 6; Medoff and Sklar 1994). Social enterprises need to form the strongest possible ties to unionised workers in mainstream production, by being unionised and by tapping into the technical expertise of mainstream workers; they can then, reciprocally, show the latter the advantages of having immediate control over one's production process. Adequate capital should be secured from the local state (including as land and buildings), from socialised finance, or from recycling of profits from other social enterprises. Economic and political economies of scale should be sought through networking of community enterprises locally, nationally and internationally. There are global networks that attempt to build cooperation between the millions of people involved in the social economy worldwide. These explicitly liberatory campaigns seek to generate synergies of alternative finance, local currencies, fair trade, ethical consumption and low impact technologies, using a variety of ownership forms. The accumulation of political strength is important since the social economy has to constantly fight against being legally marginalised by lobbying from private business. With this kind of strategy, the social economy can complement and radicalise, rather than undermine, increases in workers' influence within mainstream production and the extension of democratic state-owned production.

However, a liberatory social economy is dependent on left advance in the whole society, without which community-based organisations tend merely to manage their place within capitalist markets. Petras (1997) argues that Latin American NGOs from the 1980s moved from progressive politics to becoming neoliberalism's community face. In Argentina, the radical community-based initiatives in welfare and production of the early 2000s withered when the Kirchner government used the national scale to seize the political initiative from the left. Only 10% of the *Trueques* present in 2002 survived until 2007, and this was partly due to lack of support from and integration with local governments (Gomez and Helmsing, 2008). In the US employee ownership of firms has not made any fundamental challenge to capitalism (Williamson et al., 2002). Particularly in times of economic decline, wider left advance is needed for worker- and community-controlled enterprises to maintain their radical dynamics.

4.4   *Fighting Social Oppressions*

Various social oppressions are substantially – though never wholly – constructed within localities, and many radical struggles against them have had this scale (Craig and Mayo 1995; Gough and Eisenschitz 2006: 131–5, 224–8). The oppression of women is rooted in local relations between home, neighbourhood and waged work. Campaigns for more social care for children and the infirm, better housing, housing suitable for varied households, closer proximity of home, waged work, public and private services, more convenient and free public transport, and for women's equality within waged work, can lead to practical gains, and can show that apparently individual problems are social and have collective solutions (Rowbotham 1989; Greed 1994; Darke, Lewith and Woods 2000). Racism's deepest roots are in relations between the national and international scales. But racism is strongly expressed and developed within localities, and is fought there in campaigns for equality in housing, education and health care and against super-exploitation in waged work (Sivanandan 1990). Mainly locally-based campaigns for safety in both homes and public spaces have been waged by black people, women, and lesbians and gay men (Rowbotham 1989; Bhavnani and Coulson 2005). Neighbourhood and local scales are vital *cultural* supports to all these struggles, since antagonistic groups there confront each other not as abstractions but face-to-face and thus, potentially, as full persons. For example, campaigns to stop deportation of refugees in Britain have had their greatest success in stubborn defence of refugees by their British neighbours who have befriended them (Hayter 2000); conversely, some of the worst racism in Britain is found in regions such as Cumbria and East Anglia with very few black or immigrant residents. Local settings can thus be powerful in overcoming prejudice and developing practical solidarity.

4.5   Housing and Land

The last 40 years have seen rapid inflation in house prices throughout the high and medium income countries, resulting for the majority of the working class in drain on income, poor accommodation, overcrowding, insecurity, and blocking of inter-local migration. This crisis has been caused by insufficient new building to meet monetarily-effective demand, let alone need, plus a massive channelling of capital into property via direct investment and credit, much of it directed at speculative gain (Harvey 1989: Ch.2; Turner 2008). The socialist left internationally has been extraordinarily unsuccessful in pushing for expanded supply of affordable housing. This is in part due to the legal, institutional and financial structures of housing provision being almost entirely in the hands of *nation* states.

The most substantial local struggles around housing under neoliberalism have been to defend poor people's occupation of, or tenure in, *existing* stock. In the 1970s and 1980s, there was mass squatting by the poor in the fast-growing northern Italian cities, and in many HICs widespread squatting, mainly by young people, in high-value empty housing in central cities. However, state violence against squatters increased, and further rises in value have meant declining space available for squatting in major cities. There have also been struggles to oppose eviction of long-standing poor residents from CBD-fringe neighbourhoods to make way for commercial buildings and expensive apartments (Gough and Gundogdu, 2009); in recent years the latter has been a central part of the vaunted 'urban renaissance' (Swyngedouw, Moulaert and Rodriguez 2002). In the 1970s and 1980s these defensive campaigns had some successes (Wates 1976; Tuckett 1988); but more recently there have been few successes and many defeats; most of the successes have been in defending or setting up work and living spaces for low-income creative self-employed people (Porter and Shaw 2009). This deterioration reflects, in part, the ever-increasing profits from CBD-fringe development, and the consequent increasing ruthless of developers and state in pushing it through; creative spaces can, however, sometimes be welcomed as adding 'vibrancy'. Another form of resistance, in Britain and Germany for example, has been of social housing tenants to (semi-) privatisation of their homes; well-organised neighbourhood campaigns have had some successes here, though without reversing the national policies.

These campaigns, however, have been essentially defensive, and have not achieved new programmes to *increase the supply* of affordable housing. Yet given the manifest disaster of neoliberal housing provision, now exacerbated by the recession, left campaigns for affordable housing could be very popular, as they were in the 19th and early 20th century HICs. Left strategy should focus on the partial de-commodification of housing, through state and cooperative ownership (Bowie 2008) funded by control of the major national and international investment funds, zero-carbon construction by state-owned or cooperative building firms backed by the builders' unions, and state appropriation of empty housing. While this is essentially a national task, local actions can dramatise the housing shortage, for example through small-scale state and community building as well as resistance to city-fringe evictions, boycott by building workers of demolition of low-income housing (as in the Sydney 'green bans' in the 1970s: Mundey 1981), or coordinated mass squatting of empty property. The vast experience of self-build on squatted land in Third World cities over the last fifty years suggests another possible avenue; but this constructs slums unless tied to collective organisation of building as in Venezuela under Chavez, to legalisation of occupation, to provision of physical infrastructures by the state.

Such campaigns point towards social ownership of all land. Private ownership of land, extended by neoliberalism, is a deep, chronic generator of privatised culture (Low and Smith 2003), whereas its public ownership is a palpable assertion of the primacy of the social. Capital gains to private owners from change of land use are a gross example of unearned income, and so lack legitimacy: the left should push for their full appropriation by the state (Massey and Catalano 1978: 188–90; Sandercock 1979: Ch.6).

Again, national legislation is key. But local actions around major office and luxury-housing developments and the state's facilitation of them can make propaganda for the socialisation of land (Oudenampsen 2008; Holgersen 2008). More positively, with legislative backing social ownership of land may be developed as local community ownership, where gains from land development can be used for locally-determined social good, whether in further fixed investment or in welfare services. This was the strategy of the early 20th century Garden City movement in Britain; today the community trust in Letchworth has a property income of £6m, used for social purposes. Such land ownership can breed radical political dynamics. Thus Boston's Dudley Street Neighbourhood Initiative managed to appropriate the private landlords, and used this political momentum to develop strong policies on jobs, health, education, transport and local services (Medoff and Sklar 1994). However, the left needs to guard against governments using development values as an excuse to cut direct state funding, and in ways which exacerbate spatial uneven development. Thus in recent years in Britain, with little central state funding for social housing, local governments have been forced to negotiate social housing as 'planning gain' from private development, hence subordinating it to the market. The Development Trusts which have multiplied in poor neighbourhoods of Britain in recent years often own fixed assets; but this has been used to make anti-poverty measures a local responsibility dependent on low-value resources (Development Trusts Association 2008). Community asset management can be used in depoliticising ways (Aiken, Cairns and Thake 2008). Community land ownership needs to be an additional gain, not compensation for cuts in other fields.

4.6 *Participatory Budgeting*

Participatory budgeting, in which neighbourhood assemblies have control over the local state's spending in their neighbourhood, was pioneered in 1989 by the far-left government of Porto Alegre. It has since been taken up in many localities in Latin America and beyond (Sintomer et al. 2008), sometimes under strong pressure from the working class (Rogers 2005: 5). In Porto Alegre decisions on annual priorities for capital investment were discussed in open neighbourhood assemblies; these decisions were then centralised through delegates to boroughs and from them to the city, which then decided on distribution *between* boroughs. This method politicised local government and elicited extraordinary participation from the population, especially from previously-marginalised women, black people, those without secondary education and unskilled workers; in the first five years, 8% of the adult population was involved at some stage (Abers 1998). The process stimulated the formation of neighbourhood associations and self-organisation of blacks, disabled people and the elderly (Bairerle 2002). Over the years there was a shift from parochial defence of one's patch to support for the most needy neighbourhoods. Investment switched sharply from prestigious projects mainly used by the better-off to basic infrastructures such as street paving, sewers and schools. Spending became more efficient and less corrupt (Abers 1998).

But, even in Porto Alegre, participatory budgeting has had limitations (Baierle 2002). The delegation structure was not powerful enough to prevent the council bureaucracy continuing its control over city-wide infrastructures. The city was hemmed in by the authority of State and Federal governments which were less democratic and radical. Most importantly, democracy in the city was strongly affected by the overall political atmosphere in the locality and beyond: the Brazilian trade unions were on the offensive in the 1980s but from the 1990s were in retreat in the face of a neoliberal offensive which greatly increased unemployment. Once again we see that formal democracy of the local state cannot be effective if the working class is disempowered and unable to act in the economic and social spheres. Indeed, *under these conditions* formal democratic methods of government may function to *contain* discontent by dividing and co-opting community groups (Cockburn 1977); according to Sintomer et al. (2008) this has indeed been the most common experience of participatory budgeting in recent years.

4.7   *Alternative Accounting Systems*

Economic actors in capitalist society normally make decisions through a calculus of prices and incomes, assumed to arise from exchange in markets. This calculus tends to lock people's strategies into the order of capitalist society, and thus subordinate them to its forms of power (Mohun 1979). Conversely, alternative calculi can potentially challenge capitalist logics. In the field of local and regional politics in particular, in recent years capitalist accounting and criteria have been (increasingly) dominant; the left needs to challenge precisely these notions of 'development' (Pike, Rodriguez-Pose and Tomany 2007).

One alternative approach to accounting has been welfare economics, which uses price calculations but shifts from individual actors in markets to aggregate outcomes for social groups and the public good. Thus cost-benefit analysis puts a price on the impacts of, for example, a major infrastructure investment, including both social actors and phenomena such as noise excluded in the relevant market exchanges. Social impact assessments of (dis)investment decisions can demonstrate their wider benefits and costs, for example how closure of a large workplace imposes costs on the state in lost taxes, income support and health spending and on suppliers in lost income (Glyn 1985). Calculation of a money value of domestic work has sometimes been used to argue for feminist policies (Peterson and Runyan 2005). Such calculations can be useful in showing that capitalist society is not 'economically rational' *even in its own terms*, and in getting people to think socially. But they have limitations. Many calculations assume key prices and incomes as given, as when cost benefit analysis values people's free time as a fixed fraction of their money income (Ball 1979). More profoundly, the calculations do not in themselves reveal the *social relations* which give rise to the initial mis-calculation of costs and benefits. For example, the fact that a workplace closure imposes costs on the local state which may exceed the saving by the firm does not prevent the closure, since the state and the firm are separate social actors subject to quite different social relations. A genuinely radical dynamic here would need to *question and violate these social relations*, for example by the state taking over the firm without compensation.

Another approach to social valuation is that of LETS. LETS does indeed change social relations of production by setting up direct exchange of work without money. Though creating another money (labour time units), it enables revaluation of people's labour, skills, caring work, and even humanity through increased (self-) esteem (Walker and Goldsmith 2001).

Other alternative calculi seek to value 'the non-economic', that is, neither labour nor products of labour. One such is accounting of aspects of the ecosystem, such as green-house gases, water and agricultural land. Again, this accounting is ideologically important for the left in highlighting eco-societal impacts and long-term consequences of present actions, and in pointing the finger at both capitalist production dynamics and mindless consumption. But again, the accounting can be the basis for quite *different* political directions. Are carbon emissions to be fixed in advance, or made to respond to profits and incomes through trading of quotas? A left strategy adopts the former approach, thus violating capitalist logic.

A recently-developed strategy has been 'the economics of happiness' (Layard 2006; Michaelson et al. 2009). Like welfare economics, this starts from a critique of neoclassical economics, arguing that aspects of human wellbeing such as health, education, creativity and general happiness are mis-priced 'by markets' but nevertheless need to be accounted for in economic policy. This work can justify allocating economic resources to support these aspects of wellbeing. But the limitation of this work is that aspects of wellbeing are pictured as quasi-commodities which can be 'delivered' *to individuals*; again, the approach fails to focus on *social relations*. Thus Layard does not critique capitalist social relations of production and the low self-esteem and unhappiness that are intrinsic to exploitation (Marx 1980; Sennett 1998), nor how capitalism generates indifference to others (Geras 1998). Wellbeing is not simply something which individuals have more or less of, but rather lies *within* relations to others. Thus Wilkinson and Pickett (2009) show that the well-being of a country's inhabitants is strongly correlated with low income inequality, that is, with its relations of distribution. At a smaller scale, Baker et al. (2004: Ch.2) argue that a fundamental aspect of wellbeing is being within relationships of care.

Alternative calculi, then, can form critiques of capitalist outcomes and point to social solutions. But the left needs to act on these by challenging the *social relations* which underlie them.

5   Conclusion

Socialist tradition has emphasised solidarity and economic planning at national and international scales. The local scale has been seen as problematic because of the subordination of enterprises and local economies to competition at higher spatial scales, and because of the weaker powers of the local state compared with the national. Neoliberal globalisation is said to have exacerbated these problems. But we have argued that localities are a crucial site for left strategy, because important social and economic relations are enacted and reproduced there, because of dense local relations between economy and social life, and because daily interactions and proximity facilitate building relations of solidarity and collectivity. Transforming social relations at higher spatial scales is certainly necessary, but local struggles are a dialectical moment in this.

The left local strategy discussed here is above all a class policy, against the individualisation and division of the working class which is the foundation of all capitalist power and which has been deepened by neoliberalism. Accordingly, we have given primacy to collective self-organisation and practical collective economics rather than progressive action initiated by capital and the state. The heart of a radical local politics is a journey from individual to collective modes of thinking and acting. This implies a development of place-based community and social capital, not as the commonly-encountered self-subordination of the weak to the strong, but as the solidarity of the weak against the powerful. We hope we have shown that there are many promising tactics for carrying forward this strategy.

References

Abers, R. (1998). Learning democratic practice: distributing government resources through popular participation in Porto Alegre, Brazil. In M. Douglas and J. Friedmann. (Eds.), *Cities for Citizens*, New York: Wiley.

Agnew, J. (1997). The dramaturgy of horizons: geographical scale in the 'reconstruction of Italy' by the new Italian political parties, 1992–1995. *Political Geography, 16*(2): 99–121.

Aiken, M., Cairns, B., & Thake, S. (2008). *Community Ownership and Management of Assets*, York: Joseph Rowntree Foundation.

Allen, J. (2003). *Lost Geographies of Power*. Oxford: Blackwell.

Allen, S., & Wolkowitz, C. (1987). *Homeworking: myths and realities*. Basingstoke: Macmillan.

Allmendinger, P. (2003). From New Right to New Left in UK planning. *Urban Policy and Research, 21*(1): 57–79.

Amin, A., Cameron, A., & Hudson, R. (2002). *Placing the Social Economy,* London: Routledge.

Amin, A., & Thrift, N. (2002). *Cities*. Cambridge: Polity.

Amoore, L. (Ed.). (2005). *The Global Resistance Reader*. London: Routledge.

Arkitektkontor, AB (1974). Urban redevelopment: the Byker experience. *Housing Review, 23*(6): 149–156.

Atkinson, R. (1999). Discourses of partnership and empowerment in contemporary British urban regeneration. *Urban Studies, 36*(1): 59–72.

Baierle, S. (2002). The Porto Alegre Thermidor? Brazil's 'participatory budget' at the crossroads. In L. Panitch, and C. Leys. (Eds.), *Socialist Register 2003*, London: Merlin. 305–328.

Baker, J., Lynch, K., Cantillon, S., & Walsh, J. (2004). *Equality*. London: Palgrave.

Ball, M. (1979) Cost-benefit analysis: a critique, in F. Green and P. Nore (Eds.), *Issues in Political Economy*, London: Macmillan.

Balls, E., & Ealey, J. (Eds.) (2000). *Towards a New Regional Policy*. London: The Smith Institute.

Beck, U. (2001). Living your own life in a runaway world: individualisation, globalisation and politics. In W. Hutton, and A. Giddens (Eds.), *On the Edge: living with global capitalism*. London: Vintage.

Bhavnani, K., & Coulson, M. (2005). Transforming socialist feminism: the challenge of racism. *Feminist Review. 80*: 87–97.

Blackburn, R. (2003). *Banking on Death, or Investing in Life?* London: Verso.

Boddy, M., & Fudge, C. (Eds.). (1984). *Local Socialism*. Basingstoke: Macmillan.

Bowie, D. (2008). *Housing and the Credit Crunch*. London: Compass.

Brown, G. (Ed.). (1975). *The Red Paper on Scotland*. Edinburgh: E.U.S.P.B.

Castree, N., Coe, N., Ward, K., & Samers, M. (2004). *Spaces of Work*. London: Sage.

Caterall B, Lipietz A., Hutton, W., & Girardet, H. (1996). The Third Sector, urban regeneration and the stakeholder. *City. 5–6*: 86–97.

Chapkis, W., & Enloe, C. (1983). *Of Common Cloth: Women in the Global Textile Industry*, Amsterdam: Transnational Institute.

Coates, D. (2000). *Models of Capitalism*. London: Polity.

Cochrane, A. (2007). *Understanding Urban Policy*. Oxford: Blackwell.

Cockburn, C. (1977). *The Local State: Management of Cities and People*. London: Pluto.

Cooke, P., & Morgan, K. (1998). *The Associational Economy*. Oxford: Oxford University Press.

Cooley, M. (1987). *Architect or Bee? The Human Price of Technology*, 2nd ed. London: Hogarth.

Coventry, Liverpool, Newcastle and North Tyneside Trades Councils. (1980). *State Intervention in Industry: a workers' inquiry*. Nottingham: Spokesman.

Cowley, J., Kaye, A., Mayo, M., & Thompson, M. (1977). *Community or Class Struggle?* London: Stage 1.

Cox, K. (1998). Spaces of dependence, spaces of engagement and the politics of scale; or, looking for local politics. *Political Geography, 17*: 1–24.

Cox, R. (1999). Civil society at the turn of the millennium: prospects for an alternative world order. *Review of International Studies, 25*(1): 3–28.

Craig, G., & Mayo, M. (1995). *Community Empowerment*. London: Zed Books.

Cumbers, A., & Whittam, G. (2007). *Reclaiming the Economy*. Biggar: Scottish Left Review Press.

Dahlberg, G., & Moss, P. (2006). Introduction: our Reggio Emilia. In C. Rinaldi (Ed.), *In Dialogue with Reggio Emilia*. London: Routledge.

Darke, J., Lewith, S., & Woods, R. (2000). *Women and the City*. Basingstoke: Palgrave.

Davis, M. (2004). Planet of slums. *New Left Review, 26*: 5–34.

Development Trusts Association. (2008). *Poverty in the UK: The Role of Development Trusts*. London: Development Trusts Association.

Dinerstein, A. (2007). Workers' factory takeovers and new state policies in Argentina: Towards an 'institutionalisation' of non-governmental public action? *Policy and Politics, 35*(3): 529–50.

Direct Labour Collective. (c. 1978). *Building with Direct Labour*. London: Conference of Socialist Economists.

Eick, V. (2007). Space patrols – the new peace-keeping functions of nonprofits: Contesting neoliberalism or the urban poor? In H. Leitner, J. Peck, and E. Sheppard (Eds.), *Contesting Neoliberalism: Urban Frontiers*.

Eisenschitz, A. (2008). Town planning, planning theory and social reform. *International Planning Studies, 13*(2): 133–149.

Eisenschitz, A., & Gough, J. (1993). *The Politics of Local Economic Policy*. Basingstoke: Macmillan.

Elson, D. (1988). Market socialism or socialisation of the market? *New Left Review*, 172: 3–44.

Figart, D. (Ed.). (2004). *Living Wage Movements*. London: Routledge.

Fine, B. (2001). *Social Capital versus Social Theory*. London: Routledge.

Fuller, D., & Jonas, A. (2003). Alternative financial spaces. In A. Leyshon, R. Lee, and C. Williams (Eds.), *Alternative Economic Spaces*. London: Sage.

Galbraith, J.K. (1992). *The Culture of Contentment*. Boston: Houghton Mifflin.

Genocchio, B. (1995). Discourse, discontinuity and difference: the question of 'other' spaces. In S. Watson and K. Gibson (Eds.), *Postmodern Cities and Spaces*. Oxford: Blackwell.

Geras, N. (1998). *The Contract of Mutual Indifference*. London: Verso.

Gibson-Graham, J.K. (1996). *The End of Capitalism (As We Know It)*. Cambridge, Mass.: Blackwell.

Glyn, A. (1985). *The Economic Case against Pit Closures*. Sheffield: National Union of Mine Workers.

Glyn, A., & Harrison, J. (1980). *The British Economic Disaster*. London: Pluto Press.

Gomez, G., & Helmsing, A. (2008). Selective spatial closure and local economic development: what do we learn from the Argentine Local Currency System? *World Development*, 36(11): 2489–2511.

Gough, J. (2003). The genesis and tensions of the English Regional Development Agencies: class relations and scale. *European Urban and Regional Studies*, 10(1): 23–38.

Gough, J. (2004). *Work, Locality and the Rhythms of Capital*. London: Routledge.

Gough, J. (2010). Workers' strategies to secure jobs, their uses of scale, and competing economic moralities: rethinking the 'geography of justice'. *Political Geography*, 29(3): 130–139.

Gough, J., & Eisenschitz, A. (1997). The division of labour, capitalism and socialism: an alternative to Sayer. *International Journal of Urban and Regional Research*, 21(1): 23–37.

Gough, J., & Eisenschitz, A. (2006). *Spaces of Social Exclusion*. London: Routledge.

Gough, J., & Eisenschitz, A. (2010). Local left strategy now, in Pike, A., Rodríguez-Pose, A. and Tomaney, J. (Eds.), *A Handbook of Local and Regional Development*, Abingdon: Routledge.

Gough, J., & Gundogdu, I. (2009). Class-cleansing in Istanbul's world city project, in L. Porter and K. Shaw eds. *Whose Urban Renaissance: An International Comparison of Urban Regeneration Strategies*. London: Routledge.

Greater London Council. (1985). *London Industrial Strategy*. London: GLC.

Greater London Council. (1986). *London Labour Plan*. London: GLC.

Greed, C. (1994). *Women and Planning,* London: Routledge.

Gyford, J. (1985). *The Politics of Local Socialism.* Boston: George Allen and Unwin.

Hales, M. (1980). *Living Thinkwork.* London: CSE Books.

Hall, S., & Jacques, M. (Eds.). (1989). *New Times.* London: Lawrence and Wishart.

Harvey, D. (1989). *The Urban Experience.* Oxford: Blackwell.

Harvey, D. (1996). *Justice, Nature and the Geography of Difference.* Oxford: Blackwell.

Hayter, T. (2000). *Open Borders.* London: Pluto.

Herod, A. (1997). From a geography of labor to a labor of geography: Labor's spatial fix and the geography of capitalism. *Antipode, 29:* 1–31.

Holgate, J., & Wills, J. (2007). Organising labour in London: lessons from the living wage campaign. In Turner, L. and Cornfield, D. (Eds.), *Labour in the New Urban Battlefields.* Cornell: Cornell University Press.

Holgersen, S. (2008). *Class Conflicts and Planning.* Saarbrücken: VDM Verlag.

Hudson, R., & Sadler, D. (1986). Contesting works closures in Western Europe's old industrial regions: defending place or betraying class? In A. Scott and M. Storper (Eds.), *Production, Work, Territory.* London: Allen and Unwin.

Irazabal, C., & Punja, C. (2009). Cultivating just planning and legal institutions: A critical assessment of the South Central farm struggle in Los Angeles. *Journal of Urban Affairs, 31*(1): 1–23.

Jonas, A. (1996). Local labour control regimes: uneven development and the social regulation of production. *Regional Studies, 30:* 323–38.

Jonas, A. (1998). Investigating the local-global paradox. In Herod, A. (Ed.), *Organizing the Landscape.* Minneapolis: University of Minnesota Press.

Kakios, M., & van der Velden, J. (1984). Migrant communities and class politics: The Greek community in Australia. In G. Bottomley and M. de Lepervanche (Eds.), *Ethnicity, Class and Gender in Australia.* Sydney: George Allen and Unwin.

Laclau, E., & Mouffe, C. (1985). *Hegemony and Socialist Strategy.* London: Verso.

Lavelette, M., & Mooney, G. (Eds.). (2000). *Class Struggle and Social Welfare.* London: Routledge.

Layard, R. (2006). *Happiness.* London: Penguin.

Leitner, H., Peck, J., & Sheppard, E. (Eds.). (2007). *Contesting Neoliberalism.* New York: Guilford Press.

London Conference of Socialist Economists. (1980). *The Alternative Economic Strategy,* London: CSE.

Low, S., & Smith, N. (2003). Introduction: The Imperative of Public Space. In S. Low and N. Smith (Eds.). New York: Routledge.

MacCannell, J. (2008). The city at the 'end of history'. In BAVO (Ed.) *Urban Politics Now.* Rotterdam: NAi Publishers.

Mackintosh, M., & Wainwright, H. (Eds.). (1987). *A Taste of Power.* London: Verso.

Mance, A. (2009). Solidarity Economics. *Turbulence.* Retrieved from: http://turbulence.org.uk/turbulence-1/solidarity-economics/ (accessed 15 March 2009).

Marx, K. (1980). Alienated labour and capital. In D. McLellan (Ed.), *Marx's Gundrisse*. London: Macmillan.

Massey, D. (1993). Power-geometry and a progressive sense of place. In J. Bird, B. Curtis, T. Putnam, G. Robertson, and L. Tickner, (Eds.). *Mapping the Futures*. London: Routledge.

Massey, D., & Catalano, A. (1978). *Capital and Land*. London: Arnold.

Mathers, A. (2007). *Struggling for a Social Europe*. Aldershot: Ashgate.

Mayer, M. (2007). Contesting the neoliberalization of urban governance. In H. Leitner, J. Peck, and E. Sheppard (Eds.), *Contesting Neoliberalism: Urban Frontiers*. (Pp. 90–116).

Medoff, P., & Sklar, H. (1994). *Streets of Hope*. Boston: South End Press.

Merrifield, A. (2002). *Dialectical Urbanism: Social Struggles in the Capitalist City*. New York City: Monthly Review Press.

Meszaros, I. (1995). *Beyond Capital: Towards a Theory of Transition*. London: Merlin Press.

Michaelson, J., Abdallah, S., Steuer, N. Thompson, S., & Marks, N. (2009). *Nationa Accounts of Well-Being*. London: New Economics Foundation.

Minns, R. (1980). *Pension Funds and British Capitalism*. London: Heinemann.

Mohun, S. (1979). Ideology, knowledge and neoclassical economics: some elements of a Marxist account. In F. Green, and P. Nore (Eds.), *Issues in Political Economy*. London: Macmillan.

Monbiot, G. (2009). A better way to make money. *The Guardian*, 20 January.

Moody, K. (1997). *Workers in a Lean World*. London: Verso.

Mundey, J. (1981). *Green Bans and Beyond*. Sydney: Angus and Robertson Publishers.

Nove, A. (1983). *The Economics of Feasible Socialism*. London: Allen and Unwin.

Obi, C. (2005). Globalization and local resistance: the case of Shell versus the Ogoni. In L. Amoore (Ed.), *The Global Resistance Reader*. London: Routledge.

Oudenampsen, M. (2008). Amsterdam™, the city as a business. In BAVO (Ed.) *Urban Politics Now*. Rotterdam: NAi Publishers. pp. 100–127.

Ozarow, D. (2007). *Argentina's Nuevos Pobres since the Corralito: from despair to adapting to downward mobility*, unpublished thesis. London University – Institute for the Study of the Americas.

Panitch, L., & Leys, C. (Eds.). (2002). *Socialist Register 2003: Fighting identities*. London: Merlin Press.

Panizza, F. (2005). Unarmed utopia revisited: the resurgence of left-of-centre politics in Latin America. *Political Studies, 53*: 716–734.

Paxton, W., & Pearce, N. (2005). *The Voluntary Sector and the State*. York: Joseph Rowntree Foundation. Retrieved from: http://www.jrf.org.uk/sites/files/jrf/1859353 681.pdf (accessed 2 March 2009).

Pearce, J. (2003). *Social Enterprise in Anytown*. London: Gulbenkian Foundation.

Pepper, D. (1993). *Eco-socialism*. London: Routledge.

Peterson, V., & Runyan, A. (2005). The politics of resistance: women as nonstate, anti-state, and trans-state actors. In L. Amoore *The Global Resistance Reader.* pp. 226–243.

Petras, J. (1997). Imperialism and NGOs in Latin America. *Monthly Review, 49*(7).

Petras, J., & Veltmeyer, H. (2001). *Globalization Unmasked.* New York: Zed.

Pike, A., Rodríguez-Pose, A., & Tomaney, J. (2007). What kind of local and regional development and for whom? *Regional Studies, 41*(9): 1253–69.

Porter, L., & Shaw, K. (2009). *Whose Urban Renaissance?* London: Routledge.

Ramonet, I. (2002). The Social Wars. *Le Monde Diplomatique.* Retrieved from: http://mondediplo.com/2002/11/01socialwars (accessed 12 November 2008).

Rodgers, D. (2005). The politics of participatory budgeting in Buenos Aires. In: Romero, R. (ed.) *Democracia Participativa: una utopía en marcha.* Buenos Aires, Ediciones Cooperativas.

Ross, A. (Ed.). (1997). *No Sweat.* New York City: Verso.

Routledge, P., & Cumbers, A. (2009). *Global Justice Networks.* Manchester: Manchester University Press.

Rowbotham, S. (1989). *The Past Is Before Us.* London: Pandora.

Sandercock, L. (1979). *The Land Racket.* Melbourne: Silverfish Books.

Sanyal, B. (2008). What is new in planning? *International Planning Studies, 13*(2): 151–160.

Savage, L. (1998). Geographies of organizing: Justice for Janitors in Los Angeles, in A. Herod ed. Organizing the landscape: Geographical perspectives on labour unionism. Minneapolis: University of Minnesota press. pp. 225–252.

Sayer, A. (1995). Liberalism, Marxism and urban and regional studies. *International Journal of Urban and Regional Research, 19*(1): 79–95.

Schaumberg, H. (2008). In search of alternatives: the making of grassroots politics and power in Argentina. *Bulletin of Latin American Research, 27*(3): 368–387.

Scott, J. (2005). The infrapolitics of subordinate groups. In Amoore. (Pp. 65–73).

Sennett, R. (1998). *The Corrosion of Character: The Personal Consequences of Work in the New Capitalism.* New York: Norton.

Silver, B., & Arrighi, G. (2000). Workers, North and South, *Socialist Register 2001.* London: Merlin.

Sintomer Y., Herzberg, C., & Rocke, A. (2008). Participatory Budgeting in Europe: Potentials and challenges. *International Journal of Urban and Regional Research, 32*(1): 164–78.

Sivanandan, A. (1990). Britain's Gulags. In A. Sivanandan (Ed.), *Communities of Resistance.* London: Verso.

Sklair, L. (1998). Social movements and global politics, in Jameson, F. and Miyoshi, M. (Eds.), *The Cultures of Globalization.* Durham: Duke University Press.

Social Exclusion Unit. (2001). *Preventing Social Exclusion.* London: SEU.

Starr, A. (2005). *Global Revolt.* London: Zed.

Swyngedouw, E. (2000). Authoritarian governance, power, and the politics of rescaling. *Environment and Planning D: Society and Space, 18*: 63–76.

Swyngedouw, E. (2008). The Post-Political City. In BAVO (Ed.). Urban Politics Now. Rotterdam: NAi Publishers: 58–78.

Swyngedouw, E., Moulaert, F., & Rodriguez, A. (2002). Neoliberal urbanisation in Europe: large scale urban development projects and the new urban policy. In N. Brenner and N. Theodore (Eds.). *Spaces of Neoliberalism*. Oxford: Blackwell.

Tuckett, I. (1988). Coin Street: There is another way. *Community Development Journal, 23*(4): 249–257.

Turner, G. (2008). *The Credit Crunch*. London: Pluto Press.

Vail, J., Wheelock, J., & Hill, M. (Eds.). (1999). *Insecure Times*. London: Routledge.

Wainwright, H. (1994). *Arguments for a New Left*. Oxford: Blackwell.

Walker, P., & Goldsmith, E. (2001). Local money: a currency for every community. In E. Goldsmith and J. Mander (Ed.), *The Case against the Global Economy and for a Turn towards Localization*. London: Earthscan.

Wates, N. (1976). *The Battle for Tolmers Square*. London: RKP.

Whitfield, D. (2006). *New Labour's Attack on Public Services*. Nottingham: Spokesman Books.

Wilkinson, R., & Pickett, K. (2009). *The Spirit Level*. London: Allen Lane.

Wills, J. (2001). Community unionism and trade union renewal in the UK: Moving beyond the fragments at last? *Transactions, Institute of British Geography, 26*(4): 465–83.

Williamson T., Imbroscio, D., & Alperovitz, G. (2002). *Making a Place for Community*. New York: Routledge.

Wills, J. (1998). Space, place, and tradition in working-class organisation. In A. Herod (Ed.), *Organizing the Landscape*. Minneapolis: University of Minnesota Press.

World Bank. (2000). *World Development Report*. Washington D.C.: World Bank.

Zizek, S. (2008). Some politically incorrect reflections on urban violence in Paris and New Orleans and related matters. In BAVO (Ed.). *Urban Politics Now*. Rotterdam: NAi Publishers: 12–30.

Index

www.ingramcontent.com/pod-product-compliance
Lightning Source LLC
Chambersburg PA
CBHW070105030426
42335CB00016B/2024